The Religion Clauses of the First Amendment

The Religion Clauses of the First Amendment

Guarantees of States' Rights?

Ellis M. West

LEXINGTON BOOKS
A division of
ROWMAN & LITTLEFIELD PUBLISHERS, INC.
Lanham • Boulder • New York • Toronto • Plymouth, UK

Published by Lexington Books
A wholly owned subsidiary of The Rowman & Littlefield Publishing Group, Inc.
4501 Forbes Boulevard, Suite 200, Lanham, Maryland 20706
www.lexingtonbooks.com

Estover Road, Plymouth PL6 7PY, United Kingdom

British Library Cataloguing in Publication Information Available

Library of Congress Cataloging-in-Publication Data

West, Ellis McKinney, 1936–
The religion clauses of the First Amendment : guarantees of states' rights? / Ellis M. West.
p. cm.
Includes bibliographical references and index.
ISBN 978-0-7391-4677-4 (cloth : alk. paper) — ISBN 978-0-7391-4679-8 (electronic)
1. Freedom of religion—United States. 2. Church and state—United States. 3. States' rights (American politics) I. Title.
KF4783.W38 2010
342.7308'52—dc22 2011039843

™ The paper used in this publication meets the minimum requirements of American National Standard for Information Sciences—Permanence of Paper for Printed Library Materials, ANSI/NISO Z39.48-1992.

Printed in the United States of America

Contents

Preface

The origin of this book is as follows. In 1990, the Supreme Court handed down a very controversial decision in the case of *Employment Division, Department of Human Resources of Oregon v. Smith*. The issue raised by that case was whether the free exercise clause of the First Amendment ("Congress shall make no law . . . prohibiting the free exercise [of religion] . . . .) guarantees religion-based exemptions from valid, secular laws. In other words, the issue was whether the clause gives individuals and groups the right to be excused from having to obey a law that is itself constitutional if its application to them would prohibit or burden the practice of their religion in some way. In the *Smith* case, the specific issue was whether the free exercise clause gives Native Americans the right to use an illegal drug during a religious ceremony. In a five to four decision, the Court held that they did not have such a right because the free exercise clause does not guarantee a general right to religion-based exemptions from valid, secular laws.

The Court's opinion in that case, written by Justice Antonin Scalia, was criticized, among other reasons, for failing to provide any evidence that the free exercise clause was originally not meant to guarantee religion-based exemptions. His failure to do so was not only questionable but ironic, because Scalia is noted for being an exponent of "originalism," a theory of constitutional adjudication and interpretation that says that courts should decide constitutional law cases on the basis of constitutional provisions *as they were originally understood by the people generally at the time they were ratified.* Moreover, many of Scalia's critics assumed that if he had looked at the historical evidence, he would have discovered that it did show that the free exercise clause was originally intended to guarantee a right to religion-based exemptions.

At that time, having already done some research on the original meaning of the free exercise clause, I was fairly confident that the historical evidence would support the Court's position that the clause does not guarantee a right to religion-based exemptions. I, therefore, decided to research and write a book on the original meaning of the free exercise clause, especially because at that time, and still today, no one had published such a book. A few scholars had published law review articles, but they disagreed on their conclusions. So I set out to resolve the issue.

After a few years and after writing a couple of chapters that were published as articles, in my reading I began to encounter references to a jurisdictional or states' rights interpretation of both religion clauses of the First Amendment. (The other religion clause is generally referred to as the establishment clause, which says, "Congress shall make no law respecting an establishment of religion . . . ."). From what I could gather from my initial but second-hand introduction to this interpretation of the religion clauses, its thesis is that the clauses were not intended to protect religious freedom, a natural right of individuals, but to protect the right of states to legislate on religion as they please.

At first, because this states' rights interpretation was so contrary to the traditional interpretation of the religion clauses, including the Supreme Court's, I simply ignored it—dismissed it out of hand. No decent, self-respecting scholar, I thought, could take it seriously. The more research I did for my book, however, the more I encountered references to the jurisdictional or states' right interpretation, references by generally respected scholars that implied, if not asserted, that it was credible and should be taken seriously. At a minimum, they said that the protection of state laws on religion from Congressional legislation was *one* of the original reasons for the establishment clause, if not both religion clauses.

At that point, I decided to read for myself some of the works that advocated this novel interpretation of the religion clauses. These included, among others, some law review articles by Kurt T. Lash and the book, *Foreordained Failure* (1995), by Steven D. Smith, both men being very reputable professors of law. After reading their works, I realized that I could no longer ignore the jurisdictional account of the religion clauses and, in fact, that I would have to address it in a separate chapter of my book on the original meaning of the free exercise clause. After all, according to Smith, Lash, and others, the free exercise clause was not intended to address issues like whether religious liberty entailed a right to religion-based exemptions from valid, secular laws. In fact, according to them, originally the religion clauses did not have anything at all to say about how government should treat religion. All that they did was to give jurisdiction over that question to the states. Before attempting, therefore, to explain the original meaning of the free exercise clause, *I first had to make sure and then demonstrate to my potential readers that the clause had meaning of some sort*, other than that of giving the states jurisdiction over church-state issues.

I also realized another reason why it was so important to address the validity of the jurisdictional interpretation of the religion clauses. If it were correct, it would mean that it would be improper, even unconstitutional, for the Supreme Court to strike down state laws dealing with religion, even if those laws violated religious liberty or established a particular religion. If the original objective of the religion clauses was to protect states' rights—to prevent Congress or the federal courts from overturning state laws dealing with religion—then obviously those clauses could and should not be used by courts today to strike down such state laws. Doing such would be directly contrary to the original intent of the religion clauses. In short, if the jurisdictional interpretation of the religion clauses were correct and then to be accepted by the Supreme Court, it would have to overturn many of the decisions it has handed down during the last fifty plus years.

Upon deciding to include in my book a chapter assessing the merits of the states' rights reading of the religion clauses, I thought that it would be a relatively easy thing to demonstrate that it was without merit. Alas, the more I read and thought about the interpretation, it became more complicated and more difficult to refute. The proponents of the states' rights interpretation came up with all kinds of arguments that I was not anticipating. Some of them even attempted to show that Thomas Jefferson and James Madison subscribed to such an interpretation. Although I was not convinced by their arguments, I was certainly impressed with their ingenuity.

In any case, the result was that the chapter grew and grew in size and scope until it threatened to dwarf the rest of the book. What to do? I decided that the only feasible way of solving my problem without sacrificing the persuasiveness of what I wanted to say was not to include it in my book on the original meaning of the free exercise clause, but to reorganize, expand, and publish it as a separate book, which I have now done.

In brief, what is in this book? After explaining the jurisdictional or states' rights interpretation of the religion clauses, this book analyzes the logic of the arguments and the sufficiency of the historical evidence used to support the interpretation of the religion clauses. In doing the latter, it attempts to present all the relevant evidence—what the initial proponents of the religion clauses wanted and why, what happened at the First Congress that drafted them, and how early Americans understood the clauses after they were ratified. I have presented as much historical evidence as possible so that there will be no doubt in the reader's mind about the validity of my conclusion. Of course, I cannot claim to have included everything that should have been included, but if I have omitted a relevant piece of evidence, especially one that does not support my conclusion, it was not intentional, but simply because I never found it.

The book's main conclusion is that there is very little historical evidence to support the jurisdictional interpretation. It also shows that many of the arguments used to support it involve specious reasoning and unwarranted assumptions. Given this conclusion, the reader may have one of two reactions—either to wonder how the interpretation could ever have gained so much currency or to suspect that I have been unfair and one-sided. How could I be right and so many other scholars be wrong? Perhaps for this reason, some reviewers of my manuscript suggested I should "tone down" my criticism even though they did not disagree with it. All I can say is that I have tried to be as fair and gentle as possible in my criticism, without watering down or distorting what I believe the facts reveal. In my opinion, it is important for scholars to "call a spade a spade" even at the risk of being considered unfair or too harsh.

As for why so many respectable scholars have both advocated and accepted an interpretation of the religion clauses for which there is so little evidence, I cannot say, even though I have speculated on the question. Because of my desire to be fair and not unnecessarily critical, I have refrained from expressing my speculations. Nevertheless, I cannot refrain from saying that, in my opinion, much of what has been published to support the states' right interpretation and the extent to which scholars have accepted it as true does not reflect well on the field of American constitutional law/history. Although all interpretations of past events, including my own, are contestable, if something can be published and then accepted by other scholars as historical truth regardless of how much or little evidence supports it, then thoughtful persons cannot help but wonder what is going on.

One other point about the contents of this book—its original purpose was not to establish the original meaning of the religion clauses. Rather, it was to critically evaluate the states' right interpretation of those clauses—to see if it is supported by good arguments and sufficient historical evidence. The conclusion that it is not so supported, however, tells us only that the religion clauses were not intended to protect states' rights or state establishments of religion. It does not tell us what they were intended to do. Nevertheless, in the course of showing what the clauses were not intended to do, I necessarily suggest, if not show, what they *were* intended to do.

Most obviously and generally, they were meant to express a normative point about how the federal government should treat religion. More specifically, they were meant to protect religious liberty by prohibiting all laws of the sort associated with traditional European establishments of religion. I believe that the historical evidence shows that religious liberty and religious establishments were thought to be inversely related or polar opposites. The presence of one meant the absence of the other. In other words, the free exercise clause and establishment clause were originally understood as two different ways of saying the same thing.

Although I believe the historical evidence presented in this book shows this to have been the case, because I did not set out to show this to have been the case, I do not claim that I have conclusively shown it to be so. In order to do that, I would have to include evidence not included in this book; in short, I would have to write another book. Perhaps this is just a way of saying that I need to get back to work on my first intended book.

Now, I have a few suggestions for the reader, especially anyone who is not trained in constitutional law/history. This book was not written for members of the general public to read. Constitutional law, and thus constitutional history, is inherently complicated. It is full of legal jargon and all about making distinctions between this and that. I have tried to explain as much about the law as I could without getting side-tracked away from the main issues and arguments. Nevertheless, for many persons this book will be a challenging and slow read. Understanding that fact ahead of time, however, should help the reader get through the book. It should help one to resist putting this book aside on the assumption that it is her/his fault that s/he cannot understand what s/he is reading. If that happens, it may not be any person's fault, and hopefully that includes me. It may just be the nature of the subject matter. Even difficult passages, however, if read slowly and more than once, can be understood. So hang in there, dear reader, and do not give up without a fight.

The book also contains numerous citations at the end of each chapter. How much attention should be paid to them? On the one hand, ignoring them makes for an easier read. On the other hand, the more critical readers will want to check them out because they do contain some important points or comments, as well as sources.

More specifically, I want to warn the reader about one word—"federal" or "federalist"—that may be somewhat confusing because in this book it has at least three different meanings. At places "federal" means national, as in "federal government"; "Federalist" (with a capital F) refers to an early American who favored ratifying the Constitution of 1787 (a person who did not was called an "Anti-federalist"); and "federalist" (with a small f) means "states' rights," as in "federalist interpretation of the religion clauses." (A person favoring such an interpretation might also be called a "federalist.") The reason for mentioning this here is to establish the fact that there is no historical or logical connection between "Federalist" and "federalist." In other words, an early American could have been a Federalist without favoring a federalist interpretation of the religion clauses. This also means that today one could be a federalist (favor such an interpretation of those clauses) without being a supporter of the federal government.

Finally, I wish to acknowledge and thank those who have made (or at least attempted to make) this a better book than it would have been without their help. First, there is the Earhart Foundation, which gave me a grant that enabled me to get started on this project. I am also grateful to the following persons who at some point in its unfolding read and criticized my manuscript: Kurt T. Lash, John Dinan, and Mark McGarvie. Next, although he had nothing directly to do with this book, Douglas Laycock, one of this country's leading experts on the religion clauses, indirectly encouraged me to write it. Because he took seriously my previous publications and made use of them in his own writings, he increased my confidence in my scholarship and my desire to keep writing and publishing. I am also indebted to two persons at the University of Richmond: Beth Ann Howard, for all the technical word-processing assistance that she provided as I was getting my manuscript ready for the publisher, and my dean, Andy Newcomb, for his financial support. Last, but certainly not least, my wife, Phyllis, deserves my endless thanks for her patience and support throughout the entire process of writing this book.

Chapter One

Introduction

In America, religious freedom has often been referred to as the "first freedom,"[1] but for different reasons. Some believe it to be the most important or valuable of freedoms, and usually on the grounds that religion itself is the most important aspect of human life. After all, religion has traditionally been understood as a person or group's relationship with some kind of transcendent or supernatural power and source of meaning, and those who believe in the existence of such a reality would be very likely to consider their relationship with it to be their most important relationship. James Madison, for example, in making the case for religious freedom, wrote, "It is the duty of every man to render to the Creator such homage, and such only, as he believes to be acceptable to him. This duty is precedent both in order of time and degree of obligation, to the claims of Civil Society."[2]

For others religious freedom is chronologically the "first freedom;" it was the first freedom in the course of Western civilization to be understood as a fundamental and universal natural or human right. As such, it opened the way for other freedoms, such as freedom of expression, to be identified as fundamental, universal "rights of man."[3] Being first in this sense does not imply that religious freedom is first in rank or value, but only that efforts to establish it preceded and led to the widespread belief in the idea of natural rights in general. Some persons, however, go further and argue that religious freedom is logically, as well as historically, prior to other freedoms; their establishment depends on its establishment.[4]

A third reason that religious freedom is often called the "first freedom" is because it is the first freedom to be mentioned and guaranteed in the Bill of Rights section (first ten amendments) of the United States Constitution. The First Amendment begins with these words: "Congress shall make no law respecting an establishment of religion, or prohibiting the free exercise thereof. . . ."[5] These words are generally referred to as the religion clauses of the First Amendment. Moreover, during the course of American history most Americans have interpreted this language as protecting a very important natural or human right, i.e., the freedom of individuals, as Madison said, to render such homage to the ultimate source or ground of human existence as they believe is required of them.[6] This is certainly the way the Supreme Court of the United States has interpreted the religion clauses.[7]

In recent years, however, several constitutional law scholars have challenged this traditional interpretation of the religion clauses of the First Amendment. They argue that the rights protected by those clauses are those of states, not individuals. They contend that the clauses have no *substantive* meaning, i.e., have nothing to say about what the relationship between government and religion or government and individuals should be. Instead, the clauses are purely *jurisdictional* in nature, i.e., are simply statements that only the states, and not the national government, have the authority to determine what the relationship between government and religion should be. According to this interpretation, the religion clauses were not intended to and do not guarantee a basic, universal, natural right or express a normative principle of any sort.

This interpretation of the religion clauses has been most forcefully and influentially expressed by Steven Smith, a law professor and leading scholar in the area of religion and government, in the book, *Foreordained Failure: The Quest for a Constitutional Principle of Religious Freedom.*[8] He writes therein that "the religion clauses have nothing of substance to say on questions of religious freedom. The original meaning supplies us neither with concrete answers to particular legal questions nor with any general principle, norm, value, or theory that might serve as a basis for working out such answers." Smith explains that the clauses do not address such questions as "Should government establish one religion as the official state religion? Should the state subsidize a religion? Should it support all religions . . . on equal terms?" He concludes, "If we ask, therefore, what principle or theory of religious liberty the framers and ratifiers of the religion clauses adopted, the most accurate answer is 'None.'" Instead, the religion clauses, he says, are a declaration of states' rights, not individual rights. As such, they were intended to protect from federal legislation both the anti-establishment of religion policies of states like Virginia and the pro-establishment policies that still existed in some New England states.[9]

What is notable about Smith's states' rights or jurisdictional interpretation is that it applies to the free exercise clause as well as the establishment clause. Although some scholars have over the years argued that the sole purpose of the establishment clause was to protect states' rights, they have usually conceded that the free exercise clause has substantive meaning, i.e., was meant to prevent the federal government from passing laws that would violate the citizens' religious freedom.[10] Others have posited an even narrower interpretation of the establishment clause, namely, that it was intended to protect from Congressional legislation not states' rights as such, but state establishments of religion, but they too have thought that the free exercise clause has normative meaning, i.e., was meant to protect the religious freedom of individuals. This, for example, is the position of Supreme Court Justice, Clarence Thomas, who contends that the establishment clause, unlike the free exercise clause, "does not protect any individual right," but "is a federalism provision intended to prevent Congress from interfering with state establishments [of religion]," and for this reason should not be used by the courts to strike down state laws on religion. Such laws can be struck down only if they are coercive and thus violate the free exercise clause.[11] This idea that the free exercise clause has normative meaning, i.e., protects religious freedom, whereas the establishment clause does not, but protects only states' rights or state religious establishments, Smith labels the dualistic view of the religion clauses.

Other scholars have taken a more complicated position. They have said that the free exercise clause has entirely substantive meaning and that the establishment clause has both substantive and federalist content, i.e., it was intended to prevent the federal government from both establishing (at the national level) and disestablishing (at the state level) a church or religion.[12] This also appears to be the position of Supreme Court Justice, Antonin Scalia.[13]

In contrast, Smith argues that the free exercise clause, as well as the establishment clause, is simply a declaration that the federal government has no jurisdiction over the subject of religion. He writes:

> . . . [T]his dualistic view of the religion clauses, although virtually ubiquitous, is nonetheless mistaken. The religion clauses were not a hybrid creation—part federalism, part substantive right. They were, rather, simply an assignment of jurisdiction over matters of religion to the states—no more, no less. Consequently, perverse though it seems, the religion clauses simply do not speak to the substantive questions of religious freedom.[14]

According to Smith, the main reason that the religion clauses are purely jurisdictional in nature is the fact that early Americans were so divided in their thinking on the proper relationship between government and religion that they could not possibly have agreed on a substantive principle to encase in the clauses. He writes, "The founders *did not* answer the religion question because they *could not* have done so."[15]

Smith, however, is not the first scholar to so interpret the religion clauses. In 1964, Wilber G. Katz, a distinguished professor of law at the University of Chicago, suggested that the clauses "embodied a principle of federalism" that precluded the federal government from legislating on religion because such a power was reserved to the states. This meant, however, that the clauses did not prohibit it from legislating on religion "in areas beyond the authority of any state; for example, in the armed forces, the District of Columbia, and the territories." On the other hand, Katz speculated that the free exercise clause might have been meant to protect religious freedom from federal laws applicable *to those areas*. In all other areas, he said that the religion clauses protect only states' rights. [16](Although familiar with Katz's interpretation, Smith, for some reason, fails in his book to acknowledge it.)

Since its publication in 1995, Smith's interpretation of the religion clauses has been accepted by several other scholars. For example, Jay S. Bybee, a former law professor and now federal circuit court judge, writes:

> The Founders had their substantive views of church and state, of course, but they did not codify their views in the Bill of Rights. Thus, no coherent theory of the religious liberty or freedom of expression can be drawn from the text or the history of the First Amendment; such questions were deliberately deferred to the states. The First Amendment was the least common denominator; it was simply jurisdictional. [17]

Bybee states explicitly that the clauses neither "address church-state relations" nor guarantee "personal rights."[18] Professor of law, Daniel O. Conkle, appears to agree.[19] Kurt T. Lash, another law professor, not only agrees with, but goes beyond Smith, for he argues that the entire First Amendment was "hyper-Federalist," i.e., intended to protect "state autonomy to regulate matters like religion, speech, and press."[20]

Other scholars have accepted most, but not quite all, of Smith's thesis. Reluctant to concede that the religion clauses have *no* substantive content, they argue that they are "primarily" or "mainly" jurisdictional in meaning. Both clauses, in short, were intended primarily, if not entirely, to protect states' rights or the principle of federalism and not individuals' rights.[21] For example, Daniel Dreisbach, a leading church-state scholar, writes:

> The *principal* importance of . . . the First Amendment . . . is its clear demarcation of the legitimate jurisdictions of federal and state governments on religious matters. . . . The Bill of Rights embodied a principle of federalism; it was *essentially* a states' rights document. . . . '[T]he *principal* importance of the [First] Amendment lay in the separation which it effected between the respective jurisdictions of State and nation regarding religion, rather than in its bearing on the question of the Separation of Church and State.'. . . [T]he First Amendment, was *primarily* jurisdictional (or structural) in nature. . . [and] offered *little* in the way of a substantive right or universal principle of religious liberty.[22]

Less extreme, Arlin M. Adams and Charles J. Emmerich, whose widely used book, *A Nation Dedicated to Religious Liberty*, is an interpretation of the religion clauses, contend that there were three reasons for the religion clauses, only one of which was that the free exercise of religion was an inalienable right that needed to be protected from the federal government. The other two reasons were jurisdictional in nature. "[C]ivil authority in religious affairs resided with the states, not the national government," and Congress needed to be prevented from interfering with existing state establishments of religion. This means that the framers/ratifiers of the religion clauses, while agreeing on the need for the clauses, may have done so for entirely different reasons. Adams and Emmerich, however, fail to discuss the relative importance or popularity of these different reasons.[23]

One sign of the extent of the influence of Smith, Bybee, Conkle, and others on contemporary thinking about the religion clauses is the following comment contained in an article published in 2003:

> Recent work on the development of the First Amendment . . . confirms that the traditional goals of legal analysis require serious rethinking. The best evidence indicates that the primary if not exclusive purpose of the First Amendment's religion clauses was procedural rather than substantive, to declare that the states and not the national government were responsible for questions of religion and religious liberty.[24]

An even more recent source says, "The observation that the Religion Clauses were originally jurisdictional is commonplace."[25] Even some scholars not inclined to accept such an interpretation of the establishment clause concede that it has "true salience" and, thus, "cannot be easily ignored."[26]

As a practical matter, what difference does it make whether the religion clauses were originally meant to protect the individual right of religious freedom or the states' right to decide for themselves how to treat religion? The resolution of this issue could have a major impact on the way the Supreme Court decides cases arising on the basis of the religion clauses, especially if Supreme Court justices' interpretation of those clauses is based on their original meaning, which traditionally they have claimed to be the case. Today, moreover, certain justices, most notably Justice Antonin Scalia, continue to affirm their commitment to originalism as an important component of constitutional adjudication and interpretation.[27] If such justices were to adopt and use a jurisdictional or states' right interpretation of the religion clauses, how would that be likely to affect the way they decide religion-clauses cases?

The answer depends on whether a case being decided by the Court involves a federal law or a state law. As a practical matter, a jurisdictional interpretation of the religion clauses would still prevent the *federal* government from doing more or less what it is presently prevented from doing on the basis of the Court's traditional, substantive interpretation of the religion clauses.[28] This is because the Court has essentially said that the religion clauses prohibit the government from passing laws that have a primarily religious purpose or effect, which is almost exactly what the proponents of a jurisdictional interpretation of the clauses say that the clauses prohibit.[29] The only significant difference between the two interpretations of the clauses *as applied to the federal government* pertains not to the kind of law that the clauses prohibit, but to the reasons for their being prohibited. A substantive interpretation of the religion clauses says that federal laws dealing primarily with religion were originally prohibited in order to protect religious freedom, whereas a jurisdictional interpretation says they were prohibited in order to protect the freedom of states.

If, on the other hand, the cases being decided by the Supreme Court on the basis of the religion clauses involve *state laws* and the Court were to decide that those clauses have only jurisdictional meaning or content, then it would decide those cases in a way that would be significantly, even dramatically, different from the way it has traditionally decided them. It would not strike down state laws dealing with religion no matter what those laws said. A states' right interpretation of the clauses would allow state and local governments to pass any kind of law relating to religion that they wanted to pass. In contrast to the present situation, in which cases are decided on the basis of a substantive understanding of the religion clauses, states would be able to discriminate for or against specific religions, religious beliefs, or practices, or persons/groups because of their religion.

To understand how this could be, one must remember that originally the Bill of Rights applied only to the national government and not the state governments.[30] Thus, the First Amendment begins, "*Congress* shall make no law. . . ." It was not until the twentieth century that the Supreme Court began to apply certain provisions of the Bill of Rights to the states. The Court did this on the basis of the due process clause of the Fourteenth Amendment ("[N]or shall any State deprive any person of life, liberty, or property, without due process of law. . . ."),[31] which was added to the Constitution in 1868. Decades later, the Court decided that that clause had been added to prevent the states from violating certain substantive rights, including, but not limited to, some of those contained in the Bill of Rights, such as religious freedom. The rights in the Bill of Rights that the Court held were protected from state laws by the due process clause were said to be "incorporated" into that clause.[32] Thus, in 1940, it incorporated the free exercise clause into the clause and thereby applied it to the states, and in 1947 it did the same with the establishment clause.[33] Since then, the Supreme Court has struck down numerous state laws on the grounds that they violated the free exercise or establishment clause, as incorporated into the due process clause of the Fourteenth Amendment.

According to the proponents of a jurisdictional interpretation of the religion clauses, however, the Court's incorporating the religion clauses into the due process clause was a major mistake. If those clauses were originally intended to protect a states' right and not an individual right, then logically they can not be (and should not have been) incorporated into the due process clause of the Fourteenth Amendment and applied to the *states*. If the clauses do not express substantive principles about the proper relationship between religion and government, there is simply nothing to be incorporated into the due process clause and applied to the states. Moreover, any attempt to interpret the clauses in a substantive way and then apply them to the states would be inconsistent with what Smith (and others) say is the original purpose of the establishment clause—to allow the state governments to decide for themselves what their relationship with religion will be.[34] Thus, Akhil Amar, a professor at Yale Law School, writes, ". . . [T]o apply the [establishment] clause against a state government is precisely to eliminate its right to choose whether to establish a religion—a right clearly confirmed by the establishment clause itself."[35]

Although the Supreme Court at this time is most unlikely to reverse its decision to incorporate the religion clauses into the due process clause of the Fourteenth Amendment,[36] to the extent that individual justices accept the jurisdictional interpretation of the religion clauses, they should and will be inclined to apply those clauses to state laws more leniently than they would apply them to laws of Congress. As explained by one scholar, "because the Framers intended, and the public originally understood, the Religion Clauses to be a federalist directive, federal courts achieve some of the desirable effects of originalism . . . by deferring to the states on close church-state questions."[37] Moreover, some scholars have recently argued in favor of the Court's doing just that, i.e., applying a relaxed version of the establishment clause to the states.[38]

Whether the religion clauses are substantive or jurisdictional in content matters for one other reason. If they are the latter, they arguably would preclude Congress from passing laws that have as their objective the *protection of religious freedom*—laws like the Religious Freedom Restoration Act of 1993,[39] which gives religious persons and groups a general right to be exempt from obeying valid, secular laws, including those passed by state and local governments.[40] Although the religion clauses, if given a jurisdictional interpretation, might not prevent the federal government from granting religion-based exemptions from its own laws,[41] it is reasonably clear that they would prohibit it from requiring the states to grant such exemptions from their laws.

In summary, if the Supreme Court were to officially endorse a jurisdictional or federalist interpretation of the religion clauses, that could have a profound effect on church-state law and practice, at least at the level of state and local governments, which is the level where most church-state cases have originated.[42] Essentially the states would be completely free to pass whatever laws regarding religion they wanted to pass, except insofar as their own constitutions and courts restrained them. Neither the United States Congress nor the federal courts could intervene to protect religious freedom. Moreover, even if the Court did not officially endorse a jurisdictional interpretation of the religion clauses and did not un-incorporate the religion clauses from the Fourteenth Amendment, to the extent that it sees such an interpretation as having some validity, its decisions are likely to be affected by that interpretation. Finally, a jurisdictional interpretation would arguably preclude Congress from passing laws protecting religious liberty from state laws of one sort or another. For these reasons, the jurisdictional or states' rights interpretation of the religion clauses is not an "academic issue" and deserves careful and thorough scrutiny.[43]

Although the jurisdictional interpretation may be plausible, it can be and has been challenged, primarily on the grounds that it is based mostly, if not entirely, on circumstantial evidence and, thus, speculation.[44] Smith himself comes close to admitting this when he writes that his interpretation "is not based on any newly discovered historical evidence. . . . Rather, the conclusion results from working out the *implications* of historical facts that are already familiar to and widely accepted by scholars. . . . *implications* that I believe are plausible and even compelling once we clear away the misformulated inquiries that have caused us to overlook . . . the obvious."[45] Not surprisingly, therefore, he provides no statement from any early American that explicitly or directly supports the idea that the religion clauses are jurisdictional in nature, and, as shown in the rest of this book, he overlooks a great deal of evidence to the contrary.[46]

What is needed, therefore, to establish whether the religion clauses protect individual rights or states' rights is not assumptions or speculation, but concrete historical evidence about *why* they were sought, adopted, and applied to the new national government and *what they meant* to early Americans. Moreover, which of these two interpretations is correct should be determined by a preponderance of the historical evidence. Even if some evidence could be presented to support a federalist interpretation of the religion clauses, that interpretation should not be accepted if more and/or weightier evidence shows a normative reason for and understanding of the religion clauses, and, of course, vice versa. It also will not do for scholars to state that some framers/ratifiers of the religion clauses had normative reasons and others had federalist reasons for supporting the clauses, but then not attempt to explain how both reasons could be combined and/or what their relative importance was. If no attempt is made to do this, the clauses are left meaningless.[47]

The purpose of this book, therefore, is to present and analyze all the actual evidence pertaining to why the religion clauses were adopted and what they meant after they were adopted. Were they adopted for normative or federalist reasons? Were they understood as guarantees of individual rights or states' rights? My main conclusion is that both religion clauses have substantive or normative meaning. In order to substantiate that thesis, however, I do not need or attempt to establish precisely what that meaning is and to marshal the evidence needed to support such an interpretation. All that I need and attempt to show is that the proponents, drafters, and ratifiers of the clauses had moral or principled reasons for wanting them added to the Constitution. In presenting and explaining those reasons, however, I necessarily *suggest* what the original, substantive meaning of the religion clauses was.

Ironically, what the historical evidence presented in this book shows is that the kind of laws the religion clauses were intended to prohibit, in order to protect religious freedom, is *very similar to* the kind of laws that a jurisdictional or federalist interpretation of the clauses says they were intended to prohibit, i.e., laws dealing directly with the subject of religion.[48] I say "similar to" and not "the same as" because, as will be seen, most early Americans equated religious freedom with the absence of laws characteristic of traditional establishments of religion,[49] i.e., laws that take a position on, either for or against, certain religious beliefs and practices. Such laws, however, are not the same as laws dealing *in any way* with religion. For example, a federal law striking down a state establishment of religion could be construed as a law dealing directly with religion, but it is obviously not the kind of law that early Americans would have associated with establishments of religion or the denial of religious liberty. Under a jurisdictional or federalist interpretation of the religion clauses, such a law would violate the clauses, whereas under the substantive or normative interpretation shown in this book to have been held by early Americans, such a law would not violate the religion clauses.[50]

Nevertheless, the substantive or normative interpretation of the religion clauses that is presented herein is in one significant way like a jurisdictional or federalist interpretation of those clauses, for it, too, says that the religion clauses were intended to deny "Congress," the federal legislature, jurisdiction over a certain subject matter or the *power* to pass a certain category or class of laws.[51] For this reason, and again ironically (because it is consistent with a jurisdictional or federalist interpretation), the historical evidence also shows that the free exercise and establishment clauses have the same (albeit substantive) meaning. Contrary to what the Supreme Court has said, the evidence shows that the two clauses are redundant or two different ways of saying the same thing—that Congress cannot directly legislate on or take a position on religious issues or questions.[52]

On the other hand, the historical evidence shows that Smith and other scholars in his camp are simply incorrect in arguing that the *reason* for such a prohibition was to protect states' rights or uphold the principle of federalism. Rather, and quite clearly, as will be seen, the main reason was to protect religious freedom, which the majority of early Americans believed is threatened, if not violated, whenever *any government*—local, state, or national—legislates directly on subjects or issues that are essentially or primarily religious in nature. A secondary reason may have been to preserve national unity by preventing the *federal* government from legislating on a subject that was necessarily divisive in a religiously pluralistic nation.

The historical evidence is presented as follows. Using evidence from the ratification controversy, including the views of both Federalists and Antifederalists, chapter four explains why many early Americans wanted a religious liberty amendment added to the Constitution. The fifth chapter focuses on what happened at the First Congress, which drafted the Bill of Rights. Chapter six addresses the extent to which early Americans were divided on substantive church-state issues, and the seventh examines how the religion clauses were understood by early Americans at the time of and for several years after their adoption.

Before presenting the historical evidence relating to the issue, however, I first clarify (in the next chapter) the nature of the issue—for two reasons. First, there is confusion over exactly what the difference is between the two competing interpretations of the religion clauses, and the confusion has been caused by the use of misleading nomenclature on the part of some scholars. Steven Smith, for example, refers to the "substantive" versus the "jurisdictional" interpretation of the clauses. In the next chapter, I explain why that terminology is confusing and should be replaced by the words "normative" and "federalist." Secondly, there is considerable disagreement about what a jurisdictional or federalist interpretation would entail. For example, would it prohibit all federal laws directly pertaining to religion (a general disclaimer over religion) or only some laws (a partial disclaimer over religion)? The next chapter, therefore, also explains the different jurisdictional or federalist interpretations of the religion clauses that are possible.

Before presenting the historical evidence, I also summarize, in chapter three, the case made by Stephen Smith and others for a jurisdictional or states' rights interpretation of the religion clauses. This is necessary, I believe, so that the reader will understand what kind of historical evidence would be needed to support the various arguments for such an interpretation and can then look, in the later chapters of the book, to see if such evidence exists. On the other hand, in chapter three, I also criticize the logic of some of the arguments that are used to support a federalist interpretation of the religion clauses. Although this may strike the reader as premature (because it occurs before the presentation of the historical evidence), my criticism in chapter three does not relate to whether the historical evidence supports a federalist interpretation. Rather, it relates to the logical validity of certain assumptions that are made by some of the advocates of such an interpretation—assumptions that, in my opinion, have the effect of "loading the dice" in favor of the federalist interpretation. Before presenting the historical evidence, therefore, I attempt to clear away these false and misleading assumptions so that the evidence can speak for itself.

The book concludes with a summary of the findings presented in chapters four through seven and of the case against a federalist or states' rights interpretation of the religion clauses.

NOTES

1. Books on religious freedom that have "first freedom" or "first liberty" in their titles include William Lee Miller, *The First Liberty: Religion and the American Republic* (New York: Alfred Knopf, 1985); James E. Wood, Jr., editor, *The First Freedom: Religion & the Bill of Rights* (Waco, Tex.: Baylor Univ. Press, 1990); Gregg Ivers, *Redefining the First Freedom: The Supreme Court and the Consolidation of State Power* (New Brunswick, N. J.: Transaction Pub's, 1993); and Thomas J. Curry, *The First Freedoms: Church and State in America to the Passage of the First Amendment* (New York: Oxford Univ. Press, 1986).

2. "Memorial and Remonstrance against Religious Assessments" (6/20/1785), in *The Papers of James Madison*, ed. Robert A. Rutland et al (Chicago: Univ. of Chicago Press, 1973), 8: 299. For a more recent statement on the importance of religion, and thus religious liberty, see John T. Noonan, Jr., *The Lustre of our Country: The American Experience of Religious Freedom* (Berkeley, Calif.: Univ. of California Press, 1998), 1–2.

3. For an elaboration of this point, see George Jellinek, *The Declaration of the Rights of Man and of Citizens*, trans. by Max Farrand (Westport, Conn.: Hyperion Press, 1979 reprint of 1901 ed.), especially chap's 6 ("The Contrast between the American and English Declarations of Rights"), 7 ("Religious Liberty in the Anglo-American Colonies the Source of the Idea of Establishing by Law a Universal Right of Man"), and 8 ("The Creation of a System of Rights of Man and of Citizens during the American Revolution"), and Barry Shain, "Religious Conscience and Original Sin," in *Liberty and American Experience in the Eighteenth Century*, ed. David Womersley (Indianapolis, Ind.: Liberty Fund, 2006), 161–86.

4. See, for example, the "Williamsburg Charter," a 1988 reaffirmation of religious liberty by some of the nation's leading political and religious leaders, in *Journal of Law and Religion*, 8 (1990): 6–11.

5. *U. S. Constitution*, Amendment I.

6. For an elaboration of these and other arguments for the "firstness" of religious liberty, see Os Guinness, "Tribespeople, Idiots or Citizens?: Religious Liberty and the Reforging of the American Public Philosophy,"*Journal of Law and Religion*, 8 (1990): 35–39.

7. See, e.g., *Reynolds v. United States*, 98 U.S. 145, 164 (1879) (Court adopted Jefferson's statement that the religion clauses expressed "'the supreme will of the nation in behalf of the rights of conscience.'"); *Engel v. Vitale*, 370 U.S. 421, 430 (1962) (The two clauses "forbid two quite different kinds of governmental encroachment upon religious freedom."); and *Wallace v. Jaffree*, 472 U.S. 38, 49 (1985) (". . . [T]he First Amendment was adopted to curtail the power of Congress to interfere with the individual's freedom to believe, to worship, and to express himself in accordance with the dictates of his own conscience.")

8. (New York: Oxford Univ. Press, 1995).

9. *Foreordained Failure*, 16, 19, 21–22, 42–43.

10. See, e.g., Joseph M. Snee, "Religious Disestablishment and the Fourteenth Amendment,"*Washington University Law Quarterly*, (1954): 389; Daniel O. Conkle, "Toward a General Theory of the Establishment Clause,"*Northwestern University Law* Review, 82 (1988): 1113, 1133–34; William K. Lietzau, "Rediscovering the Establishment Clause: Federalism and the Rollback of Incorporation,"*DePaul Law Review*, 39 (1990): 1191, 1198–99; Chris Bartolomucci, "Rethinking the Incorporation of the Establishment Clause: A Federalist View,"*Harvard Law Review*, 105 (May 1992): 1700, 1703–05; Vincent P. Munoz, "The Original Meaning of the Establishment Clause and the Impossibility of Its Incorporation,"*University of Pennsylvania Journal of Constitutional Law*, 8 (2006): 600–04, 631–32; and Akhil Amar, *The Bill of Rights: Creation and Reconstruction* (New Haven, Conn.: Yale Univ. Press, 1998), 32–42, 246.

11. See *Elk Grove Unified School District v. Newdow*, 542 U.S. 1, 50–51 (2004) (J. Thomas, concurring in the judgment.) A year later, in a concurring opinion in *Cutter v. Wilkinson*, 544 U.S. 709. 727–28 (2005), Thomas re-affirmed his view that the establishment clause prohibits Congress from interfering with state laws that support religion, but he also made it clear that he does not subscribe to a completely federalist or states' rights interpretation of that clause. He said that the only kind of law that the clause prohibits Congress from passing is one that interferes with state establishments of religion. Thus, he held that the Religious Land Use and Institutionalized Persons Act of 2000, which was intended to protect religious persons and groups from certain kinds of state laws, did not violate the establishment clause. He reasoned, "It [RLUIPA] is a law respecting religion, but not one respecting an establishment of religion," and, thus, is not unconstitutional. *Cutter v. Wilkinson*, 731–33.

12. See, e.g., Kent Greenawalt, "Common Sense about Original and Subsequent Understandings of the Religion Clauses,"*University of Pennsylvania Journal of Constitutional Law*, 8 (2006): 480, 485; Arlin M. Adams and Charles J. Emmerich, *A Nation Dedicated to Religious Liberty: The Constitutional Heritage of the Religion Clauses* (Philadelphia, Penn.: Univ. of Pennsylvania Press, 1990), 46–47; Paul G. Kauper, *Religion and the Constitution* (Baton Rouge, La.: Louisiana State Univ. Press, 1964), 46–47; Robert A. Destro, "The Structure of the Religious Liberty Guarantee,"*Journal of Law & Religion*, 11 (1994–95): 371, 392; Mary Ann Glendon and Raul F. Yates, "Structural Free Exercise,"*Michigan Law Review*, 90 (1991): 477, 540–41; and Michael Malbin, *Religion and Politics: The Intentions of the Authors of the First Amendment* (Washington, D. C.: American Enterprise Institute, 1978), 10–16.

13. See *Lee v. Weisman*, 505 U.S. 577, 640 (1992) (J. Scalia, dissenting).

14. *Foreordained Failure*, 18–19.

15. *Foreordained Failure*, 26 (emphasis in original), and 19–22.

16. See his *Religion and American Constitutions* (Evanston, Ill.: Northwestern Univ. Press, 1964), 9–10.

17. "Taking Liberties with the First Amendment,"*Vanderbilt Law Review*, 48 (Nov. 1995): 1565 [citing Smith]. More precisely, Bybee subscribes to Wilber Katz's position, see note 16, that the religion clauses prohibit federal legislation on religion, *except* when it pertains to the military, the territories, and the District of Columbia. "Taking Liberties . . .," 1565–66, fn 122.

18. "Taking Liberties . . .," 1543–44.

19. See his *Constitutional Law: The Religion Clauses* (New York: Foundation Press, 2003), 16–21.

20. See "The Second Adoption of the Free Exercise Clause: Religious Exemptions Under the Fourteenth Amendment,"*Northwestern University Law Review*, 88 (Spring 1994): 1106, 1114, and "Two Movements of a Constitutional Symphony: Akhil Reed Amar's *The Bill of Rights*,"*University of Richmond Law Review*, 33 (May 1999): 485, 487, 492. Also, see Steven Waldman, *Founding Faith: Providence, Politics, and the Birth of Religious Freedom in America* (New York: Random House, 2008), 156–58. Kyle Duncan has recently written an article ostensibly to show that the establishment clause is a jurisdictional or federalist provision, but most of the arguments that he makes, including numerous references to Steven Smith's works, apply also to the free exercise clause, and several times he even refers to the federalist nature of the religion clauses and not just the establishment clause. "Subsidiarity and Religious Establishments in the United States Constitution,"*Villanova Law Review*, 52 (2007): 67–134.

21. See Edward S. Corwin, "The Supreme Court as National School Board,"*Law and Contemporary Problems*, 14 (Winter 1949): 14 ("In short, the *principal* importance of the amendment lay in the separation which it effected between the respective jurisdictions of state and nation regarding religion, rather than in its bearing on the question of the separation of church and state.") (emphasis added).

22. *Thomas Jefferson and the Wall of Separation between Church and State* (New York: New York Univ. Press, 2002), 56, 61 (quoting Edward S. Corwin), 69 (emphasis added). Dreisbach, however, is not always consistent in stating his position on this issue. Sometimes he implies that the religion clauses have *no* substantive meaning. See *Jefferson and the Wall. . .*, at 61, 68–69, and 188, fn 29. Also see below, pp. 165–66.

23. *A Nation Dedicated to Religious Liberty,* 44–47, 72. (This book, it should be noted, was published before Smith's book was published.)

24. Christopher S. Grenda, "Revealing Liberalism in Early America: Rethinking Religious Liberty and Liberal Values," *Journal of Church and State*, 45 (Winter 2003): 133–34. For an earlier, albeit less explicit version of the jurisdictional interpretation of the religions clauses, see Walfred H. Peterson, "The American Federal System and Church-State Relations," *Western Political Quarterly*, 16 (Sept. 1963): 598–601, but none of the more recent proponents of the jurisdictional interpretation appears to be aware of it.

25. Richard C. Schragger, "The Role of the Local in the Doctrine and Discourse of Religious Liberty," *Harvard Law Review*, 117 (2003–04): 1812.

26. Ira C. Lupu and Robert W. Tuttle, "Federalism and Faith,"*Emory Law Journal*, 56 (2006): 42–43. Also, see the attention given to the issue in a recently published casebook: Michael W. McConnell, John H. Garvey, and Thomas C. Berg, *Religion and the Constitution*, 2d ed. (New York: Aspen Pub's, 2006), 62–64, 74–76, 80–81.

27. Lee J. Strang, "The (Re)turn to History in Religion Clause Law and Scholarship,"*Notre Dame Law Review*, 81 (2005–2006): 1697–1716. For an excellent explanation and defense of originalism as a method of constitutional adjudication and interpretation, see Michael J. Perry, "The Legitimacy of Particular Conceptions of Constitutional Interpretation," *Virginia Law Review*, 77 (1991): 669–719. For Justice Scalia's views on originalism, see his "Originalism: The Lesser Evil,"*Cincinnati Law Review*, 57 (1989): 849–65, and *Matter of Interpretation: Federal Courts and the Law: An Essay* (Princeton, N.J.: Princeton Univ. Press, 1997).

28. See Smith, *Foreordained Failure*, 22–26.

29. See *Abbington School District v. Schempp*, 374 U.S. 203, 222 (1963) ("If either [its purpose or primary effect] is the advancement or inhibition of religion then the enactment exceeds the scope of legislative power as circumscribed by the Constitution.") and *Agostini v. Felton*, 521 U.S. 203, 222–23 (1997) (". . . [w]e continue to ask whether the government acted with the purpose. . . and . . . the 'effect' of advancing or inhibiting religion.")

30. *Barron v. Baltimore*, 32 U.S. 243 (1833).

31. *U. S. Constitution*, Amendment XIV, sec. 1 (emphasis added).

32. See Richard C. Cortner, *The Supreme Court and the Second Bill of Rights* (Madison, Wis.: Univ. of Wisconsin Press, 1981).

33. *Cantwell v. Connecticut*, 310 U.S. 296 (1940), and *Everson v. Board of Education*, 330 U.S. 1 (1947).

34. Michael A. Paulsen, "Religion, Equality, and the Constitution: An Equal Protection Approach to Establishment Clause Adjudication,"*Notre Dame Law Review*, 61 (1986): 311, 322–23; Smith, *Foreordained Failure*, 49–50; and Conkle, *Constitutional Law*, 23–25.

35. *Bill of Rights*, 33–34.

36. McConnell et al., *Religion and the Constitution*, 64. Because of the public's acceptance of the many Supreme Court decisions that states may not violate the religion clauses, Frederick M. Gedicks argues that "the very idea that it [establishment clause] might permit a classic state-established church is simply unthinkable" and would produce a "gag reflex." "The Establishment Clause Gag Reflex,"*Brigham Young University Law Review*, 2004 (2004): 999.

37. Jesse R. Merriam, "Finding a Ceiling in a Circular Room: Locke v. Davey, Federalism, and Religious Neutrality,"*Temple Political & Civil Rights Law Review*, 16 (Fall 2006): 129. Also, see Steven K. Green, "'Bad History': The Lure of History in Establishment Clause Adjudication,"*Notre Dame Law Review*, 81 (June 2006): 1717, 1751–52.

38. See Mark D. Rosen, "Establishment, Expressivism, and Federalism,"*Chicago-Kent Law Review*, 78 (2003): 669–716; Duncan, "Subsidiarity and Religious Establishments . . .," 129–33; and Schragger, "The Role of the Local . . .," generally. For a critical assessment of the argument for a relaxed application of the establishment clause to the states, see Steven H. Shiffrin, "Liberalism and the Establishment Clause,"*Chicago-Kent Law Review*, 78 (2003): 717–28.

39. 42 U.S.C. sec. 2000 bb (1993).

40. The key part of the statute states that "[g]overnment shall not substantially burden a person's exercise of religion, even if the burden results from a rule of general applicability," unless it can show that the restriction "(1) is in furtherance of a compelling governmental interest; and (2) is the least restrictive means of furthering that compelling governmental interest." 42 U.S.C. sec. 2000 bb (1993). At least as applied to state laws, the RFRA was

declared unconstitutional by the Supreme Court in *City of Boerne v. Flores*, 521 U.S. 507 (1997), but not on the grounds that it violated either of the religion clauses. For the argument that any federal RFRA violates the original meaning of the establishment clause, see Jed Rubenfeld, "Antidisestablishmentarianism: Why RFRA Really Was Unconstitutional,"*Michigan Law Review*, 95 (August 1997): 2347–84. Also, see Kurt Lash, "Power and the Subject of Religion,"*Ohio State Law Journal*, 59 (1998): 1069–1154, and Bybee, "Taking Liberties . . .," 1539–1633.

41. On this point, see Thomas C. Berg, "Religion Clause Anti-Theories,"*Notre Dame Law Review*, 72 (1997): 715, fn 94 ("Exemptions from federal laws are perfectly consistent with the federalist account of the Religion Clauses. It is not immediately clear how a decision by the federal government to refrain from interfering with religious conscience through one of its own laws would trespass on the states' power to regulate religion through their laws."). Cf. Kurt Lash, "Power and the Subject of Religion," 1110–16.

42. This is so mainly because most church-state cases deal with issues in education, which is primarily controlled by state and local governments. See Lupu and Tuttle, "Federalism and Faith," 52. According to Berg, "Religion Clause Anti-Theories," 712, fn 81, in the ten terms of the Supreme Court from 1985 to 1995, a little more than sixty percent of the Court's religion clauses decisions involved state actions.

43. Steven K. Green, "Religion Clause Federalism: State Flexibility over Religious Matters and the 'One-Way Ratchet',"*Emory Law Journal*, 56 (2006): 107, 112–13.

44. See, e.g., Donald L. Drakeman, *Church, State, and Original Intent* (New York: Cambridge Univ. Press, 2010), 229–49; Thomas J. Curry, *Farewell to Christendom: The Future of Church and State in America* (New York: Oxford Univ. Press, 2001), 43; and Noah Feldman, "The Intellectual Origins of the Establishment Clause,"*New York University Law Review*, 77 (May 2002): 346, 407.

45. *Foreordained Failure*, 17–18 (emphasis added).

46. Although he does not mention Smith by name, Thomas Curry, in a paragraph indicting "Law Office history," condemns specifically "the tendency to posit hypotheses and then proceed to act as if they were sustained by historical evidence." One example that he gives of this tendency is the contention that "the First Amendment deprived the federal government of power in religious matters because Americans wanted the states to have power over religion. . . ."*Farewell to Christendom*, 119–20, n. 29.

47. This problem, of course, is avoided with the dualistic interpretation explained earlier. See above, p. 2. In other words, if the establishment clause has federalist meaning and the free exercise clause has normative meaning, then it can logically be said that the religion clauses have both normative and federalist meaning.

48. On this point, see Berg, "Religion Clause Anti-Theories," 712–13.

49. See below, pp. 56, 103, 127–30, 141–43.

50. Another example that illustrates the difference between the federalist and normative interpretations of the religion clauses, but that is somewhat more questionable than the one given above, is a federal law requiring states to grant religion-based exemptions from valid, secular, and generally applicable laws. As explained earlier (see above, p. 7), some proponents of a jurisdictional or federalist interpretation of the religion clauses contend that such a federal law is unconstitutional. Would such a law violate the substantive or normative interpretation of the religion clauses explained in the text above? Most scholars think not, but, in my opinion, it depends on whether such a law is categorized as one associated with traditional establishments of religion, i.e., is one that favors or disfavors a specific religion or a specific religious belief or practice. For the argument that such a law should not be categorized as one characteristic of religious establishments, see Douglas Laycock, "Regulatory Exemptions of Religious Behavior and the Original Understanding of the Establishment Clause,"*Notre Dame Law Review*, 81 (2006): 1793–1842.

51. For a detailed explanation of the "power theory" of the First Amendment, including the religion clauses, see Jay S. Bybee, "Common Ground: Robert Jackson, Antonin Scalia, and a Power Theory of the First Amendment,"*Tulane Law Review*, 75 (Dec. 2000): 314–36.

52. For an elaboration of this point, see Curry, *The First Freedoms,* 216–17. Also, see Lash, "Power and the Subject of Religion," 1106, and "Two Movements of a Constitutional Symphony," 496.

Chapter Two

Clarification of the Issue

Steven D. Smith is the scholar most responsible for raising and framing the question of whether the religion clauses were originally meant to express a principled position on the proper relationship between government and religion.[1] The terms that he used for the opposing answers to this question were "substantive" (yes) and "jurisdictional" (no). Most other scholars who have "joined the fray" have accepted this terminology.

Recently, however, a few scholars have begun to question whether the words "substantive" and "jurisdictional" are the best labels for the two different ways of interpreting the religion clauses. They suggest that the terms do not work to distinguish clearly between the two different interpretations that Smith and others seem to be debating.[2] Moreover, in 2006, Smith himself published an essay that reflects at some length on how to distinguish a substantive from a jurisdictional interpretation of the religion clauses.[3] In addition to the question of whether "substantive" and "jurisdictional" are the best words to use to describe the opposing interpretations of the clauses, the scholarly debate has raised another question: what kinds of federal laws would be prohibited by a jurisdictional or states' right interpretation of those clauses? Would it be any kind of law that legislates, at least directly, on religion, or would it be, more narrowly, only certain kinds of laws that do so?

This chapter addresses these questions. It argues that the best terms for the different interpretations of the religion clauses are not "substantive" and "jurisdictional," but "normative" and "federalist." It also shows that scholars who favor the jurisdictional or federalist interpretation are divided, if not confused, on what kinds of laws such an interpretation would prevent Congress from passing.

I. THE ORIGIN OF THE "SUBSTANTIVE" VERSUS "JURISDICTIONAL" TERMINOLOGY

Early on in his book, *Foreordained Failure*, Smith writes, ". . . [T]he religion clauses were purely *jurisdictional* in nature; they did not adopt any *substantive* right or principle of religious freedom."[4] To explain these two terms, he distinguishes between two kinds of questions. The first kind he calls a "first-order or substantive" question. Essentially it asks, what is "the proper relationship between government and religion"? Smith then gives some examples of this kind of "substantive" question: "Should government establish one religion as the official state religion? Should the state subsidize a religion? Should it support all religions . . . on equal terms?. . . ." Answers to such questions, he writes, are "substantive" in nature, because they would state a "principle or theory of religious liberty." The religion clauses, therefore, have substantive meaning if originally they were meant to answer such substantive questions.[5]

The second kind of question Smith calls the "jurisdiction question." He explains it to be "one of governmental organization, or of the allocation of jurisdiction. Which level of government, state or national, should be responsible for addressing the first-order [substantive] question?"[6] Any answer to this question would not state or even imply any position on the proper relationship between religion and government; it would simply identify the level or part of government responsible for determining what the relationship between religion and government should be. The religion clauses, therefore, have purely jurisdictional meaning if they were originally meant to assign jurisdiction over substantive religious questions to the state governments.[7]

Smith explains this difference between a substantive and a jurisdictional constitutional provision in another way. If a provision says that the government should not do X, it could be, he says, for one of two different reasons. It could be because doing so would violate some moral right or norm, or it could be because some other level of government should have responsibility for doing X or at least deciding whether to do it. A provision preventing X is substantive if the reason for it is of the former kind, whereas it is jurisdictional if the reason for it is of the latter kind.[8]

Smith, of course, argues that the religion clauses have *only* jurisdictional meaning. He writes, "They were . . . simply an assignment of jurisdiction over matters of religion to the states—no more, no less. Consequently, perverse though it seems, the religion clauses simply do not speak to the substantive questions of religious freedom."[9] Later, he says, "The religion clauses kept the national government out of religion not because government support for religion was generally regarded as improper . . . but rather because the religion question was within the jurisdiction of the states." He concludes, therefore, that "it is futile to try to extrapolate or reconstruct a principle or theory of religious liberty from the original meaning of the religion clauses."[10]

II. THE PROBLEM WITH THE WORD "SUBSTANTIVE"

Smith's initial explanation of the difference between a substantive and a jurisdictional interpretation of the religion clauses seems to make perfectly good sense, but after a few pages he complicates his explanation. He writes that a constitutional provision can impose "a *substantive* restriction on one level or branch of government as a means of assigning *jurisdiction* over a subject-matter to another level of branch of government."[11] In his 2006 essay, Smith succinctly repeats this point: ". . . [A] jurisdictional provision will have substantive content and will impose substantive restrictions."[12] Regarding the religion clauses, he says, "Indeed, it seems undeniable that the religion clauses *did* have substantive content. Those clauses surely prevented the national government from establishing an official national church . . . or from doing whatever amounted to 'prohibiting the free exercise [of religion].'"[13]

How can this be? Can constitutional provisions, like the religion clauses, be both substantive and jurisdictional (non-substantive) at the same time? The only way to make sense of Smith's apparently contradictory assertions is to realize that in the various sentences quoted above "substantive" has two different meanings. When Smith says that the religion clauses have no substantive content, he is saying that they do not express a normative position (first meaning) on church-state issues; whereas when he says they do have substantive content, he is saying that they limit what the government can do in a certain area, domain, or subject-matter (second meaning), such as church-state relations. Thus, even a constitutional limitation on government that is purely jurisdictional in nature necessarily has substantive content—in the second sense of the word "substantive"—because it delimits a substantive domain or subject matter over which the government has no jurisdiction. If, however, such a delimitation "supplies or implies any answer to the 'substantive' [in the first sense of the word] questions that arise within those domains," then it cannot be a jurisdictional provision.[14] In other words, in Smith's analysis, "jurisdictional" contrasts only with the first meaning of "substantive," and the debate regarding the religion clauses is whether their meaning is jurisdictional or substantive in the first sense of the word.

Given the fact, however, that "substantive" has or can easily be given two different meanings, its use is confusing and, thus, problematic.[15] It would appear advisable for scholars to use some other word for what Smith and others had in mind when they first began to write about a substantive (versus a jurisdictional) interpretation of the religion clauses. What should that word be? In his 2006 essay, Smith suggests that the word "nonjurisdictional" be used.[16] This word, however, will not do, simply because it is too vague; it fails to indicate the ethical or principled nature of the "substantive" interpretation of the religion clauses as it was first explained by Smith. To highlight this crucial dimension, I suggest that the word "normative" be substituted for the word "substantive," and in the rest of this book I will generally use that word instead of "substantive."

One might ask, instead of "substantive" or "normative," why not call the non-jurisdictional interpretation of the religion clauses the "individual rights" interpretation? This, in fact, is a reasonable suggestion—for two reasons. First, the phrase "individual rights" clearly and sharply contrasts with "states' rights," which, according to the jurisdictional interpretation of the clauses, is what the religion clauses were intended to protect. Second, many Americans believe that religious liberty is a natural right that all humans possess and that should not be violated by any government. Therefore, it can logically be argued that the crucial issue raised by Steven Smith and addressed in this book is whether the religion clauses were intended to protect a natural right of individuals (religious liberty) or the right of states (as opposed to the national government) to legislate on the subject of religion.

Although this is a logical way of stating the issue, it is perhaps not the best way of doing so. Why? Because an individual rights interpretation is not the only possible normative interpretation of the clauses. There may have been other ethical or principled reasons for the clauses besides protecting an individual right. For example, the clauses may have been adopted to maintain unity and peace in America by preventing conflict among its competing religious groups.[17] Nevertheless, if the historical evidence actually shows that the primary purpose of the religion clauses was to protect the individual right of conscience, then it would be perfectly legitimate to refer to the individual rights, as opposed to states' rights, interpretation of the religion clauses.

III. THE PROBLEM WITH THE WORD "JURISDICTIONAL"

What about the jurisdictional side of the debate? Does it, like the substantive side, require some clarification and rephrasing? The answer is, yes. In fact, what is meant be a jurisdictional interpretation of the religion clauses is even more problematic than what is meant by a substantive interpretation. Not surprisingly, therefore, in his 2006 article, Steven Smith states that although there is "some genuine disagreement" between himself and his critics, "much of the debate reflects misunderstanding about what the jurisdictional interpretation actually holds. At least some of those misunderstandings may trace back to slipperiness in the very concept of 'jurisdiction.'"[18]

The first problem is that the word "jurisdictional," like the word "substantive," has or can easily be given two meanings. The first is the meaning that Smith and his allies give to the word. "Jurisdictional," they say, pertains to the question, which level of government—national or state—should have the authority to legislate on the subject or domain of religion? They *assume*, in other words, that if early Americans did not want the national government to have the power to legislate on religion, it was because they wanted the states to have that power. Thus, Smith writes, "The enactors of those [religion] clauses were not adding new substantive [normative] rights or principles to the Constitution; rather, they were merely reiterating what they had asserted all along—. . . that the national government had no power over religion *because the regulation of religion was within the sole jurisdiction of the states*."[19] Another scholar who makes the same assumption is Akhil Amar, who argues that the entire First Amendment was mainly about protecting state authority from federal interference. He does so partially because the language of the First Amendment ("Congress shall make no law") is different from that of the other ten amendments; according to Amar, it is a denial of Congressional jurisdiction and a reservation of state jurisdiction.[20]

Although it is certainly correct to say that the First Amendment denies Congress jurisdiction over certain subjects, it does not follow nor should one assume, as Smith and Amar do, that the jurisdiction was denied in order to give it to the states rather than for normative reasons. These scholars probably make such an assumption because they also assume that it was the states that created or established the Constitution and the resulting national government. When new constitutions and governments are established, however, they are not always or necessarily established by existing states. They can be and have been established by "the people," as were the state governments themselves after the American colonists declared their independence from England. *Moreover, in 1787, many Americans, especially Anti-federalists, thought that the proposed new national government was being created by individuals in a state of nature, and not by the states.*[21] If that were the case, then according to the "contract" theory of government, which was very influential in early America, the people creating the new national government had the right to determine, through a constitution, what powers that government would and would not have.[22] In short, they had the right to determine the subjects or domains over which it would have authority, i.e., its *jurisdiction.*

If, then, the new national government outlined by the Constitution of 1787 was widely understood as being created by the people collectively, then one cannot assume that it was denied jurisdiction over certain subjects or domains because the existing states wanted to keep jurisdiction over those subjects/domains for themselves. The *people* may have denied it jurisdiction for *normative* reasons. They may have thought that no government anywhere should be able to pass certain kinds of laws or that the government being created should not be able to do so for normative reasons peculiar to that society. Indeed, as will be seen, it was precisely for normative reasons that the Anti-federalists argued that a bill of rights needed to be added to the Constitution of 1787.[23]

In summary, a constitutional provision may deny a government *jurisdiction* over a certain subject/domain for two entirely different reasons—to protect states' rights *or* to protect a natural right, such as religious freedom, or for some other ethical or normative reason. When a government, therefore, is denied jurisdiction over a subject/domain, one cannot simply assume that it is for one or the other reason. Stated differently, the point is that even when a constitutional provision, for normative reasons, prevents the government from passing certain kinds of laws, it is still denying the government jurisdiction over those kinds of laws. Therefore, as a way of describing one side of the debate addressed in this book, "jurisdictional" is just as ambiguous and problematic as is "substantive" and should not be used.

Instead, I propose that "federalist" be used as the term for the interpretation of the religion clauses that is favored by Smith and his allies. This is an appropriate word to use because "federalism" is the theory that within a given society the powers of government should be divided between a central government and several regional governments or states. To give, therefore, a "federalist interpretation" to a constitutional provision that denies certain power to the central government is simply to say that the power was denied because it was one reserved to the states. Although the phrase "states' rights" works just as well as the word "federalist," because I propose that one word—"normative"—be used for the interpretation of the religion clauses that Smith and his allies challenge, for reasons of parallelism I propose that one word—"federalist"—be used for the interpretation of those clauses that Smith favors.[24]

Given the preceding analysis, one point stands out in importance. What determines whether a constitutional provision is substantive or jurisdictional (using Smith's terms here) is not whether it withholds a certain area, domain, or subject matter from the legislative authority of the national government. Rather the crucial factor is the *reason* for the provision or the withholding. Even if the First Amendment had been written, "Congress shall make no laws touching religion," that would not mean that it was intended to protect states' rights.[25] Rather, the crucial question would be *why* that provision was adopted. Was it intended to express a normative position on what the federal government's policy toward religion should be OR to express the position that it would simply be better if state governments were to decide how religion should be treated by government.[26] Any abbreviated way of stating this question should be worded so that it gets at this crucial distinction between two kinds of reasons for a constitutional provision, and asking if the religion clauses are "normative" or "federalist" does this much better than asking if they are "substantive" or "jurisdictional."

Although the *what* of a constitutional limitation by itself cannot tell us its *why*, and thus whether it is normative or federalist in nature, it does not follow that the way a constitutional limitation is worded is completely irrelevant to that issue. By itself, a provision's wording can sometimes imply what the reason for it is and, thus, whether it is normative or federalist in nature. Consider, for example, two provisions. One denies a government power over religion, and the other denies it the power to prohibit the free exercise of religion. Kent Greenawalt argues that because of its wording alone the free exercise clause appears to be a normative provision. He notes that its language is "distinctly one-sided," in that it forbids only laws that *prohibit* the free exercise of religion and not laws that *protect* free exercise.[27] In other words, the clause is worded too narrowly to be a federalist provision. If it were meant to be such a provision, then why did the framers deny the national government jurisdiction over only laws prohibiting the free exercise and not laws protecting the free exercise of religion? Why was the clause not worded to forbid laws in any way *relating to* the free exercise of religion? The fact that the clause forbids only laws prohibiting religion's free exercise, therefore, strongly implies that the reason such laws were forbidden is because they violate a moral right or principle and, thus, that the clause is normative in nature.[28] Nevertheless, even in this case, the important question is not what the free exercise clause prohibits, but why it prohibits it, and the normative implication of its wording might be overcome if there were enough historical evidence to support a states' rights interpretation of the clause.

In contrast to the wording of the free exercise clause, the "no law respecting" wording of the establishment clause makes it amenable to a federalist interpretation. It can legitimately be read as saying that central government should not take a normative position, pro or con, on establishments of religion, but should leave it to the states to do that.[29] Of course, whether the framers/ratifiers of the establishment clause understood it that way remains to be seen. Although its wording is broad enough to warrant its being given a federalist interpretation, early Americans may have understood it as preventing Congress from establishing a national religion or anything approaching it because they believed that religious establishments inevitably pose a threat to religious freedom.[30] In short, without evidence beyond its wording, one cannot conclude that the establishment clause was intended to protect states' rights.

The evidence that is needed, moreover, must pertain to *why* the clause was adopted. Even if it indicates that the clause was adopted to prevent a national establishment of religion, that would not be enough to make it a normative anti-establishment provision. After all, members of Congress who approved of religious establishments and wanted to protect the ones in their state, may well have opposed a national establishment, not because they disapproved of all establishments, but because any such establishment might not have been to their liking and might have undercut their own state's establishment.[31] Is this the reason early Americans gave for the establishment clause?

IV. MUST THE RELIGION CLAUSES BE EITHER NORMATIVE OR FEDERALIST?

Although it is important to distinguish clearly between the two possible interpretations of the religion clauses, does it follow that only one of them is correct? Or could the clauses have both normative and federalist meanings?

In at least one way, it is theoretically possible that they could. Because there are two religion clauses, it is certainly possible that one of them could have a normative meaning and the other a federalist meaning. Moreover, as noted in chapter one, this is the way some scholars interpret the clauses. They say that the free exercise clause has a normative meaning and the establishment clause a federalist meaning.[32] After all, they argue, many, if not most, early Americans believed strongly in both states' rights and individual rights, especially the right of conscience, and the two beliefs would seldom have to come into conflict. The *same* person could believe strongly in protecting religious liberty from federal laws (and thus want the free exercise clause) and yet also believe that each state should be allowed to determine for itself whether it would guarantee religious liberty and, if so, in what way and to what extent (and thus want the establishment clause to prevent federal laws interfering with those state laws).

Even if such a scenario were possible, was it likely to have happened? Steven Smith, of course, does not believe that the two clauses originally had separate meanings. Both were expressions of the states' right to legislate on religion. He says that the same arguments that support a states' right construction of the establishment clause also support such a construction of the free exercise clause. In other words, there were controversial issues relating to the free exercise clause as well as to the establishment clause, and early Americans could not have agreed on how to resolve either set of issues. Instead of trying to do so, therefore, the framers decided to let the states address them.[33]

Another reason for thinking that a dualistic understanding of the religion clauses would not likely have occurred is this: would persons who believed strongly in freedom of religion have wanted to prevent the federal government from protecting it from state laws that violated it? As will be seen in chapter five, in the First Congress the House of Representatives (but not the Senate) approved of an amendment to the Constitution that would have prevented states from violating religious liberty.[34] It hardly seems likely that the same House would have voted for an establishment clause that protected state laws that violated religious freedom. In short, although the free exercise clause originally may have been understood as a normative provision and the establishment clause as a federalist provision, there are at least two different reasons for thinking that they would not have been understood in that way. Only the historical evidence can tell us if the religion clauses originally had separate meanings.

Aside from the two religion clauses' having two different meanings, one normative and the other federalist, is there any other way that the religion clauses could be both normative and federalist? Could either of the religion clauses *by itself* or the clauses *collectively* have both a normative and a federalist meaning?

Some might argue that a federalist provision, i.e., one that assigns power over a certain subject to the states, is also normative because there is necessarily a moral reason for assigning that power to the states, namely, that state legislation on a given subject or on all subjects is likely to be better than federal legislation will be. More specifically, it is often argued that reserving either certain powers or as many powers as possible to state and/or local governments (and denying them to a central government) serves indirectly to protect individual natural rights—on the grounds that state and local governments are "closer" to the people and more responsive to their wishes than is a distant central government.[35]

By itself, however, the fact that a normative justification can be given for states' rights in general or a federal system of government is not enough to make a specific constitutional provision, like the religion clauses, a normative one. For that to be the case, the provision must meet the two conditions previously specified. It must take a position on a public policy issue and take it on the basis of some moral norm or principle. Thus, if the religion clauses were originally understood as expressing a normative position on the relationship between government and religion, they are normative in nature. If, on the other hand, they were passed simply to allow the states to determine what this relationship should be, then they are federalist and not normative, even if the decision to do so was based on the assumption that states will do a better job of legislating on religion than will the federal government.

Another scenario is one in which *some* early Americans understood the religion clauses as guaranteeing the individual right of religious freedom and *others* understood them as guaranteeing states' rights. In this case, however, one would not be justified in saying that the religion clauses originally had both normative and federalist meaning, because the number of persons having one interpretation would surely have been greater than the number having the other, and the interpretation with the "most votes" should be considered the authoritative interpretation of the religion clauses. Of course, it is technically possible that two interpretations could have been held by the same number of persons, more or less, but the chances of that having happened are so slim as to make the possibility irrelevant.

What about the establishment clause by itself? After all, several scholars contend that it was intended to prohibit religious establishments at the national level and to protect such establishments at the state level.[36] If that were the case, however, would it not mean that the clause was normatively schizophrenic? It would be saying simultaneously that religious establishments are both morally good (if at the state level) and morally bad (if at the national level). Surely few if any members of the First Congress would have had such a contradictory position.[37]

One scholar who appears to disagree is Kent Greenawalt. Although he concedes that the establishment clause is partially, if not primarily, normatively anti-establishment,[38] he argues that an establishment clause that was purely anti-establishment would have been unacceptable to those states that still had some elements of religious establishments, even though it would not have applied to them, because it would have implied that their state laws were morally wrong and given ammunition to the critics of those laws. He, thus, writes, "We need to understand the clause as one that people with opposing views about establishment could have endorsed. A clause that forbade establishment of a national religion *and* forbade the interference with state establishments meets this criterion."[39] The clear implication is that the establishment clause would not have passed had not a compromise been reached.

There are at least two problems with this argument. First, it assumes that persons in those New England states that had remnants of an establishment were in favor of establishments of religion and considered their laws on religion to constitute an establishment. As will be shown later, however, this is an incorrect assumption.[40] Second, even if some members of the First Congress thought that religious establishments were desirable, at least at the state level, and favored an amendment that would protect their states' "establishments," most other members are likely to have voted for the establishment clause because they believed that all religious establishments are bad. Unless there is some historical evidence to show that the members were about equally divided over establishments of religion and that a compromise was necessary in order to get the establishment clause passed, there is no reason to accept Greenawalt's interpretation of that clause. Although such a compromise could have occurred, whether there is any evidence that it actually did remains to be seen.

Another possibility is an establishment clause that prevented only a national establishment of religion, but prevented it for both normative and federalist reasons. In other words, Congressmen could have wanted such a clause because they thought a national religious establishment would threaten both individuals' freedom of religion as well as state laws on religion that would be different from a national religious establishment, and it would not matter whether those state laws established or disestablished a religion. Even persons from a state with a quasi-religious establishment could have opposed a national establishment because the religion it favored might be different from their states' favored religion.[41]

Even under this scenario, however, most Congressmen voting for the clause would have done so to protect religious freedom, and not to protect religious establishments in the states, because most of them were from states that for normative reasons, no longer had religious establishments. They would have had normative reasons, therefore, for being opposed to a national establishment because it would directly threaten religious freedom as well as indirectly threaten their states' disestablishments of religion. In short, even if some persons voted for the establishment clause to protect their state's religious establishment from a competing national establishment, the dominant reason for the clause would have been normative—to protect religious freedom.

There is, however, one way in which the establishment clause can be said to have had both a normative and a federalist meaning. Suppose that the establishment clause was clearly adopted and understood to prevent Congress from legislating *only* against existing state establishments of religion or their remnants.[42] If that were the case, would the clause be normative or federalist in nature or both? On the one hand, it would appear to be a normative provision. Because the clause's purpose is to protect the remnants of religious establishments that still existed in a few states, it expresses a normative position on the relationship between government and religion, namely, that either religion-in-general or a particular religion should be favored, encouraged, and promoted in some way by government or at least state governments. The establishment clause would be completely non-normative or federalist in nature only if it were intended to protect state laws on religion *regardless of what those laws were*, whether they were pro-or-anti-establishment of religion. In short, it would be truly federalist in nature only if its purpose were to protect states' rights as such and not a particular kind of state law or policy.

On the other hand, our hypothetical establishment clause could also be said to be federalist in nature. After all, its purpose is clearly not to prohibit Congress from establishing a religion on the grounds that such establishments are immoral. Moreover, even though its purpose is not to protect all state laws respecting religion, still because it was adopted to protect *some state laws or policies*, to that extent it could be said to be a federalist provision.

Even though an interpretation of the establishment clause that says it was intended to protect state establishments of religion can legitimately be viewed as either normative or federalist or both, in this book it will be categorized as a federalist interpretation—simply because it contrasts so clearly with the traditional, normative interpretation of the clause, whereby Congress is prohibited from doing anything like establishing a religion because that would threaten individuals' freedom of religion and the unity of the nation.

There may be other ways in which one or both of the religion clauses could have both normative and federalist meaning,[43] but at this point they are only possibilities. As stated before, whether an interpretation of those clauses is correct depends on whether it is supported by the historical evidence, and that has yet to be determined.

Finally, it should be noted that even if both religion clauses had only normative content, that would not mean that if Congress were to pass a law either "respecting an establishment of religion or prohibiting the free exercise thereof," the law could not be condemned on the grounds that it violates a right of states as well as a right of individuals.[44] If one assumes, as most early Americans surely did, that Congress has only those powers delegated to it, that all powers not delegated to it are reserved to the states, and that the power to pass laws "respecting an establishment of religion or prohibiting the free exercise thereof" is a power not delegated to Congress, then any exercise of that power by Congress can be condemned as a violation of states' rights. Moreover, one could even say that we know that such a power was not delegated to Congress because the First Amendment explicitly forbids Congress from exercising such a power.

This, however, does not warrant the conclusion that the religion clauses have federalist content. Even if most early Americans thought that certain kinds of federal laws dealing with religion violate states' rights, that alone tells us nothing about the reason for and thus the meaning of the religion clauses. *The validity of the argument that a federal law dealing with religion violates states' rights does not depend on the existence or meaning of the religion clauses. The argument could be made even if there were no religion clauses*. Therefore, even though the clauses deny Congress the power to pass certain kinds of laws, it does not follow that they do so in order to protect states' rights. In short, a federal law dealing with religion could be condemned both for violating the normative religion clauses in the First Amendment and for violating states' rights protected by the Tenth Amendment on the grounds that the power to pass such a law had never been granted to the national government.

V. THE DIFFERENT FEDERALIST INTERPRETATIONS OF THE RELIGION CLAUSES

Even if the word "federalist" were substituted for the word "jurisdictional," that would not eliminate all the confusion associated with the "jurisdictional" interpretation of the religion clauses. There would still remain the question of what kind of laws such an interpretation would prevent the national government from passing. The basic issue is whether a federalist interpretation of the clauses prohibits Congress from passing *all* laws dealing directly with religion or only *some* laws that do so. Many advocates of a federalist interpretation appear to take the position that the clauses prohibit Congress from legislating *in any way* on the subject of religion.[45] However, one can subscribe to a federalist interpretation of the religion clauses without subscribing to a no-power-over-religion interpretation.[46] There are at least two other, more limited federalist interpretations of the clauses.

A. Do the Clauses Constrain Federal Laws Applicable to Federal Domains?

The first alternative to the no-power-over-religion interpretation is one that says the clauses prohibit Congress from passing only laws that threaten or are inconsistent with the *states'* power over religion.[47] To understand the difference between this interpretation and the no-power interpretation, one must understand that not all laws on religion that Congress might pass would impact the lives of citizens within the states and thus have the potential to conflict with state powers and laws or infringe on states' rights. This is so because there are certain "federal domains" that do not fall at all under state control and for which Congress alone has the power to legislate, i.e., the national government itself, its diplomatic missions and personnel, the national military, the District of Columbia, and United States territories.[48]

Some early Americans, therefore, may have thought that from its inception the national government had the power to legislate on religion in the federal domains. They might have thought that Congress' power in this area, in contrast to its enumerated and limited powers, is inherent and plenary, and thus analogous to the inherent police powers of the state governments. Moreover, just as some early Americans thought the *states* had a duty to promote and regulate religion, they may have also thought that the *federal government* had a similar duty in the domains under its exclusive control.[49] Others, however, may have thought that even if Congress had a plenary power to legislate for the federal domains, that power needed to be limited, and they may have intended for the Bill of Rights (and the religion clauses) to do just that. Hence, the question: Does a federalist interpretation of the religion clauses prohibit Congress from legislating on religion in the federal domains?

The answer depends on which federalist interpretation one adopts. If one says that the religion clauses were meant to deny Congress all power to legislate on religion, then they would prevent Congress from legislating in any way on religion, even in the various federal domains. Thus, for example, Congress could not pass laws prohibiting or protecting religious freedom in the territories, or laws favoring or disfavoring particular religions or religion in general in the territories. On the other hand, if one says that the clauses were meant to prohibit Congress from legislating on religion only to the extent that such legislation threatens or conflicts with the states' traditional power over religion, then Congress would be free to legislate as it sees fit with respect to religion in the federal domains. It could even prohibit certain religions or establish a religion.[50]

Which is it? Do the religion clauses prevent Congress from passing any laws on the subject of religion, including laws applicable to the federal domains, or only laws that threaten or conflict with state laws on religion?

Looking at these two alternatives strictly from the perspective of federalism or states' rights, one would think that the second alternative (no laws that threaten state laws) makes the more sense. After all, if the only purpose of the clauses is to protect states' rights, there would be no reason to deny the national government power to legislate on religion in domains under its exclusive control, for its exercise of such power would not threaten or conflict with the states' control of religion within their borders. This second interpretation, however, would allow the national government to pass laws discriminating for or against certain religions, at least in its own domains, and even the strongest advocate of a federalist interpretation of the religion clauses might find it difficult to accept that the religion clauses allowed such laws to be passed.[51] Moreover, the text supports the first interpretation of the clauses more than it supports the second. "That is because nothing in the clauses themselves indicates that they are irrelevant for federal domains."[52]

On the other hand, if the first or "no power over religion" interpretation is accepted, it would logically imply that the religion clauses were originally understood as having some normative content, at least when they were being used to challenge a federal law that applied only to persons or groups within the federal domains. What, other than a normative reason, could be the justification for limiting the federal government's power over religion in its own domain? Given the "no power over religion" interpretation, therefore, the religion clauses could have both a normative meaning (when used to protect persons in the federal domains) and a federalist meaning (when used to protect states' rights). In both cases, the clauses would prohibit all federal laws on the subject of religion, but would do so for quite different reasons.[53]

On this issue of whether the religion clauses prohibit all federal laws pertaining to religion or only those that would threaten the states' control over religion, federalist interpreters of the religion clauses have not taken a clear and consistent position. Consider the case of Steven Smith, the leading proponent of a federalist interpretation. At the beginning of his book, *Foreordained Failure*, he writes, "The religion clauses were not a hybrid creation—part federalism, part substantive right. They were, rather simply an assignment of jurisdiction over matters of religion to the states—no more, no less."[54] Such an explanation of the clauses clearly implies that the religion clauses were intended to deny the national government *all* power over religion.

Later, Smith contends that the drafters of the Bill of Rights were oblivious to the fact that Congress would have to legislate for the federal domains and, thus, did not consider and take a position on the issue of whether there were certain kinds of laws for those domains that it could not pass.[55] He gives two reasons for their oversight. First, they were "worried about national power vis-à-vis *the states*; Congress's power to regulate religion in the territories was not their concern." Second, they were apathetic about the Bill of Rights generally because they believed they had more important business to attend to.[56] In any case, Smith concludes: "The religion clauses were understood as a federalist measure, not as the enactment of any substantive principle of religious freedom. Consequently, when later forced to deal with issues of religion in an area in which it *did* have jurisdiction, Congress acted in an ad hoc manner dictated by the particular circumstances; it did not seem to regard itself as being legally constrained by any substantive principle of religious freedom."[57] If that were the case, however, it would mean that Congress thought that it *could* legislate on religion in the federal domains—in spite of the religion clauses and regardless of whether they were normative or federalist in content.

A few pages later Smith explicitly takes this position. Here, contrary to his earlier position, he suggests that the framers of the religion clauses did address the issue of whether the federal government could legislate on the subject of religion in its domains. He notes that the framers considered but ultimately rejected a proposed amendment that would have clearly stated that Congress could not legislate on the subject of religion.[58] Smith says that when the First Congress replaced this proposed wording with the religion clauses as we know them, it was replacing "a *general disclaimer of jurisdiction* over religion" with "a more limited or *partial disclaimer of jurisdiction* over religion."[59] He then explains why it did this: "Even though the religion question was regarded as one for the states rather than the national government to address, . . . *reflection might have made it clear* that the national government would not be able to avoid matters of religion altogether."[60] As examples of legislation that the First Congress might not have wanted to prohibit, Smith mentions legislation on religion in the federal territories and its decision to appoint chaplains for each of its houses.[61] In short, after initially implying otherwise, Smith eventually concludes that the religion clauses do not preclude all federal laws on religion but only those that might threaten or be inconsistent with state laws on religion.

In his 2006 article, however, Smith takes a different position on the issue of which federalist interpretation of the religion clauses he favors; he contends that it does not matter. He writes, "It is an interesting question, though likely one for which no definitive answer is possible. For present purposes, . . . the crucial point is that either answer is perfectly compatible with the basic position being argued for here."[62] Then, after making a good argument for both interpretations—no-power-over-religion and no-power-over-religion-except-in-the-federal-domains—he repeats that either one is acceptable. How so? Because under neither interpretation, he says, were the religion clauses "meant to constrain the national government, even in the domain in which it *did* have authority to act, by adopting some right or principle of religious freedom," and under both interpretations the clauses were "merely intended to deprive the national government of jurisdiction over the subject (either categorically or vis-á-vis the states)."[63]

Unfortunately, Smith's position here will not do for two reasons. First, for persons in the federal domains, it certainly does matter whether the federal government can legislate on religion. Second, as explained earlier, if the religion clauses were intended to deprive Congress of *all* power over religion, even in the federal domains, such a complete deprivation of power can not be explained on the grounds of states' rights or federalism. After all, the federal government's regulation of religion in the federal domains poses no threat to the states' regulation of religion within their borders. If, therefore, the religion clauses were meant to prevent the federal government from legislating on religion in the federal domains, the only reason for their doing so would have been a normative one, e.g., to protect religious freedom. Logically, therefore, neither Smith nor anyone else can avoid having to choose between the no-power-over-religion interpretation and the partial-power-over-religion interpretation of the religion clauses.

Kurt Lash is another scholar who struggles to maintain a clear and consistent position on which federalist interpretation of the religion clauses he favors. Like Smith, he begins by defending the position that as a result of the First and Tenth Amendments, "*all power over the subject of religion* was denied to the federal government and reserved to the states. . . ."[64] Lash, however, admits that after the adoption of the religion clauses "the federal government involved itself with religion and religious exercise in a variety of ways" and that this raises a question about the validity of the no-power-over-religion interpretation of the religion clauses.[65] How does he respond? He argues that those acts should "be presumed to be *inconsistent* with the most plausible understanding" of the clauses—the no-power-over-religion understanding—"unless such unambiguous activity is so pervasive and consistent that it overcomes the most plausible understanding. . . . In other words, sporadic unambiguous action inconsistent with the no power theory will be presumed to be *in violation* of the most plausible interpretation" of the religion clauses.[66] Then, Lash reviews the federal government's actions involving religion in the federal domains after 1791 and concludes that, with one exception, they "are ambiguous in regard to their use of religion either as a means or an end" and "do not clearly contradict the conclusions . . . that Congress had neither express power over religion, nor the option of using religion as a means to advancing an enumerated end."[67] The one exception—the appointment of military and congressional chaplains—Lash concludes was unconstitutional.[68]

Although one might very well quarrel with Lash's characterization of the federal government's early dealings with religion as ambiguous and sporadic, he does try to be consistent in arguing for the no-power-over-religion interpretation of the religion clauses. Even on this score, however, he falters when he introduces and relies on other grounds for dismissing the evidence inconsistent with the no power interpretation of the religion clauses. For example, he says that many of the legislators who voted for federal laws promoting religion in the federal domains may have done so because they believed that "government promotion of religion was a good thing." Although such persons, he explains, would have "voted for the religion clauses in order to protect the autonomy of the states," they "might be open to some degree of federal promotion of religion as long as the federal activity did not imply that the federal government had power to interfere with state regulation of religion."[69] Well, yes, but if that is the way the framers understood them, then the religion clauses do *not* stand for the proposition that Congress cannot legislate on religion in the federal domains.

In summary, in explaining which federalist interpretation of the religion clauses they favor, both Smith and Lash are ambiguous, if not inconsistent.

B. Does a Federalist Interpretation of the Religion Clauses Prohibit *All* Federal Laws on Religion Applicable to the States?

To repeat—the general issue raised by a federalist interpretation of the religion clauses is whether they prohibit all or only certain kinds of laws pertaining directly to religion. As we have seen, one reason this is an issue is the fact that some federal laws—those applying to the federal domains—do not threaten state powers or laws. Are they constrained by the religion clauses? This general issue, however, would still exist even if our analysis were limited to national laws applying to persons/groups in the states. After all, the basic question a federalist interpretation must answer is what kinds of laws pertaining to religion did the framers/ratifiers of the religion clauses think that only the states, and not the national government, should be able to pass. Do the clauses prohibit *all* or only *some* laws dealing directly and explicitly with religion? Smith phrases the issue as follows: ". . . [W]as the disclaimer of national power over religion total, or merely partial?"[70]

The position taken by most federalist scholars is that the clauses were meant to prevent Congress from passing any law dealing directly with religion.[71] If, however, that is what they were intended to do, one would also think that the religion clauses would have been worded so as to make that intention perfectly clear, but they were not.[72] Instead, the religion clauses prevent only laws "respecting an establishment of religion, or prohibiting the free exercise of thereof."[73] Are laws "respecting an establishment of religion" the same as laws "respecting religion"? Although early Americans may have thought so, if they did, then why did the framers add the free exercise clause? It was not needed. Moreover, the free exercise clause, in contrast to the establishment clause, is worded in a one-sided way. It does not prohibit all laws "respecting" the free exercise of religion, but only laws that "prohibit" its free exercise. In short, the wording of the religion clauses clearly implies that it was not all laws on religion that Congress could not pass, but only laws that deal with religion in certain specific ways.[74]

This begs the crucial question: if the religion clauses are not a complete denial of federal power over religion, then what kinds of laws touching religion do they allow Congress to pass and what kinds can only the states pass? Steven Smith gives two different answers to this question, and both are extremely brief and unsatisfactory. In *Foreordained Failure*, his answer is that the religion clauses constitute a "partial disclaimer of jurisdiction over religion." "This solution would effectively assign to the states the *major, controversial* issues of religion—issues regarding the 'establishment' and regulation of religion—and it would defer the residual, nonassignable issues of religion to the future."[75] Apparently, Smith believes that the religion clauses do not prohibit Congress from passing all laws touching religion, but only laws that address "the major, controversial issues of religion."[76] And what kinds of laws might the framers have considered minor and uncontroversial and, thus, within Congress' power to pass? The only example that Smith gives is the authorization of Thanksgiving proclamations.[77]

In his 2006 article, however, Smith appears to retreat from his partial-jurisdiction-over-religion interpretation of the religion clauses because he refuses to take a clear position on the issue. He simply says that it is not clear what the framers intended and that "either choice [complete or partial disclaimer] is compatible with the basic claim of the jurisdictional interpretation."[78] Later he continues his "fence-sitting" when he says that "the core purpose of the Establishment Clause was to confirm that jurisdiction over religion—*or at least over the central concerns of religious establishment and free exercise of religion*—would remain with the states."[79] In short, on the rather important issue of what kind of laws the religion clauses prohibit, Smith is equivocal.

As we have seen, one way of interpreting the religion clauses is to say that the establishment clause is federalist in meaning and the free exercise clause is normative in meaning. Under such an interpretation, Congress could not prohibit the free exercise of religion in either the states or the federal domains, but could establish a religion in the federal domains (unless one assumes that religious establishments necessarily violate the free exercise of religion).[80] What kinds of federal laws dealing with religion and applying to persons in the states, however, would a federalist interpretation of the establishment clause prevent? Clearly Congress could not pass laws respecting an establishment of religion, but, to repeat, are such laws the same as laws respecting religion? If not, what constitutes a law "respecting an establishment of religion"?[81] Does the establishment clause prohibit all laws on religion or only those that address major, controversial religious issues? Does it prohibit, as Justice Thomas claims, only laws that aim to eliminate or weaken state laws establishing or promoting religion in non-coercive ways, or does it also prohibit laws that threaten or weaken state laws *disestablishing* religion? In either case, does it prohibit only federal laws that are directly aimed at certain state laws, or does it also prohibit federal laws that only indirectly threaten state laws simply by virtue of being different from those state laws, e.g., a federal law that favors a particular church that is different from the church favored by a state?

What about a federal law that in some way protects religious freedom in the states, e.g., a statute that guarantees a general right to religion-based exemptions from valid state laws or a treaty that prohibits discrimination against members of a certain religious minority in the states? If the establishment clause prohibits any and all laws on religion, then even a federal law protecting religious freedom in the states would probably be unconstitutional.[82] If the clause prohibits only major, controversial laws on religion or laws respecting establishments of religion, including those in the states, then it is simply not clear whether a federal law protecting religious freedom would be constitutional.[83]

In summary, what the various federalist scholars are proposing as an alternative to the traditional, normative interpretation of the religion clauses is conceptually confusing. Although all of them agree that the religion clauses were intended to protect states' rights to some degree and in some way, they do not agree on what that degree or way is. There is, thus, more than one possible federalist interpretation. Which one should replace the traditional normative interpretation of the clauses?

If scholars who favor a federalist interpretation of the religion clauses believe that the answer to this question should be based on the original meaning of the clauses (and most, if not all, of them do), then the question cannot be answered solely on the basis of logic or the text of the religion clauses. Logic and text give us only "possibilities"—interpretations that are plausible. Consider, for example, Smith's defense of his "partial disclaimer of jurisdiction" interpretation of the clauses. He writes that "in the historical context such a course might have seemed sensible and attractive and that if Congress *had* made a decision in favor of a partial disclaimer of jurisdiction, the religion clauses as adopted would have been a suitable way of expressing that decision."[84] Well, yes, but this hardly amounts to a convincing conclusion about the original meaning of the clauses. All that can be said about such an interpretation is that it is a plausible possibility. More is needed, and that "more" is historical evidence that would support one federalist interpretation over the others.

On the other hand, saying that whichever federalist interpretation one chooses should be dictated by historical evidence assumes that there is a fairly significant amount of historical evidence supporting *any* kind of federalist interpretation of the religion clauses. If there is no or very little such evidence, and most, if not all, of the evidence supports a normative interpretation of the clauses, then the issue of which federalist interpretation of the religion clauses should replace the traditional, normative interpretation becomes moot, for the answer is that none of them should.

NOTES

1. See his *Foreordained Failure: The Quest for a Constitutional Principle of Religious Freedom* (New York: Oxford Univ. Press, 1995).
2. See, e.g., Kent Greenawalt, "Common Sense about Original and Subsequent Understandings of the Religion Clauses,"*Univ. of Pennsylvania Journal of Constitutional Law*, 8 (2006): 479–512.
3. "The Jurisdictional Establishment Clause: A Reappraisal,"*Notre Dame Law Review*, 81 (2005–06): 1843–93. Unfortunately, as this chapter shows, Smith's attempt to clarify the issue was unsuccessful.
4. *Foreordained Failure*, 17 (emphasis added).
5. *Foreordained Failure*, 19.
6. *Foreordained Failure*, 19.
7. *Foreordained Failure*, 19.
8. *Foreordained Failure*, 25–26.
9. *Foreordained Failure*, 18–19.
10. *Foreordained Failure*, 21.
11. *Foreordained Failure*, 25 (emphasis added).
12. "Jurisdictional Establishment Clause," 1874, fn 123.
13. *Foreordained Failure*, 23 (emphasis in original).
14. *Foreordained Failure*, 25. Also, see Smith, "Jurisdictional Establishment Clause," 1876.
15. The confusion caused by the use of the word "substantive" is clearly revealed in the debate between Smith and his critics, who argue that the religion clauses are substantive in nature and, therefore, cannot be jurisdictional. When they make that argument, of course, they are using the word "substantive" in its first or normative sense. To this argument, Smith gives a

purely semantic response. Instead of forthrightly denying that the religion clauses have any ethical or normative content, he says, well, of course, the clauses have substantive content because all jurisdictional clauses have substantive content, and, thus, he claims there is no disagreement between himself and his critics. When Smith presents this kind of response, however, he is using the word "substantive" in its second sense as a synonym for area, domain, or subject matter. Moreover, by responding in this way, he both obfuscates and evades the issue. See "Jurisdictional Establishment Clause," 1870–80.

16. "Jurisdictional Establishment Clause," 1876–77.

17. This is how the religion clauses are interpreted by John Courtney Murray in *We Hold These Truths: Catholic Reflections on the American Proposition* (Garden City, N. Y.: Doubleday & Co., 1964), 65–66.

18. "Jurisdictional Establishment Clause," 1844–45. Later, at 1874, fn 124, Smith adds, "I think that the concept of 'jurisdiction' becomes more elusive the more closely we consider it. . . ."

19. *The Constitution and the Pride of Reason* (New York: Oxford Univ. Press, 1998), 56 (emphasis added).

20. *The Bill of Rights: Creation and Reconstruction* (New Haven, Conn.: Yale Univ. Press, 1998), 36–39. Smith reasons similarly in "Jurisdictional Establishment Clause," 1856.

21. See James H. Hutson, "The Bill of Rights and the American Revolutionary Experience," in *A Culture of Rights: The Bill of Rights in Philosophy, Politics, and Law—1791 and 1991*, ed. Michael J. Lacey and Knud Haakonssen (New York: Cambridge University Press, 1991), 80–84 and Leslie F. Goldstein, "Popular Soveriegnty, the Origins of Judicial Review, and the Revival of Unwritten Law,"*Journal of Politics*, 48 (Feb. 1986): 51–71.

22. The Declaration of Independence, for example, says that ". . . Governments are instituted among Men, deriving their just Powers from the Consent of the Governed, that whenever any Form of Government becomes destructive of these Ends, it is the Right of the People to alter or to abolish it, and to institute new Government, laying its Foundation on such Principles, and Organizing its Powers in such Form, as to them shall seem most likely to effect their Safety and Happiness." For an excellent discussion of the contract theory's influence on eighteenth century American thought, see Hutson, "Bill of Rights," 70–80.

23. Hutson, "Bill of Rights," 83. An excellent example of this point comes from Melissa Rogers, who explains that Isaac Backus and John Leland, the leaders of early American Baptists, had a "jurisdictional" understanding of government's relationship to religion, i.e., it had no legitimate power over religion matters, but took such a position for normative or theological reasons. "Traditions of Church-State Separation: Some Ways They Have Protected Religion and Advanced Religious Freedom and How They Are Threatened Today,"*Journal of Law & Politics*, 18 (2002): 284.

24. In fairness to Smith, it should be noted that he frequently uses the word "federalist" as well as the word "jurisdictional" to describe the interpretation of the religion clauses that he favors. See, e.g., *Foreordained Failure*, 22–27, 30. Nevertheless, my point is that to avoid the confusion associated with the word "jurisdictional," he and other like-minded scholars should avoid using it to stand for the interpretation of the religion clauses that they favor.

25. Among the scholars making such an assumption are Gerard V. Bradley, *Church-State Relationships in America* (Westport, Conn.: Greenwood Press, 1987), 76, 92, and Akil Amar, *Bill of Rights,* 33.

26. This point is emphasized above because at times Smith seems to affirm it and at other times to deny it—thus making his position quite confusing. Thus, he affirms it when he writes, "The question is not whether the clauses imposed substantive restrictions on the national government—plainly, inevitably, they did—but instead whether these restrictions were adopted to effect a positive national policy on the subject of religious freedom or, more modestly, were calculated merely to assign jurisdiction over matters of religion to the states."*Foreordained Failure*, 26. He appears to deny it when he writes, "The fact that a provision disclaimed jurisdiction over a substantive [moral] right—and that it did so for the conscious purpose of protecting that right against outside interference—need not negate the provision's jurisdictional character." "Jurisdictional Establishment Clause," 1878. Not surprisingly, Smith immediately adds, "Abstractly stated, this point may seem confusing; and, coming from a proponent of the

jurisdictional interpretation, it may also seem like a piece of backsliding." "Jurisdictional Establishment Clause," 1878. Indeed! Moreover, if true, his point would mean that there is no issue with respect to how the religion clauses should be interpreted, but, of course, there is. Unfortunately, Smith, instead of coming up with two words that will clearly represent the two interpretations, confuses the issue by using the words "substantive" and "jurisdictional," each of which has two different meanings, and arguing that the clauses can be both "substantive" and "jurisdictional." To say the least, this is not helpful.

27. "Common Sense," 483.

28. Greenawalt concedes, however, that if the framers had intended to draft a purely federalist provision, it may not have been necessary for them to word the free exercise clause so as to forbid laws *protecting* the free exercise of religion, because such laws may have been considered laws "respecting an establishment of religion" and therefore forbidden by the establishment clause. In other words, the religion clauses combined could have been intended to forbid laws both prohibiting and protecting the free exercise of religion. "Common Sense," 484–86.

29. "Common Sense," 485. Note that this way of interpreting the establishment clause is quite different from one that says, as Justice Thomas does, that it was "intended to prevent Congress from interfering with state establishments [of religion]." *Elk Grove Unified School District v. Newdow*, 542 U.S. 1, 49 (2004) J. Thomas, concurring. Such an interpretation is as much normative as it is fedearalist, because it clearly implies that the framers/ratifiers of the clause thought that religious establishments are morally good and should be protected. The text of the establishment clause, moreover, does not support such a narrow interpretation, for it does not prohibit Congress from legislating only *against* state establishments of religion.

30. For a concisely, but eloquently worded argument to this effect, see Douglas Laycock, "Theology Scholarships, the Pledge of Allegiance, and Religious Liberty: Avoiding the Extremes but Missing the Liberty,"*Harvard Law Review*, 118 (Nov. 2004): 155, 242–43.

31. Greenawalt, "Common Sense," 493. Even critics of a federalist interpretation of the religion clauses sometimes fail to see this possibility. For example, Donald L. Drakeman argues that the sole purpose of the establishment clause could not be to protect state establishments of religion, because there is so much evidence that proponents of the religion clauses wanted to prevent a national religious establishment. *Church, State, and Original Intent* (New York: Cambridge Univ. Press, 2010), 229–30. He fails to consider that they could have opposed a national establishment simply because it might have jeopardized existing state establishments.

32. See above, p. 2.

33. *Foreordained Failure*, 37–39.

34. See below, p. 93.

35. For an explanation of the original normative justification of federalism, see Thomas B. McAffee, "The Federal System as Bill of Rights: Original Understandings, Modern Misreadings,"*Villanova Law Review*, 43 (1998): 17–154.

36. See, e.g., Arlin M. Adams and Charles J. Emmerich, *A Nation Dedicated to Religious Liberty* (Philadelphia, Penn.: Univ. of Pennsylvania Press, 1990), 46–47.

37. This argument assumes, of course, that early Americans who would have opposed a national religious establishment or anything like it would have done so for normative reasons.

38. "Common Sense," 504–5.

39. "Common Sense," 494.

40. See below, pp. 104–5.

41. Greenawalt, "Common Sense," 493.

42. This, of course, is Justice Thomas' understanding of the original meaning of the establishment clause; it was "intended to prevent Congress from interfering with state establishments [of religion]."*Elk Grove Unified School District v. Newdow*, 542 U.S. 1, 49 (2004)(J. Thomas, concurring). There are, moreover, two ways in which such a clause could be interpreted—narrowly or broadly. According to a narrow interpretation, the clause prevents only federal laws intentionally and directly aimed at eliminating or weakening state establishments of religion. According to a broad interpretation, the clause prohibits not only these kinds of laws, but laws establishing a religion at the national level, not, however, because such an establishment is morally wrong, but because any national religious establishment might be

different from and thus a threat to one or more of the existing state establishments of religion. Unfortunately, persons like Justice Thomas usually fail to specify which of these two interpretations they have in mind when they say the establishment clause was originally understood only to protect state establishments of religion.

43. See below, p. 28.

44. As will be seen in chapter seven, this is exactly the kind of argument that Thomas Jefferson and James Madison used against the Sedition Act of 1798. They said it violated both the First Amendment (free press clause) and the Tenth Amendment ("The powers not delegated to the United States by the Constitution, nor prohibited by it to the States, are reserved to the States respectively, or to the people.").

45. See, e.g., Kurt T. Lash, "Power and the Subject of Religion,"*Ohio State Law Journal*, 59 (1998): 1080, and Smith, *Foreordained Failure*, 47. According to Daniel O. Conkle, the establishment clause alone was intended "to make it plain that *Congress* was not to legislate on the subject of religion." "Toward a General Theory of the Establishment Clause,"*Northwestern University Law Review*, 82 (1988): 1113, 1133.

46. On this point, see Smith, "Jurisdictional Establishment Clause," at 1881, where he cogently explains why a jurisdictional or federalist limitation does not have to be "an all-or-nothing affair."

47. Greenawalt, "Common Sense," 481–82, refers to this as a "*purely* jurisdictional interpretation."

48. Greenawalt, "Common Sense," 481–82. In agreement is Jed Rubenfeld, "Antidisestablishmentarianism: Why RFRA Really Was Unconstitutional,"*Michigan Law Review*, 95 (Aug. 1997): 2347, 2357.

49. Lash, "Power and Religion," 1119–21.

50. Greenawalt, "Common Sense," 481, and Smith, "Jurisdictional Establishment Clause," 1859–60.

51. Greenawalt writes: "It would be an extremely odd reading of the clause's language to conclude that Congress could have prohibited free exercise within domains such as the federal military and the District of Columbia. . . . [T]he notion that the First amendment had *no* application to territorial governance . . . is intrinsically much less plausible than the alternative," "Common Sense," 484, 498.

52. Greenawalt, "Common Sense," 489. On this point Thomas Berg writes, "But the notion that Congress would be entirely unconstrained in making laws in the territories . . . is simply too inconsistent with the text, which says 'Congress shall make *no* law,' to serve as a legal standard. Since it is the text that was enacted and that we are interpreting, no principle accounting for historical actions is acceptable as a legal standard if it is flatly inconsistent with the text." "Religion Clause Anti-Theories,"*Notre Dame Law Review*, 72 (1996–1997): 717.

53. Of course, there are additional possibilities. When relied on by persons/groups within the federal domains, the religion clauses might be understood as prohibiting not all laws on the subject of religion in those domains, but, more narrowly, only laws prohibiting the free exercise of religion or respecting an establishment of religion. If it were the latter, Congress would be free to pass laws for the federal domains that directly affect religion in some ways, such as laws protecting religious freedom. A final possibility is that with respect to persons and groups in the federal domains, only the free exercise clause, but not the establishment clause, has normative content. According to this interpretation, Congress could not violate religious freedom in the federal domains, but could establish a religion—assuming that establishing a religion does not inherently violate religious freedom.

54. *Foreordained Failure*, 18.

55. "Jurisdictional Establishment Clause," 1859–60.

56. *Foreordained Failure*, 28–29.

57. *Foreordained Failure*, 30 (emphasis in original).

58. The amendment, proposed by Representative Samuel Livermore of New Hampshire, said, "Congress shall make no law touching religion, or infringing on the rights of conscience." Although initially approved by the House of Representatives, it was later replaced with other wording. See below, chap. 5, pp. 91–92.

59. *Foreordained Failure*, 33.

60. *Foreordained Failure*, 33 (emphasis added).
61. *Foreordained Failure*, 33.
62. "Jurisdictional Establishment Clause,"1860.
63. "Jurisdictional Establishment Clause," 1861.
64. "Power and Religion," 1093 (emphasis added). He later adds, at 1099, that the religion clauses express "a single proposition: Congress has no power to address the subject of religion (either to prohibit or promote)."
65. "Power and Religion," 1116.
66. "Power and Religion," 1117.
67. "Power and Religion," 1123.
68. "Power and Religion," 1132–38, 1142.
69. "Power and Religion," 1118.
70. "Jursidictional Establishment Clause," 1861.
71. See, e.g., Lash, "Power and Religion," 1093, and Conkle, "Toward a General Theory," 1133.
72. Greenawalt, "Common Sense," 489.
73. U. S. Constitution, Amend. I.
74. Greenawalt, "Common Sense," 488–89. For Smith's attempt to counter the argument that because of its one-sided wording, the free exercise clause is normative in nature, see "Jurisdictional Establishment Clause," 1881–85.
75. *Foreordained Failure*, 33–34 (emphasis added).
76. And what about laws that are "major" but not "controversial" and vice versa? Or to be precluded, must a law be both "major" and "controversial"?
77. *Foreordained Failure*, 34. Because Smith's criterion for determining what laws respecting religion the federal government can and cannot pass is only briefly mentioned and not explained, it is missed by some scholars. David Steinberg, for example, does not understand what Smith's position is on the meaning or scope of the federal government's jurisdiction. "Gardening at Night: Religion and Choice,"*Notre Dame Law Review*, 74 (March 1999): 1006 ("I'm not entirely certain what Professor Smith means by the phrase 'partial renunciation of jurisdiction'.")
78. "Jurisdictional Establishment Clause," 1862–63.
79. "Jurisdictional Establishment Clause," 1870 (emphasis added).
80. Greenawalt, "Common Sense," 482.
81. Although Daniel Conkle writes that the establishment clause was intended to prevent all federal legislation on the subject of religion, in the same article he later concedes that the framers/ratifiers did not necessarily agree on "how to effectuate the basic policy of federalism on which they all agreed." Thus, it could allow either the no-preference-to-religion-over-irreligion or the no-preference-to-any-one-religion-over-others interpretation of the establishment clause. "Toward a General Theory," 1133, 1135.
82. Greenawalt, "Common Sense," 482.
83. Greenawalt, "Common Sense," 485.
84. *Foreordained Failure*, 34 (emphasis in original). Even critics of Smith are guilty of relying mostly, if not entirely, on logic and text. Thus, Kent Greenawalt, "Common Sense," 487, in defending a more normative interpretation of the religion clauses, writes, "I am by no means claiming that most of the textual implications I have drawn generally were perceived at the time, or indeed that all of them were perceived by anyone. As with all legislation, the text had implications that no one may have seen. And certainly with regard to the understanding of the two religion clauses, we have examined some subtleties that would have been far from anyone's attentions."

Chapter Three

A Critical Analysis of the Federalist Interpretation

The first part of this chapter summarizes the main arguments that have been made to support the federalist or states' rights interpretation of the religion clauses. They total six in number. Some of them, however, overlap to a degree, and not all of the exponents of the federalist interpretation subscribe to all of the arguments. Some of the arguments are based on the wording of the religion clauses, some on historical evidence, and some on a combination of both.

The second part of the chapter contains a preliminary and partial evaluation of the arguments for a federalist interpretation of the religion clauses. The evaluation is preliminary and partial because it pertains only to the validity of the arguments' logic and not to the historical evidence supporting them. As stated in chapter one, most of the arguments for a federalist interpretation are based on indirect or circumstantial evidence. Even if that evidence itself is factually correct, the conclusions drawn from it may be incorrect, if they are based on false assumptions or illogical reasoning. The second purpose of this chapter, therefore, is to indicate the ways in which the arguments for a federalist reading of the religion clauses are based on faulty assumptions and logic. This by itself, however, is not enough to show that the federalist reading is invalid, but it should indicate that much more in the way of historical evidence than its advocates present is needed before one can conclude that it is valid. It should also remove any blinders that would prevent a fair and accurate assessment of the material presented in the remaining chapters of this book.

I. AN OVERVIEW OF THE ARGUMENTS

The first argument is that the religion clauses are primarily federalist in content because they, like the other provisions in the Bill of Rights, limit the federal government but not the states. James McClellan, for example, argues that the Bill of Rights is "*essentially* a states' rights document" and "could thus be construed as a *guarantee* to the states that they were free to *deny* civil liberties to their citizens—to deny them the free exercise of religion. . . ." To support this claim, he simply cites the fact that originally the Bill of Rights did not apply to and, thus, limit the states.[1] Similarly, to support the claim that the establishment clause was meant to protect state establishments of religion from federal legislation, Akil Amar cites statements by various early Americans, such as Joseph Story, to the effect that the states are legally free to establish a religion because the Constitution does not prohibit them from doing so.[2]

The second argument builds on the first one. According to it, the religion clauses were intended simply to confirm what the Federalists, defenders of the Constitution, had said when, during the ratification debate, its critics began to demand that a religious liberty amendment be added to the document. The Federalists had supposedly responded that such an amendment was unnecessary because the original Constitution gave the national government no power to legislate on religion—that power being reserved to the states. When it became clear that the Constitution's critics could not be convinced of that fact, its defenders agreed to add an amendment that would make clear that the national government had no jurisdiction over religion.[3] This interpretation, according to its proponents, is supported by the absolute nature of the ban imposed on Congress by the First Amendment: "Congress shall make *no* law . . . ," in contrast to the partial restraints imposed by the other provisions in the Bill of Rights. "Such language," according to Steven Smith, "seems nicely calculated to express a denial of jurisdiction over a subject" for the purpose of confirming "the jurisdictional arrangement that preexisted the Constitution . . . in which religion was a subject within the domain of the states, not the national government."[4] In addition, federalist scholars emphasize the fact that Madison originally intended his proposed amendments to be placed in Art. I, Sec. 9, of the Constitution, which prohibits the national government from passing certain types of laws and which follows the section that grants powers to the national government, including the power "[t]o make all Laws which shall be necessary and proper for carrying into Execution" all the other powers given to it.[5] For this reason, Amar calls the First Amendment an inverted or reverse Necessary and Proper Clause, "meaning that Congress simply had no enumerated power over either speech or religion."[6] Thus, the entire First Amendment, not just the religion clauses, was originally a federalist provision.[7]

The third reason given to support the federalist interpretation of the religion clauses is that early Americans generally, and the framers of the First Amendment specifically, were so divided in their views on what the principle of religious freedom means or prohibits that they could not possibly have agreed on the meaning of a normative constitutional provision intended to protect it. One scholar writes, ". . . [T]he only consensus among the Framers of the First Amendment about the appropriate relationship between church and state was to allow the states to decide the issue themselves."[8] Steven Smith goes so far as to say that early Americans "fundamentally and passionately disagreed about the proper relation between religion and the state."[9] To some, religious liberty precluded government support of any religion (what Smith calls the voluntarist position), while to others such support was permissible, provided all other religions were free to practice their faith (the traditional position).[10] More specifically, Americans were divided on "monetary subsidies [to an approved religion], laws prohibiting blasphemy and Sabbath-breaking, exclusion of the religiously heterodox from public office."[11] Given the division on these issues, the framers of the religion clauses, according to Smith and others, could not have settled them and, therefore, did not even try to do so, but wrote the clauses simply to express their desire to leave it up to the states individually to decide what the principle of religious liberty did and did not prohibit.[12]

Fourth, as evidence of the existence of a deep division of opinion on the proper relationship between religion and government, Smith (and others) cite the "desultory and superficial" quality of the debate over the religion clauses in the First Congress.[13] He notes that "there was virtually no discussion at all of what we now call the free exercise clause." Given the fact that the earlier debates over church-state issues in the states had been "extensive" and "spirited," Smith reasons that if the proposed religion clauses had been understood by members of the First Congress as normative or principled in nature, they would have generated the same degree and kind of debate there as similar provisions had generated in the states. The fact that they did not generate such debate, Smith reasons, can only be explained on the premise that "the enactors believed that they were not answering the difficult [church-state] questions at all but were merely deferring those questions to someone else—the states. . . ." They did not need to debate anything, because they all agreed that the original Constitution had not or should not have given Congress any power over religion. All they needed to do was make that point clear.[14]

The fifth argument is that a states' rights interpretation of the religion clauses best explains Congress' legislative record on religion in the first few years after the ratification of the religion clauses. During that time Congress passed several laws that did aid religion, even specific religions, in the federal domains—the territories, the military, and the District of Columbia.[15] Although the fact that Congress passed such laws would appear to indicate either that the religion clauses were not intended to deny Congress all jurisdiction over religion or that Congress was willfully violating the Constitution, Smith rejects both conclusions. Instead, he argues that when the religion clauses were adopted by the First Congress, it was concerned only with protecting states' rights, and "was not concerned with, and hence paid no attention to, the subject of Congress's powers over religion in the territories." With respect to areas legitimately under its control, members of the First Congress were just absent-minded and said nothing.[16] (Needless to say, if this is true, it does not reflect well on the framers; it means they created a sizable lacuna in the Constitution.)

For this reason, when Congress later legislated on religion in the federal domains, it did not seem "to have regarded itself as bound by any adopted constitutional principle controlling the relationship between government and religion." Rather it acted in an ad hoc manner. Such behavior, Smith says, can best be explained not on the assumption that the religion clauses impose normative restrictions on Congress, but on the assumption that they (and other provisions of the First Amendment) prohibit only federal legislation that affects persons within the states or conflicts with state laws/policies. As for legislation on religion in areas under its control, Congress simply did not consider what it could and could not do.[17]

The sixth and final argument pertains only to the establishment clause. According to it, because some states in 1789 had elements of religious establishments, i.e., laws that favored certain religions (or persons because of their religion) over other religions (or persons),[18] that clause was worded in a way that would prevent the central government from legislating in any way against those state laws. Specifically, the establishment clause prohibits laws "*respecting an* establishment of religion," language that on its face arguably precludes Congress from trying to undermine state laws favoring/promoting particular religions over others. Although this language also precludes national laws favoring/promoting some religion or religions and, thus, could be said to have normative content, some scholars argue that because the language "respecting an establishment of religion" is "peculiar" and unique to the U. S. Constitution, i.e., is not contained in any earlier state constitutional provisions pertaining to religion, and because the clause refers to "an [existing?] establishment of religion," the establishment clause must have been intended only to protect state establishments of religion.[19] Thus, it "does not express a value of 'nonestablishment.'"[20] If it had been intended to do so, the clause would, according to these scholars, have been worded differently. It would have prohibited laws "respecting religion," "establishing a religion," "aiding [or advancing] a religion," "discriminating in favor of or against a religion," or even "respecting the establishing of a religion."[21] The clause is not only not worded in any of the above ways, but some of these wordings were considered and rejected by the First Congress that drafted the First Amendment.[22] The conclusion, therefore, is that the establishment clause was worded the way it was in order to protect existing state establishments of religion.

II. AN ASSESSMENT OF THE ARGUMENTS' LOGIC

Now, the most striking aspect of all the above arguments is their speculative nature. None of them is based on historical evidence that directly and unequivocally supports a federalist or states' rights interpretation of the religion clauses. More specifically, the federalist scholars fail to cite a single statement by any early American that the religion clauses were meant to protect states' rights or establishments of religion. Rather, all the evidence is circumstantial in nature. In other words, the evidence is consistent with, but by itself does not establish or dictate a federalist interpretation of the clauses. There could very well be another "explanation" for the historical evidence besides the federalist interpretation. In addition, some of the historical evidence used to support such an interpretation is either questionable or misleading because it ignores other evidence. Finally, some of the facts used to support the federalist interpretation are simply irrelevant, and any conclusions based on them are the result of illogical reasoning. Each of the six arguments for a federalist reading of the religion clauses can be criticized on one or more of these grounds.

Take the first argument that the provisions of the Bill of Rights were intended to protect the states from federal legislation because they did not apply to the states. As a matter of logic, the conclusion that the religion clauses *themselves* were meant to give the states a constitutional right to legislate as they please with respect to religion simply does not follow *from the fact that the Bill of Rights, including the religion clauses, was not intended to apply to the states*. After all, the states had such a right even before the addition of the religion clauses to the Constitution and continued to have it after their addition, even if the clauses were intended to protect individual rights. The only conclusion that follows is that the religion clauses per se, i.e., without the Fourteenth Amendment, cannot be used by *courts* to prevent the states from legislating as they please on religion. One simply cannot say, however, that because the clauses were not intended to apply to the states, they have little or no normative meaning or content, such as protecting religious freedom from federal legislation.[23]

Congress, of course, may not have the power to pass laws that would limit what the states can do in the area of religion, but if it does not, it is because the power was never delegated to it and is thus reserved to the states or to the people[24] OR because some specific provision in the Constitution, possibly the establishment clause, prohibits it from doing so.[25] It cannot be argued, however, that Congress has no such power simply because the Bill of Rights, including the religion clauses, does not apply to and restrict the states. As one scholar has said, "It would be more than naïve to suggest that Congress was unable to protect the religious liberty of American citizens against state action on the ground that it was forbidden 'to prohibit the free exercise' of religion!"[26] On the other hand, the fact that Congress cannot establish a religion or prohibit its free exercise does not, by itself, mean that it *can* pass laws *prohibiting* religious establishments or *protecting* the free exercise of religion. Whether it can or cannot pass such laws is simply an issue unrelated to the fact that the religion clauses were not intended to apply to the states.

The second argument—that the religion clauses were adopted simply to make it clear, as some Federalists allegedly argued during the ratification debates, that the Constitution had never given the national government the power to legislate in any way with respect to religion in the states—is just as questionable as the first argument is. It is based entirely on the *assumption* that it was religion per se over which the Federalists said Congress has no jurisdiction. It is understandable, of course, why an exponent of a federalist reading of the religion clauses would make such an assumption, for, if true, it would certainly imply that the religion clauses have no normative content, but were intended to make clear that the states alone have jurisdiction over questions relating to religion.

What, however, if that assumption is incorrect? What if the Federalists thought that it was only the rights of conscience, and not religion in general, over which the new Constitution had no jurisdiction? What if both the original Constitution and the religion clauses were meant to preclude not *all laws violating religion, but only laws relating to religious liberty or equality?* If that were the case, it would imply that the clauses have a normative purpose—to protect religious liberty/equality, an individual right. Many defenders of a federalist interpretation of the religion clauses, however, simply assume that both Federalists and Anti-federalists wanted to prevent the passage of all laws in any way relating to religion or at least religion in the states,[27] but is that assumption warranted by the historical evidence?[28]

Even if it could be established that the original Constitution gave the national government no power whatsoever over *religion* per se and that the religion clauses were simply meant to make that clear, that fact alone would not be nearly enough to prove that the clauses have little or no normative content, i.e., that they were adopted to protect the states' power to legislate with respect to religion. It only raises the question as to *why* the original

Constitution failed to give the national government power over religion and *why* many, if not most, early Americans wanted an amendment to affirm that fact. *Was it because they thought that this was a power more appropriately exercised by state governments rather than the federal government OR because they believed that no government—national, state, or local—should exercise such a power, given the threat that such a power posed to liberty of conscience*?[29] Again, one cannot simply assume that it was the former. As explained in chapter two, the mere fact that a constitutional provision removes an area from the jurisdiction of the federal government does not at all indicate that it is a federalist provision, i.e., a provision that does not address any normative questions but simply transfers to the states the power to decide them. Even a purely normative provision deprives the federal government of jurisdiction over some subject.

Moreover, the fact that the First Amendment begins with the words, "Congress shall make *no* law . . .," has no bearing whatsoever on the issue. What *is* relevant are the remaining words in the sentence—what do they mean and *why* were they chosen? In order to answer those questions, one must look at the historical evidence, such as that presented in this book, which, I believe, clearly demonstrates that the reason for the religion clause was normative in nature.

Finally, coupling the Tenth to the First Amendment adds nothing to the argument. That amendment simply affirms that whatever power is denied the federal government by the religion clauses (and for whatever reason) is not denied the state governments. Although the Tenth Amendment clearly has a federalist or states' rights meaning, that is no reason for thinking that the religion clauses themselves have federalist meaning. If it did, it would mean that all provisions in the Constitution that limit the federal government's powers have federalist meaning, which is patently absurd. Is the federal government, for example, forbidden to inflict cruel and unusual punishments[30] because the framers wanted only the states to have the right to inflict such punishments?[31] The answer is obvious.

The third argument—that the framers of the religion clauses and the persons they represented were too divided over church-state issues to have agreed on any normative amendment—is obviously very speculative in nature. What is missing from the federalism argument is detailed evidence about how closely early Americans were divided and how significant the issues were that divided them. One cannot simply assume that they were evenly divided or unable to reach a compromise on the issue of the proper role of government in relation to religion. Moreover, even if the founding generation was divided to a significant degree over this issue, that fact by itself would hardly support the argument being made. After all, disagreement among legislators or their constituents is "par for the course" in American politics and does not always, or even usually, prevent laws, constitutional or statutory, from being passed.[32] Consider, for example, the fact that a provision was inserted into Article VI of the Constitution[33] that prohibits the use of religious tests as a means of determining whether a person is qualified to hold office in the national government—even though at that time many Americans favored such tests and most states used them.[34] If division of public opinion on an issue did not prevent the framers of the Constitution from including a religious liberty provision that they favored on principle, why should it have prevented framers of the Bill of Rights from doing likewise? (This issue is discussed more thoroughly in chapter six.)

The main problem with the fourth argument is that it assumes that the *only* possible explanation of the alleged "apathy," "complacency," and "carelessness" of the framers of the religion clauses is that those clauses were understood by the framers to be primarily, if not purely, federalist in nature. As will be seen in chapter six, however, there are other more credible explanations for the desultory nature of the debate over the religion clauses. This is clearly indicated by the fact that it was not just the debate pertaining to them but the debate pertaining to *all* of the proposed amendments to the Constitution, that was brief and lackluster.[35] This indicates that whatever accounted for the nature of the discussion, it was not something pertaining just to the religion clauses or church-state issues. Moreover, as already explained, most of the proposed amendments that were included in what we now call the Bill of Rights were not federalist in nature.[36]

The fifth argument for a federalist interpretation of the religion clauses—that it *best* explains the laws on religion passed by Congress after the adoption of the First Amendment—is very speculative and questionable. First, as for the First Congress' failure to discuss its jurisdiction over religion in areas under its control, like the territories, although Smith's absent-mindedness explanation is a possibility, that is all it is, for there is an even more plausible explanation for the framers' silence on the matter. In drafting and adopting the religion clauses, the framers could have been intending to protect individual rights, not states' rights. If so, the limitations placed on the national government by those clauses would have protected individuals whether they were in the states, the territories, the military, or the District of Columbia. If this is what the framers were doing, obviously there would have been no need for them to discuss the issue of the federal government's power over religion in the territories and other federal domains.

Secondly, the fact that the first few Congresses passed some laws promoting religion *in the territories, the military, or the District of Columbia* works to support a states' rights interpretation of the religion clauses ONLY if they did not pass laws promoting religion *in the states*, but the fact is that the early Congresses did pass such laws. Most notably, they passed laws authorizing the President to issue proclamations establishing national days of prayer[37]—laws which are clearly inconsistent with a states' rights interpretation of the religion clauses because such proclamations had traditionally been issued by state officials. Because of such laws, Gerard Bradley, among others, argues that "it is not true that the federal government has no power over religion in the states."[38]

One can argue, therefore, that whatever explains legislation establishing days of prayer also explains why Congress occasionally passed laws promoting religion in the territories, the military, and DC. For example, Congress could have done so on the basis of a narrow but normative understanding of what the religion clauses prohibit.[39] Although Kurt Lash argues that federal laws aiding religion in the territories were consistent with a federalist reading of the religion clauses, his explanation shows, unintentionally, how they could have been passed on the basis of a normative but narrow understanding of what the clauses prohibit. He writes: ". . . [T]he number of congressional acts that actually regulated religion *as religion* in the territories was quite small. Most of the federal government's involvement with religion came in the form of educational aid to religious organizations serving Native Americans. Although there was a religious component to this education, this by itself is not enough to make such aid an exercise of power over the subject of religion."[40] In other words, early Americans could have thought (in contemporary terminology) that such laws did not violate the normative principle encased in the religion clauses because their "primary" purpose and effect were secular, not religious, in nature.

Another possibility—Congress could have passed laws promoting religion in the federal domains without even considering whether they were consistent with the Constitution or in the belief that the Constitutional violation was relatively minor and outweighed by what it considered a more pressing priority.[41] Douglas Laycock, for one, rejects the assumption that early American lawmakers never violated the religion clauses. He explains that during this period of transition from established churches to free churches, customs or traditions that in principle were inconsistent with the new religion clauses did not end abruptly and completely, mainly because lawmakers would not have the time or inclination to consider whether each and every one of them violated the Constitution.[42]

In short, the fact that Congress passed some laws promoting religion in areas outside the states does not necessarily support a federalist interpretation of the religion clauses, because there are other possible explanations of such laws.

In the face of this counter-argument, which Smith concedes is "common" and "plausible," he takes the position that unless there is no other way of explaining the early federal laws promoting religion in the states and territories, one ought not assume that they were the result of the early lawmakers' being thoughtless or hypocritical. He believes that "there is something troubling, and more than a little presumptuous" in an argument that depicts early

American lawmakers "as lacking in reflection, or [being] weak-willed, or hypocritical."[43] If, however, one should not make such an assumption, then Smith should forsake his original account of the religion clauses, because it attributes absentmindedness to members of the First Congress (for not addressing Congress' power to legislate on religion in the federal domains).

Perhaps because he does not want to be inconsistent in this way, Smith, in fact, posits another interpretation that does not rely on the First Congress' being absentminded. He modifies his original assertion that the religion clauses are "*purely* jurisdictional in nature." He says that the clauses do not call for a total renunciation of the federal government's jurisdiction over religion, but only for "a more limited or *partial disclaimer of jurisdiction* over religion," which would allow Congress to legislate on religion in areas under its control *and* on some other matters pertaining to religion .[44] He explains as follows:

> Even though the religion question was regarded as one for the states rather than the national government to address, . . . reflection [by members of First Congress] might have made it clear that the national government would not be able to avoid matters of religion altogether. Such responsibility would arise not only in the governance of the territories . . . but also in . . . Congress's management of its own operations. . . . The . . . alternative was to opt for a partial renunciation of jurisdiction over religion. This solution would effectively assign to the states the major, controversial issues of religion—issues regarding the "establishment" and regulation of religion—and it would defer the residual, non-assignable issues of religion to the future.[45]

There are several problems with this move on Smith's part. First, it makes the meaning of the religion clauses vague, if not meaningless, and difficult, if not impossible, to enforce. According to Smith, they prohibit the federal government from passing only laws that involve "major, controversial issues of religion," but what is the difference between such laws and those that involve minor, not-so-controversial issues? What would it take for a court to say that a policy is controversial? How many persons would have to be opposed to it? Also, what is unconstitutional would obviously change with the times, depending on how controversial it was at any given time. It will not do to answer, as Smith does, that major issues are those involving the establishment and regulation of religion, for that simply begs the question. After all, if, as Smith argues, early Americans were divided over what constitutes the forbidden establishment and regulation of religion, then how could they (and later courts) agree on whether a federal law was one that dealt with a "major, controversial" issue of religion?[46] In short, Smith's partial disclaimer interpretation of the religion clauses raises too many questions.[47]Second, and ironically, in adopting the partial-jurisdiction-over-religion interpretation of the religion clauses, Smith, unintentionally, comes close to providing a normative interpretation of those clauses. To restate a point made several times already, the crucial issue is *why* did the framers of the First Amendment deprive Congress of jurisdiction over religion (not how much, whether completely or partially, they deprived it). On this crucial issue, Smith, when explaining which policies toward religion the federal government could and could not adopt, clearly implies that the framers did not want the federal government to legislate on religion if and when *it would be divisive* to do so. Why else would the framers have wanted Congress to avoid the "major, controversial issues of religion"? Although this may be more of a practical and less of a principled reason for having the religion clauses than is the protection of religious liberty, *it is nonetheless a normative reason.* It is a reason that says that all national legislation on religious matters that would threaten the unity of the nation should be avoided. This is certainly more normative in nature than saying that the national government was not given jurisdiction over religion in order to protect states' rights or state establishments of religion.[48] In short, contrary to his own argument that there can be no principled or normative interpretation of the religion clauses,[49] Smith's own final interpretation appears to be just that.

Smith's partial-disclaimer-of-jurisdiction interpretation of the religion clauses is not convincing for a third and final reason. It is entirely speculation based on limited, circumstantial evidence—a point that Smith himself concedes: "The historical evidence is too sparse to permit a definitive conclusion in favor of this specific aspect of the original understanding, [which] . . . may simply attribute to the enactors greater attention and thought than they actually gave to those clauses." Ultimately all that Smith claims is "that in the historical context such a course might have seemed sensible and attractive and that if Congress *had* made a decision in favor of a partial disclaimer of jurisdiction, the religion clauses as adopted would have been a suitable way of expressing that decision."[50] If, however, this is the best argument that Smith can make for his limited federalist interpretation, i.e., that it is a possibility, surely it does not deserve to be accepted.

The sixth and final argument for a federalist reading of the religion clauses relates only to the meaning of the establishment clause. It rests on two facts. One is the existence at that time in a few states of what might be called quasi-establishments of religion. By itself, of course, this proves nothing, as some defenders of a federalist interpretation of the establishment clause concede.[51] The second fact is the literal wording of the establishment clause ("no law respecting an establishment of religion"), which, admittedly, can be interpreted as prohibiting the federal government from disestablishing a religion in one of the states, as well as from establishing a national religion.[52]

The argument, however, that the establishment clause was intended to protect state religious establishments because it does not use obviously anti-establishment language (such as no laws "respecting religion," "establishing a religion," "aiding a religion," "discriminating for or against a religion," or "respecting the establishing of a religion") is not convincing because there is another possible explanation for the "respecting" language besides an intent to protect state establishments of religion. What if the framers, for normative reasons, had wanted to prevent *all* the above kinds of laws and perhaps other kinds as well, and not just one of those kinds of laws? If they had, they would have needed wording that is more general and inclusive than any of the above wordings—*a wording that would prohibit all the different kinds of laws associated with traditional establishments of religion.*[53] Although "respecting an establishment of religion" may not have been the ideal phrase for the framers to have used, surely it works well enough for that purpose, and if it does, it means that one cannot say that the clause was obviously or necessarily intended to protect state establishments of religion. In short, its wording alone cannot tell us the original meaning of the establishment clause.

To determine, therefore, which of these two plausible readings of the establishment clause is correct or more nearly so, one must look for historical evidence about how the framers and early Americans understood it. In this regard, it is significant that the states' rights scholars present no evidence beyond its wording to support their claim that the clause was originally understood as protecting the quasi-establishments of religion that existed at the time the clause was drafted. Their failure to do so suggests that there is no historical evidence to support the states' rights interpretation of the clause, but that remains to be seen.

One final brief point—this sixth argument, even if true, applies only to the establishment clause and, thus, in no way shows that the free exercise clause was intended to protect states' rights.

The preceding analysis hopefully makes it clear why the case for the states' rights interpretation of the religion clauses is mostly speculative in nature and, without additional support, unconvincing. It is based mostly on inferences and not on a thorough and careful examination of the historical evidence bearing on the issue. What is missing, above all, is evidence on whether early Americans, including the framers of the religion clauses, understood and described them as protecting individual rights or states' rights. For example, what did the proponents of a religious liberty amendment want, and why did they want it? This question is addressed in the next chapter.

NOTES

1. *Joseph Story and the American Constitution* (Norman, Okla.: Univ. of Oklahoma Press, 1971), 146–47 (emphasis added to "essentially" and "guarantee"). Also, see McClellan's "Hand's Writing on the Wall of Separation: The Significance of *Jaffree* in Future Cases on

Religious Establishment," in *How Does the Constitution Protect Religious Freedom?*, ed. Robert A. Goldwin and Art Kaufman (Washington, D. C.: American Enterprise Institute, 1987), 47–49.

2. *The Bill of Rights: Creation and Reconstruction* (New Haven, Conn.: Yale Univ. Press, 1998), 33–35. To support the same contention, Michael Paulsen quotes Philip Kurland, "The states had not forfeited, by the promulgation of the amendment, any of their rights to establish a state religion or to afford preferences to one religious sect over others." "Religion, Equality, and the Constitution: An Equal Protection Approach to Establishment Clause Adjudication,"*Notre Dame Law Review*, 61 (1986): 317. For other examples of this "logic," see Christopher Grenda, "Revealing Liberalism in Early America: Rethinking Religious Liberty and Liberal Values,"*Journal of Church and* State, 45 (Winter 2003): 134, fn 10, and Daniel Dreisbach, *Thomas Jefferson and the Wall of Separation between Church and State* (New York: New York Univ. Press, 2002), 60–61, 65, 68–69.

3. For this argument, see Steven D. Smith, *The Constitution and the Pride of Reason* (New York: Oxford Univ. Press, 1998), 56, and below, pp. 57–59.

4. Steven D. Smith, "The Jurisdictional Establishment Clause: A Reappraisal,"*Notre Dame Law Review*, 81 (2006): 1843, 1856, 1858.

5. U. S. Constitution, Art I, sec. 8.

6. "Anti-Federalists, *The Federalist Papers*, and the Big Argument for Union,"*Harvard Journal of Law & Public Policy*, 16 (1993): 115. Smith, in "Jurisdictional Establishment Clause," 1856, agrees with Amar.

7. See Steven D. Smith, *Foreordained Failure: The Quest for a Constitutional Principle of Religious Freedom* (New York: Oxford Univ. Press, 1995), 30–31, and Amar, *Bill of Rights*, 35–39. In *Constitutional Opinions: Aspects of the Bill of Rights* (New York: Oxford Univ. Press, 1986), 132–33, 162–66, Leonard Levy gives this same states' rights interpretation to the free speech and press clauses of the First Amendment. Given what has been presented thus far, it is clear that proponents of a federalist interpretation of the religion clauses disagree over whether it is the entire Bill of Rights, just the First Amendment, just the religion clauses, or just the establishment clause that has federalist meaning.

8. Chris Bartolomucci, "Rethinking the Incorporation of the Establishment Clause: A Federalist View,"*Harvard Law Review*, 105 (May 1992): 1705.

9. "The Religion Clauses in Constitutional Scholarship,"*Notre Dame Law Review*, 74 (March 1999): 1040.

10. Although Smith states that the dividing issue was whether the principle of religious liberty precludes government "support for religion," he fails to explain exactly the kind of government support that was at issue. *Foreordained Failure*, 19–22. Was it support of religion in general (or all religions equally) or support of one religion (or some religions) to the exclusion of others? The answer to this question is crucial because whether there was a *significant* difference of opinion among early Americans on the meaning of religious liberty depends on which of these kinds of government support for religion one is talking about. In other words, early American would have been much more likely to accept the proposition that government cannot support certain religions over others than they would the proposition that government cannot support religion in general or a very general, nonsectarian civil religion. See John Witte, Jr., "'A Most Mild and Equitable Establishment of Religion': John Adams and the Massachusetts Experiment,"*Journal of Church and State*, 41 (Spring 1999): 213–52.

11. Smith, "Religion Clauses," 1046.

12. Smith, *Foreordained Failure*, 6–8, 11–12, 19–21, 26–27, 30–34, 37–43; Jay S. Bybee, "Taking Liberties with the First Amendment: Congress, Section 5, and the Religious Freedom Restoration Act,"*Vanderbilt Law Review*, 48 (Nov. 1995): 1565; William K. Lietzau, "Rediscovering the Establishment Clause: Federalism and the Rollback of Incorporation,"*DePaul Law Review*, 39 (1989–1990): 1200; Daniel O. Conkle, *Constitutional Law: The Religion Clauses* (New York: Foundation Press, 2003): 19–20; Kurt Lash, "Power and the Subject of Religion,"*Ohio State Law Journal*, 59 (1998): 1117; Amar, *Bill of Rights*, 246–47; and Paulsen, "Religion, Equality," 318–22.

13. Smith, *Foreordained Failure*, 26. Smith adds that "[m]ost state ratifying conventions approved the measure with even less reflection or discussion."*Foreordained Failure*, 26. How

he can say that is puzzling, for we have no record of what happened in "most" state ratifying conventions. Chester J. Antieau et al., *Freedom From Federal Establishment: Formation and Early History of the First Amendment Religion Clauses* (Milwaukee, Wis.: Bruce Pub., 1964), 143–58.

14. *Foreordained Failure*, 26–27, 29, 31.

15. For examples, see Robert L. Cord, *Separation of Church and State: Historical Fact and Current Fiction* (New York: Lambeth Press, 1982), 38–39, 47, 57–80, 261–70.

16. *Foreordained Failure*, 28–29.

17. Smith, *Foreordained Failure*, 8–9, 27–30. In contrast, Kurt T. Lash argues that Congress' actions after the adoption of the First Amendment are consistent with, if not explained by, a "no power over religion" interpretation of the religion clauses. "Power and the Subject of Religion," 1116–43.

18. Because scholars disagree over what constitutes an establishment of religion, they also disagree over the number (from two to eight) of states that had established religions in the late eighteenth century. Compare Jed Rubenfeld, "Antidisestablishmentarianism: Why RFRA Really Was Unconstitutional,"*Michigan Law Review*, 95 (Aug. 1997): 2351 ("The truth is that by the standards of modern doctrine, almost every state in post-Revolutionary America had laws establishing religion.") with David Barton, "The Image and the Reality: Thomas Jefferson and the First Amendment,"*Notre Dame Journal of Law, Ethics & Public Policy*, 17 (2003), 399, 420–22, who argues that eight states had enacted *disestablishment* laws prior to Virginia's doing so in 1785. Compare both with what John Leland, a leading Baptist minister in early America, had to say in 1791: ". . . [A]ll the states now in union, saving two or three in New England, have no legal force used about religion, in directing its course or supporting its preachers." "The Rights of Conscience Inalienable," in *Political Sermons of the American Founding Era, 1730–1805*, ed. Ellis Sandoz (Indianapolis, Ind.: Liberty Press, 1991), 1086.

19. Jonathan P. Brose, "In Birmingham They Love the Governor: Why the Fourteenth Amendment Does Not Incorporate the Establishment Clause," *Ohio Northern University Law Review*, 24 (1998): 1, 7; Arlin M. Adams & Charles J. Emmerich, *A Nation Dedicated to Religious Liberty: The Constitutional Heritage of the Religion Clauses* (Philadelphia, Penn.: Univ. of Pennsylvania Press, 1990), 46–47; Kurt Lash, "The Second Adoption of the Free Exercise Clause: Religious Exemptions Under the Fourteenth Amendment,"*Northwestern University Law Review*, 88 (Spring 1994): 1111–12; and Daniel O. Conkle, "Toward a General Theory of the Establishment Clause,"*Northwestern University Law Review*, 82 (1988): 1134–35, & fn 109, and *Constitutional Law*, 20.

20. Lash, "Second Adoption," 1111.

21. William C. Porth & Robert P. George, "Trimming the Ivey: A Bicentennial Re-examination of the Establishment Clause,"*West Virginia Law Review*, 90 (1987): 109, 137, and Brose, "In Birmingham," 7–8.

22. Brose, "In Birmingham," 7–15.

23. Also making this point are Donald L. Drakeman, *Church, State, and Original Intent* (New York: Cambridge Univ. Press, 2010), 235, fn 130; William E. Nelson and Robert C. Palmer, *Liberty and Community: Constitution and Rights in the Early American Republic* (New York: Oceana Pub's, 1987), 133; and Steven K. Green, "Federalism and the Establishment Clause: A Reassessment,"*Creighton Law Review*, 38 (2004–2005): 767–68. This same criticism can be and has been made of the argument that the free speech/press clauses are guarantees of states' rights. See David A. Anderson, "The Origins of the Press Clause,"*U. C. L. A. Law Review*, 30 (1983): 455, at 506–09. To his credit, Steven Smith rejects the first argument for a federalist reading of the religion clauses. *Foreordained Failure*, 22 ("The religion clauses . . . might have applied only to the national government and yet have embodied a substantive [normative] principle or right of religion freedom.").

24. U. S. Constitution, Amend. X.

25. See Joseph M. Snee, "Religious Disestablishment and the Fourteenth Amendment,"*Washington University Law* Quarterly, (1954): 388 ("Congress could not prohibit the free exercise of religion, but it was left powerless to interfere with the states if they chose to do so. *Only* the *establishment* clause, as an application of the general reservation of power in the Tenth Amendment, explains this Congressional impotence.") (emphasis added to "Only"). Of

course, it is debatable whether the establishment clause was intended to have this effect—an issue discussed below, pp. 101–7

26. Snee, "Religious Disestablishment," 388. To his credit, Smith acknowledges this point. *Foreordained Failure*, 22, 26.

27. See, e.g., Bybee, "Taking Liberties," 1539–71, and Amar, *Bill of Rights*, 36.

28. See below, pp. 57–58.

29. On this point, see Lash, "Power and the Subject of Religion," 1117–18.

30. *U. S. Constitution*, Amend. VIII.

31. That the Eighth Amendment expresses a normative principle and that "[t]he religion clauses, similarly, *might* have applied only to the national government and yet have embodied a substantive [normative] principle or right of religious freedom" is conceded by Steven Smith in *Foreordained Failure*, at 22 (emphasis added).

32. Green, "Federalism and Establishment Clause," 774.

33. ". . . [N]o religious Test shall ever be required as a Qualification to any Office or public Trust under the United States." U. S. Const., Art. VI.

34. Adams & Emmerich, *Nation Dedicated*, 13–16.

35. Even Smith notes this in *Foreordained Failure*, 29.

36. A point conceded by Smith, *Foreordained Failure*, 22.

37. Cord, *Separation of Church and State*, 27–29, 34, 51; and Lash, "Power and the Subject of Religion," 1123–27.

38. *Church-State Relationships in America* (Westport, Conn.: Greenwood Press, 1987), 96. In contrast, Lash attempts to show that these laws are consistent with the no-federal-power-over-religion interpretation of the religion clauses, but in doing so, he undercuts his federalist interpretation of the religion clauses. He writes, "In general, the Founders' position on the federal government's use of religious symbols seems to depend on their position on the more general issue of the proper relationship between church and government—*federal or state*. There being no consensus on *that* issue in the early decades of the Constitution, each administration followed its own policy." "Power and the Subject of Religion," 1126 (emphasis in original). Such an explanation obviously implies that the issue of whether the federal government's use of religious symbols violates the religion clauses was understood at that time as a normative, not a federalist, issue.

39. For an extended elaboration of this point, see Kent Greenawalt, "Common Sense about Original and Subsequent Understandings of the Religion Clauses,"*University of Pennsylvania Journal of Constitutional Law*, 8 (2006): 499–503.

40. "Power and the Subject of Religion," 1121.

41. Greenawalt, "Common Sense," 400, 497.

42. "'Nonpreferential' Aid to Religion: A False Claim about Original Intent,"*William & Mary Law Review*, 27 (1986): 913–14.

43. *Foreordained Failure*, 8–11.

44. Smith, *Foreordained Failure*, 17, 33 (emphasis in original). Jed Rubenfeld, another federalist interpreter of the religion clauses, agrees with Smith that the religion clauses do not make Congress "wholly powerless over the subject of religion." "Antidisestablishmentarianism," 2357.

45. Smith, *Foreordained Failure*, 33–34.

46. Thomas C. Berg, "Religion Clause Anti-Theories,"*Notre Dame Law Review*, 72 (1997): 717.

47. Like Smith, Rubenfeld agrees that the religion clauses allow the federal government some power over religion and attempts to explain what that power is and is not. He writes,

> There may be distinctively federal domains—say, in the issuance of money, in regulating the armed forces, in making rules for its own legislative sessions, in governing territories, and so on—in which Congress can constitutionally make *laws intermeddling with religion*. But the question becomes very different when Congress tries to *regulate matters of faith directly* or to tell states what relation their laws must have to the fostering of one or all religions. . . . Congress has no power to *dictate a*

position on religion for individuals, and it has no power to dictate a position on religion for states." "Antidisestablishmentarianism," 2357 (emphasis added).

Although one can fairly clearly distinguish between a law telling individuals what to do and one telling states what to do, Rubenfeld's attempt to explain what laws *affecting individuals* in the federal domains the federal government can and cannot pass is no better than Smith's is. What is the difference between "laws intermeddling with religion" and those that "regulate matters of faith" or "dictate a position on religion?"

48. Moreover, it is a reason that would allow the religion clauses to be applied to the states, although perhaps via the privileges and immunities Clause, rather than the due process clause, of the Fourteenth Amendment. Although some early Americans may have thought that legislation on religion at the state level might not be divisive, at least in those states with a religiously homogeneous population, as states became more religiously pluralistic, one of the reasons for not allowing the federal government to legislate on religion—to avoid controversy and division—could legitimately be used to disallow such legislation by the states.

49. Smith, *Foreordained Failure*, chap. 1.

50. Smith, *Foreordained Failure*, 34 (emphasis in original).

51. Vincent P. Munoz, "The Original Meaning of the Establishment Clause and the Impossibility of Its Incorporation."*Univ. of Pennsylvania Journal of Constitutional Law*, 8 (2006): 585, 601–2.

52. For such an interpretation, see Bradley, *Church-State Relationships*, 95.

53. See John Witte, Jr., *Religion and the American Constitutional Experiment*, 2d ed. (Boulder, Col.: Westview Press, 2005), 94–95 ("On this . . . reading of the disestablishment clause, the word 'respecting' . . . becomes something of an umbrella term for . . . [all] features of a religious establishment. Congress could not agree on what specifics of religious establishment to outlaw—and so they simply outlawed the establishment of religion altogether and anything that 'pointed to' or 'moved toward' the same." 95).

Chapter Four

The Ratification Debate and Proposed Religion Clauses

The Bill of Rights, including the First Amendment, had its origin in some of the state conventions that met in 1787–1788 to consider whether to ratify the proposed new Constitution that had been written during the summer of 1787. As it turned out, the Constitution was ratified, but only by a slim margin and after considerable public debate. One of the main objections to it, made by both its opponents, the Anti-federalists, and some of its supporters, like Thomas Jefferson and John Adams, was that it did not contain a bill of rights.[1] Although its proponents, the Federalists, were generally strong supporters of the freedoms of religion, speech, and press,[2] they contended that a bill of rights was not needed or desirable and would not effectively protect basic rights.[3] They said, for example, that a guarantee of religious freedom was not needed because the only powers that the central government had were those delegated to it by the Constitution and the power to legislate on the subject of religion (or its free exercise) had not been one of those delegated to it.[4]

The Anti-federalists, however, were not convinced by the Federalists that a Bill of Rights should not be added to the Constitution—primarily because they were not convinced that the Constitution gave the national government no power over religion or its exercise. They reasoned that even if no such power had been explicitly delegated to Congress, it could still pass laws dealing with religion on the basis of the last clause in Article I, section 8, which authorized it to pass laws "necessary and proper for carrying into Execution" powers that *were* delegated to it—especially if that clause were liberally or loosely interpreted by the courts.[5] Some Anti-federalists also pointed out that the ban on religious tests contained in Article VI implied that the central government had power to legislate with respect to religion. If it did not, why was the ban needed?[6] The Anti-federalists, therefore, demanded that the proposed Constitution not be ratified until a bill of rights, including a religious liberty provision, was added to it.[7] This was one of their most powerful arguments against the Constitution, a fact recognized by many Federalists.[8]

Because of the Anti-federalists' demands for a bill of rights, and in order to obtain enough votes in favor of the Constitution, the Federalists, in some of the crucial ratifying conventions, proposed a compromise. They promised that if the Constitution as written were approved, either a constitutional convention or the first congress of the new government would draft amendments and submit them to the states for their approval. At each of the conventions where such a promise was made in order to secure an affirmative vote (Massachusetts, New Hampshire, New York, and Virginia), a list of proposed amendments to the Constitution was drawn up.[9] Also, in Pennsylvania and Maryland, where the proponents of the Constitution were able to win without having to make any such promises, the Anti-federalists on their own published a list of proposed amendments.[10] Another list of amendments came from the North Carolina ratifying convention, which, dominated by Anti-federalists, refused to ratify the Constitution until after it had been amended.-[11] It was these proposed amendments that the First Congress, under the leadership of James Madison, had in mind when it drafted the Bill of Rights.[12] Among these suggested amendments, "no subject was of greater concern than religion."[13]

I. THE SIGNIFICANCE OF THE DEBATE

The importance of these proposed amendments for our understanding of the religion clauses of the First Amendment cannot be overstated. One group of scholars has said:

> As men versed in the public affairs of the day, the members of the First Congress . . . certainly attempted to honor the wishes and demands of the states for additional safeguards of religious freedom through amendments. It is impossible to believe that the senators and representatives did not pay special heed to the amendments proposed by the states, at least from their respective states. Hence, any study of the First Amendment must include the state proposals.[14]

Other scholars, however, have challenged the importance of the amendments proposed by the Anti-federalists on the grounds that the Anti-federalists were either insincere or tepid in advocating that a bill of rights be added to the Constitution. They argue, for example, that the Anti-federalists' attack on the Constitution for not having a bill of rights was simply a smoke-screen that masked their real reasons for demanding a bill of rights, e.g., to prevent the ratification of the Constitution or to protect their political/economic interests, but one that worked effectively to arouse the people against the Constitution.[15] Although this point is surely valid in relation to certain leaders of the Anti-federalists, it in no way diminishes the importance of the amendments they proposed as indicators of the meaning of the provisions that were eventually included in the Bill of Rights. After all, regardless of the motives of individual Anti-federalist leaders, their argument that a bill of rights, including a religious freedom provision, should be added to the Constitution did, in fact, capture the popular imagination, and ultimately it was what the people wanted that counted in the minds of James Madison and other framers of the Bill of Rights.[16]

In summary, both the Federalists and Anti-federalists agreed that the soon-to-be-created national government should not be able to legislate on religion, at least not directly or in a threatening way. They disagreed, at least initially, on whether an amendment to the Constitution was needed to prevent the national government from doing what neither group wanted it to do. By agreeing to the Anti-federalists' demand for an amendment that would protect religion and religious freedom, the Federalists, in effect, conceded that the Constitution either conferred or might be interpreted as conferring powers that could be used to justify Congress' legislating on religion or religious freedom.[17] They then became the allies of the Anti-federalists, at least in this area, and took the initiative in drafting and passing such an amendment. What, however, did both groups want the amendment to say, and why?

II. ISSUES: WHAT KIND OF LAWS PERTAINING TO RELIGION DID BOTH FEDERALISTS AND ANTI-FEDERALISTS WANT TO PROHIBIT, AND WHY?

Given the sequence of events just summarized, some scholars contend that the proposed amendments relating to religion that came out of the ratification controversy can best be understood as attempts to say that the new national government should have no power whatsoever to legislate directly on the subject of *religion*, at least within the states beacuse that power should be reserved for the states.[18] This interpretation of the proposed amendments, however, is problematic for two reasons. First, it conflates legislation in any way relating directly with *religion* with legislation denying or threatening *the rights of conscience or freedom of religion*. In other words, it ignores the possibility that the proponents of an amendment may have wanted to prohibit not all laws directly relating to religion, but only those directly *endangering* religion, a particular religion, or a person or group because of her/his/its religion. After all, some laws directly relating to religion might be beneficial to religion and/or religious freedom.[19] For example, what about a federal statute that makes it illegal for private individuals and groups or agencies of government to violate religious freedom or to discriminate against persons or groups because of their religion? Also, what about laws that provide some sort of non-preferential aid to all religions?[20] In short, the first issue raised by what happened during the ratification controversy is whether the Federalists and Anti-federalists were opposed to *all* federal laws directly relating to religion or only those laws directly endangering religion or religious freedom.

Most of the scholars who favor a federalist or states' rights interpretation of the religion clauses seem to be unaware that there is an issue here. In other words, they simply assume that it was religion in general, and not more narrowly religious *rights*, that both Federalists and Anti-federalists wanted to remove from the jurisdiction of the federal government.[21] Although they sometimes use language that implies that it was religious rights that both groups wanted to protect, they then ignore the logical implications of such language. For example, Steven Smith writes:

> . . . [T]he Federalists' position might have been described something as follows: "We believe . . . that explicit constitutional *protection for religion* is unnecessary, because the national government has no power to *regulate or establish religion* in the first place. You (the Anti-Federalists) fear that Congress *does* have such power, perhaps under the 'necessary and proper' clause. We disagree; but just in case you are right, and in order to demonstrate our good faith, we consent to make the lack of congressional power over religion explicit through a constitutional amendment." By this view, the religion clauses served a clarifying and still jurisdictional purpose; they did not enact any substantive right or principle.[22]

Except for its last sentence, this quotation clearly implies that both Federalists and Anti-federalists wanted to *protect religion, not a state's right*, by preventing the national government from regulating or establishing it.

The quotation, however, concludes illogically. If the original proponents of the religion clauses wanted to *protect religion*, how does it follow that what they wanted was not substantive or normative in nature? If the purpose of an amendment is to protect religion, the natural, logical inference is that the amendment has normative meaning, and because of this inference, the burden of proof certainly rests on Smith or any other federalist scholar to come up with additional evidence to overcome the inference.[23] For example, is there any evidence that shows that the Federalists and Anti-federalists sought amendments pertaining to religion in order to ensure that the states had exclusive jurisdiction over religion in general?

Secondly, if it were true that both Federalists and Anti-federalists agreed that it was religion in general and not just religious freedom over which the national government should have no jurisdiction, that by itself hardly means that the amendment "did not enact any substantive [normative] right or principle." Whether such a conclusion is warranted depends on *why* both Federalists and Anti-federalists did not want to give the central government power to legislate with respect to religion. They could have done so either for reasons of federalism (to protect states' rights) or for a normative reason (because *no* government—national, state, or local—should have such a power). To determine which of these reasons was paramount, one needs to have additional historical evidence.

If the preceding analysis is correct, it means that the issue of *what* power the Federalists and Anti-federalists wanted to withhold from the federal government, while important, is not as important or relevant as the issue of *why* they wanted that power withheld. In short, as explained in chapter two, what determines whether the religion clauses have normative meaning is the *reason* for their enactment. What was their purpose? What problem were they trying to solve or prevent?[24]

Of course, the two issues are related. Just as the *why* determines the *what*, the *what* implies a *why*. If both the Federalists and Anti-federalists thought that the federal government could legislate with respect to religion, provided it did not harm it, e.g., by establishing a religion or prohibiting its free exercise, that would imply that some normative principle was responsible for the restriction on federal power. On the other hand, if the Federalists and Anti-federalists thought that the federal government should not legislate at all with respect to religion, that would imply that it was a concern for states' right that accounted for the religion clauses. After all, why else would they want to prevent federal legislation respecting religion that posed no threat to religion or religious freedom?

In any case, as with the first issue, scholars favoring a federalist interpretation of the religion clauses simply assume that both Federalists and Anti-federalists opposed the federal government's having jurisdiction over religion *because* they wanted the states alone to have that jurisdiction. For example, Steven Smith writes: "The enactors of those [religion] clauses were not adding new substantive rights or principles to the Constitution; rather, they were merely reiterating what they had asserted all along—. . . that the national government had no power over religion *because the regulation of religion was within the sole jurisdiction of the states.*"[25]

By itself, however, this assertion is not enough. What is needed in relation to both issues is historical evidence—evidence that shows whether it was religion or religious liberty on which both Federalists and Anti-federalists did not want the federal government to legislate and, in either case, evidence that shows *why* both groups did not want the federal government to legislate on that subject. What does the evidence show?

III. THE VIEWS OF THE FEDERALISTS

On the first issue, the Federalists themselves were not entirely clear, but were clear enough. Some of them said explicitly that Congress had not been given any power over "religion,"[26] but in most of those cases, accompanying comments make it clear that what they were talking about was power to establish a religion or prevent its free exercise. James Iredell, for example, in the North Carolina ratifying convention, asked, "Is there any power given to Congress in matters of religion?" This question, however, was in the middle of a reply to the fears expressed by another delegate that under the proposed Constitution the people "would be deprived of the privilege of worshipping God according to their consciences. . . ." Iredell, therefore, explained at some length that the national government has "no authority to interfere in the establishment of any religion whatsoever" or to "pass a single act to impair our religious liberties. . . ." He added: "If they could, it would be a just cause of alarm. . . . Happily no sect here is superior to another."[27] For Iredell, it was not really legislating on "religion," but the establishing of a religion and the denying of religious liberty that Congress had no power to do.

Other Federalists explicitly said that Congress had no power over the exercise of religion or the "rights of conscience" or words to that effect.[28] Consider what Madison said at the Virginia Ratifying Convention (the statement most relied upon by scholars who contend that the federal government was given no power over religion): "There is not the shadow of right in the general government to intermeddle with religion. Its least interference with it would be a most flagrant usurpation."[29] Does this statement support the conclusion that Madison thought the federal government was given no power over religion?[30] What Madison literally said was that it had no power to "intermeddle" or "interfere" with religion—words that clearly imply a harmful effect on religion.[31] Moreover, Madison immediately went on to say, "I can appeal to my uniform conduct on this subject, that I have warmly supported religious freedom."[32] A few years later, Madison said that it was "rights," not "religion," over which the federal government had no power.[33] Like Madison, Jefferson also said that the original Constitution gave the federal government no power "over the freedom of religion" or "its free exercise."[34] Another Federalist, Nicholas Collin wrote that what was not warranted by the original Constitution was "[p]artiality to any sect, or ill treatment of any. . . ."[35]

Some Federalists, in explaining why an amendment protecting rights of conscience was not needed, stated not only that the Constitution gave Congress no power to pass laws that might threaten such rights, but that Congress was explicitly prohibited from passing such laws by the provision in Article VI of the Constitution that prohibited the use of religious tests for determining persons' eligibility for holding office in the national government.[36] For example, Isaac Backus, the leader of Baptists in New England and an outspoken critic of the religious establishments that existed in that region, made this argument in explaining why a provision banning religious establishments did not need to be added to the Constitution.[37] In his opinion, the "no religious test" provision already in the Constitution precluded any religious establishment because "no such way of worship can be established without any religious test."[38] James Iredell was another Federalist who viewed Article VI ban on religious tests "as one of the strongest proofs that could be adduced, that it was the intention of those who formed this system, to establish a general religious liberty in America."[39] In short, all the Federalists cited above thought it was laws aimed at denying religious freedom or establishing a religion, not laws pertaining in any way to religion, that Congress could not pass.

If this correctly states the Federalists' understanding of the powers over religion that the Constitution did not delegate to the federal government, it obviously means that they thought the federal government could legitimately pass some laws respecting religion, provided they did not threaten the rights of conscience or the free exercise of religion. What might these laws have looked like? First, they could have been laws that prevented religious freedom from being violated by the federal government itself or by private individuals or groups. This point is strongly argued by Philip Hamburger, whose recent book, *Separation of Church and State*, presents numerous examples of Americans who believed that "not only constitutions but also . . . governments should protect individuals in the free exercise of their religion." More specifically, Hamburger writes that "the evangelical opponents of establishments had no desire for an antiestablishment clause so strong as to forbid laws protecting their property or recognizing their marriages, and Quakers hardly wanted a guarantee that would have nullified legislative exemptions."[40] Given these facts, it would have been foolish for the Federalists to have claimed that the original Constitution deprived the federal government of *all* power over the subject of religion.

Secondly, unobjectionable federal laws respecting religion could have included even laws protecting religious freedom from state laws. Kent Greenawalt gives the example of Congress' using its treaty-making power to enter into a treaty with a country in which it promised to protect the religious worship of persons of non-Christian faith coming to America from that country. He also gives the example of Congress' enlisting the support of a Catholic country during a war by promising to protect the religious freedom of Catholics in America. Thirdly, the federal government, according to Greenawalt, had the power to pass laws relating to religion in federal domains, such as the District of Columbia and the territories, over which Congress had plenary authority. He gives the specific example of a treaty that guaranteed all persons in a newly acquired territory the right to freely practice their religion.[41]

The one piece of evidence that has been cited against the preceding conclusion is the fact that at the North Carolina ratifying convention the leader of the Federalists in that state, James Iredell, said, "Had Congress undertaken to guarantee *religious freedom*, or any particular species of it, they would then have had a pretence to interfere in a subject they have nothing to do with."[42] In saying this, Iredell was responding to a critic of the Constitution, who, after noting that the Constitution contained a clause (in Article IV) guaranteeing to every state in the union a republican form of government,[43] asked "why a *guarantee of religious freedom* was not [also] included." Iredell answered by explaining that the "Guarantee Clause" was intended to "prevent any state from establishing any government but a republican one." In contrast, regarding religious freedom, he said, "Each state . . . must be left to the operation of its own principles."[44] This clearly implies that Iredell believed that Congress could not pass a law guaranteeing or protecting religious freedom *from state laws*.

The only problem with accepting this conclusion is that earlier in the very same speech, in response to the contention that Congress' treaty-making power could be used to establish the Roman Catholic Church in America, Iredell had said, "The power to make treaties can never be supposed to include a right to establish a foreign religion among ourselves, *though it might authorize a toleration of others*."[45] Obviously, if Iredell believed that Congress, by a treaty, could authorize the toleration of different religions, he did not believe that Congress had been denied *all* power over religion. Was Iredell simply contradicting himself, or is there some way of reconciling his two statements on the power of Congress to protect religious freedom? Although the former explanation may very well be the correct one, one could argue that there is a difference between a constitutional provision giving explicit jurisdiction over religious freedom to Congress and one, e.g., treaty-making power, giving only implicit jurisdiction over religious freedom to Congress, and that Iredell's position was that the latter kind of provision, but not the former, was acceptable. In any case, given their ambiguity, Iredell's comments are not enough to warrant the conclusion that Federalists generally thought the national government had, and should have, *no power whatsoever* over the subject of religion.

It only makes sense, therefore, to interpret the Federalists' statements about the federal government's lack of power over religion to mean that it lacked power to violate the rights of conscience or the free exercise of religion. As shown above, what the Federalists clearly and uniformly opposed were laws that attempted to control or influence what persons believed and practiced in the area of religion. It was not difficult for them, therefore, to accede to the request of the Anti-federalists for an amendment that would explicitly prevent such laws from being passed.[46]

As for the second issue, i.e., *why* the Federalists did not want the federal government to have jurisdiction over religious questiosn or religious liberty, the evidence, although limited, clearly supports a normative explanation. First, there is the record of the Constitutional Convention of 1787. Although nothing therein explicitly explains why the proposed national government was not given the power to legislate on religious matters, Frank Lambert makes a convincing case based on circumstantial evidence that the "founding fathers" considered the issue and consciously decided not to give the national legislature any power to legislate on religious matters. He emphasizes, first, that Charles Cotesworth Pinckney of South Carolina proposed a provision that would have explicitly prohibited the legislature from passing any laws "on the subject of religion" (but there is no recorded discussion of it) and, second, that the Convention approved the Article VI prohibition against religious tests for holding federal office.[47] Lambert says that there were several different reasons why the delegates did not want the national government to have direct jurisdiction over religious issues. They thought that it would have been wrong in principle, unnecessary, and in violation of states' rights. "[T]he prevailing sentiment," however, "was a desire to avoid dissension that would undermine union. To these delegates, religion was a divisive, not a unifying, force in pluralistic America. Any hope of obtaining ratification would be dashed if the new constitution attempted to define or support religion, because one or more sects would construe any formulation as violating their freedom of conscience. Better to make no mention of religion at all."[48]

Second, during the ratification debate, several influential Federalists explained why the national government had not been given power to legislate on religion or religious issues,[49] but, in contrast to Lambert's pragmatic explanation, they said that it was because it would be morally wrong for it, and by implication any government, to have such jurisdiction. For example, in the North Carolina ratifying convention, James Iredell stated:

> Is there any power given to Congress in matters of religion? Can they pass a single act to impair our religious liberties? If they could, it would be a just cause of alarm. If they could, sir, no man would have more horror against it than myself. Happily, no sect here is superior to another. As long as this is the case, we shall be free from those persecutions and distractions with which other countries have been torn.[50]

Iredell added that another reason Congress was given no power over religion was because "[t]he divine author of our religion never wished for its support by worldly authority. . . . It made much greater progress for itself [without such support], than when supported by the greatest authority upon earth."[51] Likewise, Tench Coxe, in explaining why the President, unlike the King of

England, had no power to influence religion, cited "the principle of perfect equality" and added that the "danger from ecclesiastical tyranny, that long standing and still remaining curse of the people—that sacrilegious engine of royal power in some countries, can be feared by no man in the United States."[52] In the Virginia ratifying convention, James Madison and Edmund Randolph gave similar reasons for why the national government did not and should not have jurisdiction over religion.[53]

After the Constitution was ratified and he was elected president, George Washington, in a letter to Virginia Baptists, explained that the national government had no powers that might threaten the liberty of conscience because the drafters of the Constitution, especially himself, wanted to avoid "the horrors of spiritual tyranny, and every species of religious persecution."[54] Most revealing is Washington's response to a group of Presbyterians in New England who in a letter to him expressed regret that there was no acknowledgment of God and Christ in the Constitution. He replied, ". . . [T]he path of true piety is so plain as to require but little political direction. To this consideration we ought to ascribe the absence of any regulation, respecting religion, from the Magna-Charta of our country. To the guidance of the ministers of the gospel this important object is, perhaps, more properly committed."[55] Notice that Washington did *not* say that religion should be left to the guidance of state governments!

Finally, the Federalists' explanation of why the Constitution gave the national government no power over religion paralleled their explanation of why it gave the national government no power over the press. As William T. Mayton has shown, the framers of the Constitution subscribed to "an eighteenth-century political philosophy that in a mature and sophisticated way contained most of the elements of modern free speech theory." Moreover, they believed in freedom of expression for normative or principled reasons—because it is "essential to preserving 'all the civil, political, and religious rights of an Englishman,'" because government is "a very poor judge of error in comments on public matters," because laws regulating expression tend to be indeterminate and grant sweeping discretion to officials, and because suppression of political speech is incompatible with democratic government.[56] The framers, however, did not consider freedom of expression to be absolute or unlimited. Although they thought that expression critical of the government should not be punished, they were willing to allow expression injurious to private persons, e.g., defamation, to be punished, but only by state governments and not the central government. If expression had to be regulated, the diverse regulations of the states, they thought, posed less of a threat to freedom of expression than would a national law applicable to everyone.[57]

The evidence that is available, therefore, indicates that the framers of the Constitution and prominent Federalists had normative, not federalist, reasons for denying the federal government any power over religious issues or religious freedom.[58] Although their statements may have been "after-the-fact" explanations, that does not make them invalid or hypocritical. Without evidence to the contrary, the statements must be taken as sincere expressions of why the framers and leading Federalists did not want the federal government to have jurisdiction over religious issues. More importantly, the reasons they gave have nothing to do with protecting states' rights or state establishments of religion. In fact, *there is no record of any Federalist's stating that the reason the federal government was not given or should not be given the power to interfere religion is because the states should have exclusive control over religion.*

Because of this fact, it is unwarranted for proponents of a federalist interpretation of the religion clauses to claim or even imply that the Federalists agreed to add religion clauses to the Constitution in order to make clear that the states had sole jurisdiction over religion. One example of such a claim comes from Steven Smith, who writes that "virtually everyone in the country—supporters and opponents of the Constitution alike—agreed from the outset that religion had been and should continue to be a matter within the domain of the states: it should not be transferred to the jurisdiction of the national government."[59] This claim, moreover, has been repeated so often that it is now assumed, even by its critics, to be one of the main historical arguments that can be made for a federalist interpretation of the religion clauses. Kent Greenawalt, for example, in explaining why at least the establishment clause has federalist meaning, writes: "A consistent theme of Federalist defenders was that speech and religion were subjects of state authority, not within the delegated powers of the federal government."[60] Such a claim, however, is simply not supported by the evidence, and repeating it will not change that fact. Although the Federalists certainly argued that the power to regulate speech and religion was not among the powers granted to the federal government , *they did not say that the reason for this was because such a power rightfully belonged to the states. Rather, they said that the reason was because such a power would be harmful to religion, a threat to religious freedom, and thus morally wrong.*

IV. THE VIEWS OF THE ANTI-FEDERALISTS

A. The Religious Liberty Amendments Sought by the Anti-federalists

What about the Anti-federalists? What kind of laws pertaining to religion did they not want the federal government to be able to pass and why? Here the evidence is voluminous and consistent, albeit somewhat complicated. Most of it is related to the religious liberty amendments that were proposed by either the majority or the minority at six of the ratifying conventions—Virginia, North Carolina, New York, New Hampshire, Pennsylvania, and Maryland.[61]

Presaging the First Amendment, five of the six proposed amendments contained both a "free exercise" or "rights of conscience" clause and a "no establishment" clause. Both the Virginia and North Carolina ratifying conventions submitted the following: "That religion, or the duty which we owe to our Creator, and the manner of discharging it, can be directed only by reason and conviction, not by force or violence, and therefore all men have an equal, natural and unalienable right to the free exercise of religion according to the dictates of conscience, and that no particular religious sect or society ought to be favored or established by Law in preference to others."[62] The provision proposed by New York's convention was similar but shorter: "That the people have an equal, natural and unalienable right, freely and peaceably to exercise their religion according to the dictates of conscience; and that no religious sect or society ought to be favored or established by law in preference of others."[63] Of the three remaining proposed amendments, two referred to "rights of conscience." The one from New Hampshire's convention said: "Congress shall make no laws touching religion, or to infringe the rights of conscience."[64] The provision proposed by Pennsylvania's Anti-federalist minority was the most unusual because it proposed to protect from federal law not only the rights of conscience but the various state constitutional provisions guaranteeing religious liberty. It read, "The rights of conscience shall be held inviolable, and neither the legislative, executive, nor judicial powers of the United States shall have authority to alter, abrogate or infringe any part of the constitutions of the several states, which provide for the preservation of liberty in matters of religion."[65] The remaining amendment was proposed by Maryland Anti-federalists and said, "That there be no national religion established by law; but that all persons be equally entitled to protection in their religious liberty."[66]

Were these proposed amendments to the Constitution expressions of states' rights, i.e., simply jurisdictional statements about what the new national government, as distinguished from the states, could not do, or were they expressions of individual, natural rights that no government, state or national, could violate?

Part of the answer to this question can be found in the wording of the proposed amendments. First, the amendments proposed by Virginia, North Carolina, and New York refer to the free exercise of religion as "an equal, natural and unalienable right," which, by definition, means it is a right *no* government can violate. Moreover, they include an explanation of why such rights are natural and unalienable: "That religion, or the duty which we owe to our Creator, and the manner of discharging it, can be directed only by reason and conviction, not by force or violence [laws]." Obviously these are normative reasons for adopting the amendments, and they have nothing to do with protecting states' rights or state establishments of religion. In fact, the amendment proposed by Pennsylvania's Anti-federalists implies an anti-states' rights position, for it prohibits the federal government from interfering not with any church-state arrangement or with a religious establishment in the states, but only with those state constitutional provisions "*which provide for the preservation of liberty in matters of religion*." This wording clearly implies that Pennsylvania Anti-federalists would not have objected to a federal law overruling a state law that *violated* religious liberty.[67]

Secondly, the amendment proposed by Virginia and North Carolina is taken verbatim from the religious liberty provision of the Virginia Declaration of Rights, which obviously states normative, not federalist, limitations on the Virginia government. If, therefore, the delegates at the Virginia and North Carolina ratifying conventions were proposing only federalist limitations on the federal government's power to control religion, then they picked a strange and misleading way of wording their proposals. Surely no other persons in Virginia or North Carolina at that time would have considered the proposals as imposing federalist restraints on the national government.

Finally, in the proposed amendments from Virginia, North Carolina, New York, and Maryland, the prohibitions against religious establishments are linked to and justified by the "right" to the free exercise of religion. In other words, the proposed amendments clearly imply that the normative "right" to religious liberty requires the absence of establishments of religion. This is most clearly implied in the request from Maryland's Anti-federalists that there be "no national religion established by law; *but* that all persons be *equally* entitled to protection in their religious liberty."[68] The crucial words here are "but" and "equally." The latter is important because it links religious liberty with the principle of equality, and the former is important because it indicates that an establishment of religion is the opposite of *equal* religious liberty. Although the proposals from the other three states connect their free exercise and anti-establishment clauses with "and" rather than "but," it is a fair inference that their authors also understood establishments of religion as necessarily or inherently inconsistent with the free exercise of religion. In all three proposals, the free exercise and anti-establishment clauses are linked by the principle of equality. The free exercise of religion is called an "equal" right, and what is condemned by the other clause is the "favoring" or "preferring" of one religious sect or society over others.[69]

Also important in establishing the equivalence of the free exercise and anti-establishment clauses is the addition (in the amendments proposed by Virginia, North Carolina, and New York) of the phrase "according to the dictates of conscience" after "free exercise of religion." Why was such a phrase added? Although this phrase may have been intended to emphasize the inviolability of one's conscience and, thus, that persons should not be compelled to act in ways inconsistent with the dictates of their consciences, it also makes sense to see the phrase "dictates of conscience" as simply the opposite of "dictates of government." In other words, religion should be exercised according to the dictates of individual consciences and not according to the dictates of law or government. Understood in this way, the phrase means that the free exercise of religion and the establishment of religion are exact opposites and that free exercise clauses and no establishment clauses are simply two different ways of prohibiting the same thing—government's dictating religion.[70]

If this way of interpreting the two clauses—as one—is correct, it means that the proposed anti-establishment amendments have just as much normative content as do the proposed free exercise amendments. One cannot argue, as some scholars do,[71] that the proposed free exercise or religious freedom amendments were intended to protect a normative, natural right, and the proposed anti-establishment amendments were intended to protect states' rights and, even, state establishments of religion. Such an interpretation is perverse—the exact opposite of how the proposed amendments were originally understood. To the Anti-federalists who proposed the amendments, the free exercise of religion meant no establishment of religion.[72]

B. Explanations of the Proposed Religious Liberty Amendments

These conclusions derived from the wording of the proposed religious liberty amendments are supported by what the Anti-federalists in Pennsylvania, New York, Virginia, North Carolina, and Maryland said in explaining and defending their proposed religious liberty amendments. Most of them were even more explicit than the amendments themselves were in equating religious freedom with an inalienable, natural right and with the complete disestablishment of religion.[73] In Pennsylvania, which at that time was generally considered the most religiously tolerant polity in America, if not the world,[74] the address of the ratifying convention minority refers to the rights of conscience as one of "those inalienable and personal rights of men, without the full, free, and secure enjoyment of which there can be no liberty, and over which it is not necessary for a good government to have the control."[75] The clear implication is that *no* government should have control over such rights.

Other leading Anti-federalists made it quite clear that the "rights of conscience" meant both "the free exercise of religious worship" and no establishment of religion.[76] One essay, most likely written by the leading Anti-federalists in the state, gave normative reasons for protecting the rights/liberty of conscience from federal laws. Without such protection, there would be (1) persecution "to promote the unity of the faith, in matters which pertain to our final salvation in a future world," (2) the establishment of "a form of religion, for the good people of this continent, with all the pains and penalties which in other countries are annexed to the establishment of a national church," and (3) the forcing of those "conscientiously scrupulous of bearing Arms" to serve in the military.[77]

At least two Anti-federalists proposed that the liberal religious liberty provisions in the Pennsylvania Declaration of Rights be added to the Constitution.[78] This is important because those provisions unquestionably contain detailed normative limitations on state government.[79] It is difficult to see how they, as applied to the federal government, could have been understood as stating anything other than normative restraints. More importantly, most of their writings indicate that Pennsylvania Anti-federalists viewed the Constitution as a contract or compact with the national government that was no different from the contract or compact that any people might make when founding a government. In other words, they thought that it should withhold from government control certain natural, inalienable rights, the first of which "it is of the utmost importance for the people to retain to themselves, which indeed they have not even the right to surrender . . . the LIBERTY OF CONSCIENCE."[80]

In New York, Virginia, and North Carolina, all of which proposed both a free exercise and a no establishment clause, leading Anti-federalists argued that an amendment was needed to protect religion and its free exercise. It was not enough that power to regulate religion had not been explicitly delegated to Congress. They also equated the free exercise of religion, the rights of conscience, and disestablishment of religion.[81] In Virginia, the leading Anti-federalist, Patrick Henry, said, "That sacred and lovely thing Religion, ought not to rest on the ingenuity of logical deduction. [Without explicit protection in the Constitution] Holy Religion . . . will be prostituted to the lowest purposes of human policy."[82] Although its ratifying convention proposed a "free exercise provision," individual Virginians often used "rights" or "liberty of conscience" language to refer to what the Constitution failed to protect.[83]

Others linked the free exercise of religion in a general way with religious equality.[84] For example, John Leland, the leader of Baptists in that state and the one who extracted from Madison a promise to secure the passage of a Bill of Rights, argued that the absence of a religious liberty provision was "Very Dangerous" to "religious liberty" because it would allow Congress to "favour one System more then another, . . . [and] oblige all others to pay to the Support of their System . . .," which, he said, would constitute "Oppression."[85] However religious liberty was explained, Baptists in Virginia were troubled, for normative reasons, by its lack of protection in the Constitution.[86]

As was done in Pennsylvania, moreover, it was argued that religious freedom was an inalienable right that *no* government had the right to violate.

For example, in a widely published letter that included a list of proposed amendments to the Constitution, Richard Henry Lee wrote:

> It having been found from universal experience, that the most express declarations and reservations are necessary to protect the just rights and liberty of mankind from the silent, powerful and ever active conspiracy of those who govern. . . . it is submitted—That the new constitution proposed for the government of the United States be bottomed upon a declaration or bill of rights, clearly and precisely stating the principles upon which this social compact is founded, to wit: That the rights of conscience in matters of religion ought not to be violated. . . .[87]

At about the same time, Thomas Jefferson made exactly the same argument in a letter to James Madison.[88] The preamble to the constitutional amendments submitted by the Virginia convention also makes quite clear that it considered the Constitution to be a "social compact" of the people, not states, and that a bill of rights was needed to protect certain unalienable rights, including "liberty of conscience."[89]

Similarly, in New York, which also proposed a "free exercise" provision, a leading Anti-federalist, Governor George Clinton, argued prior to the ratifying convention that the Constitution should protect the "rights of conscience" by making it impossible for "rulers . . . to establish particular forms of religion, and make every body worship God in a certain way, whether the people thought it right or not, and punish them severely, if they would not. . . ."[90] At the convention itself, one delegate expressed the wish that the Constitution had "prevented the general government from tyrannizing over our consciences by a religious establishment—a tyranny of all others most dreadful. . . ."[91] More importantly, according to "Brutus," a very influential spokesperson for Anti-federalists, such a provision was needed on the normative grounds that religious freedom was a natural right that "cannot be surrendered" to any government. To him, the establishment of the new national government and Constitution was no different from the establishment of a political society by persons in a state of nature. It required the clear and precise statement of the "principles . . . upon which the social compact is founded" and "the most express and full declaration of rights. . . ."[92] The convention itself echoed this sentiment by including similar language in its resolution ratifying the Constitution and calling for amendments.[93]

In North Carolina, another "free exercise" state, two of the Anti-federalist leaders, William Lenoir and Samuel Spencer, argued that the Constitution did not protect the "rights of conscience" because it allowed one particular religion, including its "ecclesiastical courts," to be established by the national government.[94] Again, religious liberty was equated with the absence of an established religion. Also, as in Virginia and New York, North Carolina's proposed religious freedom amendment was defended on the grounds that the new central government was the same as or analogous to the creation of a government by individuals in a state of nature. As such, it could not be given any power to control or regulate religion.[95] Spencer made the point in these terms: "It was observed, that as the Constitution is to be a delegation of power from the several states to the United States, a bill of rights was unnecessary. But it will be noticed that this is a different case. The states do not act in their political capacities, but the government is proposed for individuals. . . . The expression, 'We the people of the United States,' shews that this government is intended for individuals; there ought therefore to be a bill of rights."[96]

In contrast, it is not very clear what happened at the Maryland and New Hampshire ratifying conventions and how their proposed religious liberty provisions were generally understood, mainly because in both cases the record of the debates is incomplete. The evidence that does exist indicates relatively little concern in those conventions about the threat posed to religious liberty by the proposed new government.[97] Although the Maryland ratifying convention, for example, approved thirteen amendments and the Anti-federalists proposed others that were not approved, none of them pertained to religious freedom. It was only after the convention adjourned that the Anti-federalists published a list of proposed amendments that included a religious liberty provision.[98] Outside the convention, moreover, there was little commentary on the proposed provision. Luther Martin, the state's leading Anti-federalist, argued that a bill of rights, including a guarantee of liberty of conscience, should have been included in the proposed constitution, but he did not explain why he wanted such a guarantee.[99]

There was, however, one extremely influential Anti-federalist publication that made a very compelling case for adding a Bill of Rights, including a "liberty of conscience" provision, to the Constitution. "Essays by A Farmer," most likely written by John Francis Mercer, a non-signing member of the Constitutional Convention and a leader of the Maryland Anti-federalists,[100] insisted that some rights, including liberty of conscience, were fundamental, natural, inalienable, and personal. They were not rights vested in society or in the majority thereof, but "reserved to each member thereof." A bill of rights Mercer associated with the social contract that should be the basis of any society, a contract whereby it was agreed that "*no power*, which they [the people] thus conditionally delegated to the majority (*in whatever form organized*) should be so exercised as to infringe and impair these their natural rights. . . ." Most strikingly, like some Federalists, e.g., Madison, Mercer argued that these rights were threatened most, not by kings, but by majority-rule democracies, such as those of the state governments. "In such government the *tyranny* of the legislative is most to be dreaded." His conclusion was that "if these rights are not clearly and expressly ascertained, the *individual* must be lost."[101] Clearly, Mercer was arguing for a bill of rights, including liberty of conscience, in order to protect not states' rights, but individual rights—rights that *no* government has the authority to violate.[102]

According to extant records, neither at nor outside the New Hampshire convention was concern expressed over the lack of a provision in the Constitution protecting religious freedom.[103] This suggests that the only reason the New Hampshire convention proposed that a "rights of conscience" provision be added to the Constitution was because it wanted a Bill of Rights added and a guarantee of religious liberty was normally included in such a document.

It is also unclear why New Hampshire worded its proposed provision so that it prohibited laws "touching religion." At least three explanations are possible. First, it can be construed as a normative attempt to protect religious liberty on the basis of the contract theory of government, which was widely accepted and, as noted earlier, was used by Anti-federalists in other states to justify adding a religious freedom amendment to the Constitution. In other words, governments can exercise lawfully only those powers that are delegated to them by the people, and religion is a subject on which the people could never authorize *any* government to legislate. If a government were to do so, it would violate the principle of religious freedom.[104] A second, less radical interpretation is that the provision was simply a way of stating the Federalist position that no power to regulate religion had ever been delegated to the *central* government, but for a reason unrelated to protecting religious freedom, i.e., because that power resided exclusively in the states. Thirdly, although the New Hampshire Constitution of 1784 had a rather liberal guarantee of "rights of conscience,"[105] because it also contained a provision authorizing, but not requiring, towns to make payments to "protestant teachers of piety, religion and morality" and another requiring that officeholders be Protestants,[106] the proposed amendment to the U. S. Constitution that prohibited laws "touching religion" may even have been intended to prevent the national Congress from interfering with the state's support of the Protestant religion.[107] If that were its purpose, it would mean that the New Hampshire delegates understood their proposed "rights of conscience" provision conservatively, i.e., as not precluding all laws associated with traditional establishments of religion. This interpretation of the provision is certainly credible.

There is no explicit evidence to support it, however,[108] and some evidence that does not support it. First, because their constitution also said that "no subordination of any one sect or denomination to another, shall ever by *established* by law,"[109] it may be that the people of New Hampshire did not consider their limited support of religion to constitute an establishment of religion. Second, the Federalist delegates at the New Hampshire ratifying convention played an important, if not controlling, role in the drafting of the proposed amendments,[110] and one of them, the Reverend Samuel Langdon, was extremely influential. According to the president of the convention, his "preaching" changed the minds of about thirty delegates who had been instructed to vote against the Constitution.[111] At the convention, Langdon used the contract theory of government to defend religious freedom. He praised the prohibition of a religious test in the U. S. Constitution as "one of the greatest ornaments to the new constitution" and defended it on the grounds that religion should be "unconnected with and detached from civil power." He added that "[r]eligion must stand upon its own ground . . . if it could not, he should never think of calling upon the civil arm for its support . . . It would be arguing that its great author was insufficient." Finally, he insisted that the Constitution proposed no threat to either "the cause of religion" or "the free exercise of our religion" guaranteed by the New Hampshire Constitution.[112] If Langdon spoke for most Federalist delegates, then it is certainly possible, if not likely, that the provision prohibiting laws "touching religion" proposed by the New Hampshire ratifying convention was intended to be a normative or principled guarantee of religious freedom.[113]

Finally, there is the fact that one contemporary observer of the amendments proposed by the various states made no distinction, in terms of their purpose, between the religious freedom amendment proposed by New Hampshire's ratifying convention and those proposed by the Anti-federalist minorities in Pennsylvania and Maryland. He understood all three as prohibitions against the establishment of "any religious system in the United States."[114]

C. Summary: The Normative Nature of the Proposed Religious Liberty Amendments

In summary, except possibly for New Hampshire's, the proposed amendments relating to religious freedom, whether worded in terms of religious freedom, rights of conscience, the free exercise of religion, or no establishment of religion, were clearly understood by their authors and advocates as normative guarantees of religious equality. They wanted to prohibit the establishment of one religion over another and the passage of laws of the sort traditionally associated with establishments of religion.[115] Most importantly, the Anti-federalists often explained the need for a religious liberty amendment on the grounds that all governments, not just the federal government, should be limited by such a constitutional provision. Persons urged that religious liberty and no-establishment provisions be added to the Constitution because of a genuine fear of what might happen to the integrity of religion and its free exercise if the new central government could pass laws like those associated with traditional establishments of religion. Finally, there is very little, if any, evidence that they wanted such provisions in order to protect states' rights or state establishments of religion from federal legislation. Surely it is telling that the states that would have benefited the most from an amendment protecting state quasi-establishments of religion, i.e., Massachusetts and Connecticut, failed to propose or even consider such an amendment. The inescapable conclusion, therefore, is that early Americans wanted religious freedom amendments that had normative, not federalist, meaning.[116]

If any doubt remains about the truth of this claim, perhaps the following passage from one of the more influential Anti-federalist writings will remove it:

> There are certain rights which we have always held sacred in the United States, and recognized in all our constitutions, and which, by the adoption of the new constitution, its present form will be left unsecured. . . . It is proper the national laws should be supreme, and superior to state or district laws; but then the national laws ought to yield to *unalienable or fundamental rights*. . . . In fact, the 9th and 10th Sections in Art. I. in the proposed constitution, are no more nor less, than a partial bill of rights; they establish certain principles as part of the compact upon which the federal legislators and officers can never infringe. . . . [T]his bill of rights ought to be carried farther, and some other principles established, as a part of this fundamental compact between the people of the United States and their federal rulers.
>
> It is true, we are not disposed to differ much, at present, about religion; but when we are making a constitution, it is to be hoped, for ages and millions yet unborn, *why not establish the free exercise of religion, as a part of the national compact.*[117]

This passage, along with many others like it,[118] illustrates that Anti-federalists and other proponents of a Bill of Rights considered certain rights, especially religious freedom, to be so fundamental that *no government* should be allowed to violate them. Their arguments, in fact, assume that the creation of the new central government was the same as or analogous to the creation of a government by individuals in a state of nature. Using explicit contract or compact language, the proponents of a religious freedom provision argued that the rights of conscience were natural and inalienable, and thus could/should not be restricted by any government whatsoever.[119] Nowhere is it implied, let alone stated, that it is only the central government that should not violate them or that state governments were morally free to have whatever policy toward religion that they wanted to have. The proposed religious liberty amendments, in short, expressed a normative principle about the proper relationship between religion and government, and that principle was government non-involvement in religious beliefs and practices, i.e., neutrality toward different religions and perhaps even religion in general.[120]

Of course, none of the proposed amendments was worded precisely the same as the amendment later framed by the first Congress and ratified by the American people—the First Amendment. Given the fact, however, that in the

First Congress the main reason that was given for adding a guarantee of religious liberty to the Constitution was to satisfy the demands of so many persons and states,[121] it only makes sense to assume that whatever language was ultimately approved was thought to have satisfied those demands. In any case, if someone had told the Anti-federalists and the other proponents of a provision protecting religious freedom that the amendment that was ultimately approved had no normative content, but was merely federalist in nature and intended to protect states' rights, surely their response would have been one of shocked incredulity.[122]

There is, nevertheless, always the possibility that the First Congress adopted religion clauses with no normative content and, thereby, betrayed those who had demanded the clauses in the first place. Is there any evidence from the proceedings of the First Congress that such a turn of events actually occurred? This question is addressed in the next chapter.

NOTES

1. See Jefferson's letter to James Madison, 12-20-1787, in *The Papers of James Madison*, ed. Robert A. Rutland et al (Chicago: Univ. of Chicago Press, 1977): 10:337, and Adams' letter to Cotton Tufts, 2-12-1788, in *The Documentary History of the Ratification of the Constitution* (hereafter cited as *DHRC*), Vol. XIV, *Commentaries on the Constitution, Public and Private* (hereafter cited as *CC*), Vol. 2, ed. John P. Kaminski & Gaspare J. Saladino (Madison, Wis.: State Historical Society of Wisconsin, 1983): 463 n. 4.

2. Federalists "held advanced civil libertarian ideas for their times. . . ." Charlene B. Bickford and Kenneth R. Bowling, *Birth of the Nation: The First Federal Congress 1789–1791* (Madison, Wis.: Madison House Pubs, 1989), 52. For examples of eloquent defenses of religious freedom by Federalists, see Rev. Phillips Payson, at Massachusetts Ratifying Convention, 1/31/1788, in *The Debates in the Several State Conventions on the Adoption of the Federal Constitution*, ed. Jonathan Elliot (New York: Burt Franklin, 1965 rep. of 1888 ed.), 2:120, and Tench Coxe, "A Friend of Society and Liberty,"*Pennsylvania Gazette*, 7/23/1788, in *DHRC*, XVIII, *CC*, 6:281–82. Owen S. Ireland convincingly demonstrates that in Pennsylvania the Federalists had much the better record in terms of defending religious freedom and other civil liberties. *Religion, Ethnicity, and Politics: Ratifying the Constitution in Pennsylvania* (University Park, Penn.: Pennsylvania State University Press, 1995), 79–86, 273–74. See, however, Morton Borden, "Federalists, Antifederalists, and Religious Freedom,"*Journal of Church and State*, 21 (Autumn 1979): 469–82, for the case that the Federalist record on religious freedom was no better than that of the Anti-federalists.

3. For the argument that adding a bill of rights was both unnecessary and dangerous, see James Wilson's speech of 10/6/1787 in Philadelphia, in *DHRC*, XIII, *CC*, 1:339–40; *Federalist*, No. 84; and Madison's speeches of 6/24/1788 in the Virginia Ratifying Convention, in *DHRC*, Vol. X, *Ratification of the Constitution by the States* (hereafter cited as *RCS*): *Virginia*, ed. John P. Kaminski & Gaspare J. Saladino (Madison, Wis.: State Historical Society of Wisconsin, 1993), 1498–1505, 1507. For the ineffectiveness argument, see A Countryman [Roger Sherman], New Haven *Gazette*, 11/22/1787, in *DHRC*, III, *RCS: Delaware, New Jersey, Georgia, Connecticut*, ed. Merrill Jensen (Madison, Wis.: State Historical Society of Wisconsin, 1978), 471–73, and Madison's letter to Jefferson, 10/17/1788, *PJM*, 11:297–300. For an account of all the arguments (six) made by the Federalists against adding a bill of rights to the Constitution, see Paul Finkelman, "Between Scylla and Charybdis: Anarchy, Tyranny, and the Debate over a Bill of Rights," in *The Bill of Rights: Government Proscribed*, ed.

Ronald Hoffman & Peter J. Albert (Charlottesville, Va.: Univ. Press of Virginia, 1997), 123–36.

4. For examples of this argument, see The Landholder VI [Oliver Ellsworth], Connecticut *Courant*, 12/10/1787, in *DHRC*, III, *RCS: Delaware, New Jersey, Georgia, Connecticut*, 490; A Freeman II [Tench Coxe], Pennsylvania *Gazette*, 1/30/1788, in *DHRC*, XV, *CC*, 3:508; Edmund Randolph's speech in the Virginia Ratification Convention, 6/10/1788, in *DHRC*, IX, *RCS*: *Virginia*, 1100; An Independent Freeholder [Alexander White?], Winchester Virginia *Gazette*, 1/18/1788, in *DHRC*, VIII, *RCS: Virginia*, 311; James Madison's speeches in the Virginia Ratification Convention, 6/6/1788, in *DHRC*, IX, *RCS: Virginia*, 994, and 6/12/1788, in *DHRC*, X, *RCS: Virginia*, 1223–24; and Cassius II, "To Richard Henry Lee, Esquire," *Virginia Independent Chronicle*, 4/9/1788, in *DHRC*, IX, *RCS*: *Virginia*, 715.

5. For examples of this argument, see Letter IV from the Federal Farmer [unknown] to "The Republican," New York, 10/12/1787, in *DHRC*, XIV, *CC*, 2:44; James Monroe, "Some Observations on the Constitution" (pamphlet), 5/25/1788, in *DHRC*, IX, *RCS: Virginia*, 859; and Deliberator (essay), Philadelphia *Freeman's Journal*, 2/20/1788, in *The Complete Anti-Federalist*, Vol. 3, ed. Herbert J. Storing (Chicago: Univ. of Chicago Press, 1981), 179. Also, see Kurt T. Lash, "Power and the Subject of Religion,"*Ohio State Law Journal*, 59 (1998): 1081–86.

6. See "The Government of Nature Delineated, or An Exact Picture of the New Federal Constitution by Aristocrotis," in *Complete Anti-Federalist*, 3:207–8; Cincinnatus [Arthur Lee], "Reply to Wilson's Speech, III,"*New York Journal*, 11/15/1787, in *DHRC*, XIV, *CC*, 2:125; and Edmund Randolph, "Letter to James Madison," 2/29/1788, in *DHRC*, VIII, *RCS: Virginia*, 437.

7. See, e.g., "An Old Whig V," [George Bryan?] *Independent Gazetteer* (Philadelphia), 11/1/1787, in *DHRC*, XIII, *CC*, 1:538–43. For excellent summaries of all the arguments that the Anti-federalists made for adding a bill of rights to the Constitution, see Saul Cornell, "Mere Parchment Barriers? Antifederalists, the Bill of Rights, and the Question of Rights Consciousness," in *Bill of Rights*, 175, 191–208; Michael Lienesch, "Reinterpreting Rights: Antifederalists and the Bill of Rights," in *Bill of Rights*, 245–73; and Finkelman, "Between Scylla and Charybdis," 146–70.

8. Saul Cornell, "Mere Parchment Barriers?," 193.

9. See Michael Allen Gillespie, "Massachusetts: Creating Consensus," in *Ratifying the Constitution*, ed. Michael A. Gillespie and Michael Lienesch (Lawrence, Kan.: Univ. Press of Kansas, 1989), 138–67; Jean Yarbrough, "New Hampshire: Puritanism and the Moral Foundations of America," in *Ratifying the Constitution*, 235–58; Lance Banning, "Virginia: Sectionalism and the General Good," in *Ratifying the Constitution*, 261–99; and Cecil L. Eubanks, "New York: Federalism and the Political Economy of Union," in *Ratifying the Constitution*, 300–40. The South Carolina convention also proposed some (four) amendments, but not in order to win enough votes for the Constitution. The Anti-federalists attempted to get the convention to recommend other amendments, including a bill of rights, but they were easily defeated. Robert M. Weir, "South Carolina: Slavery and the Structure of the Union," in *Ratifying the Constitution*, 224.

10. See George J. Graham, Jr., "Pennsylvania: Representation and the Meaning of Republicanism," in *Ratifying the Constitution*, 52–70, and B. C. Steiner, "Maryland's Adoption of the Constitution,"*American Historical Review*, 5 (Oct. 1899): 22–44, 207–24.

11. See Michael Lienesch, "North Carolina: Preserving Rights," in *Ratifying the Constitution*, 343–67. In Rhode Island, where sentiment was overwhelmingly against the new constitution, the legislature refused to call a ratifying convention until well after the new national government was organized and the Bill of Rights was drafted and submitted to the states by the First Congress. See John P. Kaminski, "Rhode Island: Protecting State Interests," in *Ratifying the Constitution*, 368–90. For an excellent summary of what happened in all the states, see John P. Kaminski, "The Making of the Bill of Rights: 1787–1792," in *Contexts of the Bill of Rights*, ed. S. L. Schechter and R. B. Bernstein (Albany, N.Y.: New York State Commission on the Bicentennial of the United States Constitution, 1990), 18–38.

12. See below, pp. 87–88.

13. John E. Semonche, *Keeping the Faith: A Cultural History of the U. S. Supreme Court* (Lanham, Md.: Rowman & Littlefield, 1998), 30.

14. Chester J. Antieau, et al, *Freedom from Federal Establishment: Formation and Early History of the First Amendment Religion Clauses* (Milwaukee, Wisc.: Bruce Pub., 1964), 111. In agreement is Gerard V. Bradley, *Church-State Relationships in America* (Westport, Conn.: Greenwood Press, 1987), 70, and Gary D. Glenn, "Forgotten Purposes of the First Amendment Religion Clauses,"*Review of Politics*, 49 (Summer 1987): 340, 341.

15. Perhaps the most notable example of such a scholar is Leonard W. Levy. See his *Emergence of a Free Press* (New York: Oxford Univ. Press, 1985), 220–66, and "The Bill of Rights," in *The American Founding: Essays on the Formation of the Constitution*, ed. J. Jackson Barlow et al (New York: Greenwood Press, 1988), 296–97. For other scholars who view the Anti-federalists as uncommitted to individual rights, see James H. Hutson, "The Birth of the Bill of Rights: The State of Current Scholarship,"*Prologue*, 20 (Fall 1988): 143, 146–51; and Bradley, *Church-State Relationships*, 71–72.

16. Hutson, "Birth of Bill of Rights," 157 (". . . [T]he convictions of his [Madison's] constituents in Orange County, Virginia, and of common people in other parts of the country that arbitrary power could be arrested by a bill of rights generated the pressure that helped produce the document.") Also, see David A. Anderson, "The Origins of the Press Clause,"*U.C.L.A. Law Review*, 30 (1983): 470–71. Even Levy concedes that "[t]he single issue that united Anti-Federalists throughout the country was the lack of a bill of rights."*Emergence of a Free Press*, 233. Also, see David Rabban, "The Ahistorical Historian: Leonard Levy on Freedom of Expression in Early American History,"*Stanford Law Review*, 37 (Feb. 1985): 813–14, 831; Richard W. T. Martin, *The Free and Open Press* (New York: New York Univ. Press, 2001): 110; and Semonche, *Keeping the Faith*, 30.

17. Douglas Laycock, "'Nonpreferential' Aid to Religion: A False Claim about Original Intent,"*William and Mary Law Review*, 27 (1986): 908.

18. See, e.g., Leonard W. Levy, *The Establishment Clause: Religion and the First Amendment* (Chapel Hill, N. C.: Univ. of North Carolina Press, 1994, 2d ed. rev.), 93; John F. Wilson, "Religion, Political Culture, and the Law,"*DePaul Law Review*, 41 (1992): 824; T. Jeremy Gunn, *A Standard for Repair: The Establishment Clause, Equality, and Natural Rights* (Hamden, Conn.: Garland Pub. Co., 1992), 66; Jay S. Bybee, "Taking Liberties with the First Amendment: Congress, Section 5, and the Religious Freedom Restoration Act,"*Vanderbilt Law Review*, 48 (Nov. 1995): 1562; Jed Rubenfeld, "Antidisestablishmentarianism: Why RFRA Really Was Unconstitutional,"*Michigan Law Review*, 95 (Aug. 1997): 2354–57; Steven D. Smith, *Foreordained Failure: The Quest for a Constitutional Principle of Religious Freedom*, (New York: Oxford Univ. Press, 1995), 31; Steven D. Smith, *The Constitution and the Pride of Reason*, (New York: Oxford Univ. Press, 1998), 56; and Lash, "Power and Religion," 1088–93.

19. On this point, one early American minister said, "Religion and civil government, are not one and the same thing . . . [and] the former . . . hath rights and prerogatives, with which the latter may not intermeddle. Still, there are many ways, in which civil government may give countenance, encouragement, and even support to religion, without invading the prerogatives of the Most High; or . . . tho [sic] sacred rights of conscience. . . ." Timothy Stone, "Election Sermon," 5/10/1792, Hartford, Conn., in *American Political Writing during the Founding Era: 1760–1805*, ed. Charles S. Hyneman and Donald Lutz (Indianapolis, Ind.: Liberty Fund, 1983), 2:851–52.

20. Gerard Bradley, for example, rejects the proposition that "the federal government has no power over religion in the states" precisely because he believes the religion clauses were not intended to preclude laws aiding all religions equally. *Church-State Relationships*, 96–98. Of course, other scholars, such as Douglas Laycock (see his "'Non-preferential' Aid to Religion" cited above, fn 17), reject such a non-preferentialist interpretation of the religion clauses.

21. For examples of scholars who fail to distinguish between "religion" and "religious rights," see Akhil Amar, *The Bill of Rights: Creation and Reconstruction* (New Haven, Conn.: Yale Univ. Press, 1998), 36 (". . . Federalists of all stripes . . . declared that the federal government simply had no jurisdiction over religion in the several states."); and Rubenfeld, "Antidisestablishmentarianism," 2354 ("Federalists replied to all such objections by saying that Congress had no legislative power over religious matters one way or the other."). At least one

proponent of a federalist interpretation of the religion clauses, however, does consider the possibility that the two groups wanted only to protect religious liberty and not to prohibit all laws dealing with religion. Kurt Lash concedes that "certain laws passed on behalf of religious freedom" might not have been prohibited by the religion clauses, and he even gives evidence from the drafting of the clauses that supports such an interpretation. "Power and Religion," 1089–90. He goes on, however, and attempts to explain away this evidence and presents other evidence that he believes supports the idea that it was religion, and not just religious rights, on which Congress was precluded from legislating. "Power and Religion," 1090–93. All of the evidence that Lash discusses is examined above at pp.44–45, and below at p. 174–75.

22. Smith, *Foreordained Failure*, 31 (emphasis on "protection for religion" and "regulate or establish religion" added).

23. Remarkably, Smith argues that the natural inference is otherwise. He writes: "By itself, . . . the fact that the Federalists acknowledged possible federal implied power over religion does not entail the conclusion that the religion clauses adopted any substantive [normative] right or principle of religious freedom. On the contrary, the more natural inference is that the religion clauses were calculated simply to make explicit the jurisdictional division that both the Federalists and their opponents had professed to favor but that the Anti-federalists thought was not clearly expressed in the Constitution itself."*Foreordained Failure*, 31.

24. On the importance of this question, see Laycock, "'Nonpreferential' Aid," 908–9.

25. *Constitution and Pride,* 56 (emphasis added).

26. See, e.g., Edmund Randolph, Speech in the Virginia Ratification Convention, 6/10/1788, in *DHRC*, IX, *RCS: Virginia*, 1100.

27. Speech in the North Carolina Ratifying Convention, 7/30/1788, in *The Debate on the Constitution: Federalist and Antifederalist Speeches, Articles, and Letters During the Struggle over Ratification*, 2 vols, ed. Bernard Bailyn (New York: Library of America, 1933), 2:904.

28. See, e.g., An Independent Freeholder, Winchester Virginia *Gazette*, 1/18/1788, in *DHRC*, VIII, *RCS: Virginia*, 311; Cassius II, "To Richard Henry Lee, Esquire," *Virginia Independent Chronicle*, 4/9/1788, in *DHRC*, IX, *RCS: Virginia*, 715; and others cited by Daniel Dreisbach, *Thomas Jefferson and the Wall of Separation between Church and State* (New York: New York Univ. Press, 2002), 190–91, n. 37.

29. Speech in Virginia Ratifying Convention, 6/12/1788, in *DHRC*, X, *RCS: Virginia*, 1223–24. Similarly, on 7/30/1788, the North Carolina Federalist, Richard Spaight, said, "As to the subject of religion. . . . no power is given to the general government to *interfere* with it at all." Speech at the North Carolina Ratifying Convention, in *The Founders' Constitution*, 5 vols, ed. Philip B. Kurland & Ralph Lerner (Chicago: Univ. of Chicago Press, 1987), 5:92 (emphasis added). In addition, the South Carolina Federalist, Charles C. Pinckney, said, ". . . [T]he new government possessed no power of *interference* in religion." (emphasis added). Speech in S. C. House of Representatives, 1/18/1788, reported in *The American Herald*, 7 (2/28/1788): 1.

30. As alleged, e.g., by Bybee, "Taking Liberties,"1563 (. . . [H]e [Madison] continued to believe the federal government lacked any power to address religion, speech, or press. . . .)

31. Earlier at the same convention, Madison had been somewhat ambiguous as to the "subject" over which "[t]he Government has no jurisdiction." He said, "I confess to you, Sir, were uniformity of religion to be introduced by this system, it would, in my opinion, be ineligible; but I have no reason to conclude, that uniformity of Government will produce that of religion. This subject is, for the honor of America, perfectly free and unshackled: The Government has no jurisdiction over it—The least reflection will convince us, there is no danger to be feared on this ground." Speech in Virginia Ratifying Convention, 6/6/1788, in *DHRC*, IX, *RCS: Virginia*, 994. His remarks in toto, however, make it clear that what he feared was uniformity of religion, which he considered a threat to religious freedom.

32. Speech in Virginia Ratifying Convention, 6/12/1788, in *DHRC*, X, *RCS: Virginia*, 1224. Indeed, a few years earlier Madison had used almost identical language to explain why he condemned a Virginia law incorporating the Protestant Episcopal Church: "Because the law admits the power of the Legislative Body to interfere in matters of Religion which we think is not included in their jurisdiction." "A Petition Relating to Church Establishment" (1786), in *Church and State in American History*, ed. John E. Wilson & Donald L. Drakeman (Boulder, Col.: Westview Press, 2003, 3rd ed.), 69.

33. See his "Report on the Virginia Resolutions" (Jan. 1800), in *Founders' Constitution*, 5:141, 143, 146.

34. Quoted in Lash, "Power and Religion," 1094.

35. "Remarks on the Amendments to the Federal Constitution" (No. 9), in Philadelphia *Federal Gazette*, (11/18/1788): 2.

36. ". . . [N]o religious Test shall ever be required as a Qualification to any Office or public Trust under the United States."*U. S. Constitution*, Article VI.

37. Backus was a member of the Massachusetts ratifying convention, and although he had been elected as an Anti-federalist, at the convention he changed his mind about the proposed Constitution and thought it should be ratified.

38. Speech in Massachusetts Ratifying Convention, 2/4/1788, in *Debate on the Constitution*, 1:931.

39. Speech in North Carolina Ratifying Convention, 7/30/1788, in *Debate on the Constitution*, 2: 903.

40. *Separation of Church and State* (Cambridge, Mass.: Harvard Univ. Press, 2002), 101–7. For several examples of legislature-granted, religion-based exemptions from valid laws, see Michael W. McConnell, "The Origins and Historical Understanding of Free Exercise of Religion,"*Harvard Law Review*, 103 (1990): 1466–73, 1500–3, and Douglas Laycock, "Regulatory Exemptions of Religious Behavior and the Original Understanding of the Establishment Clause,"*Notre Dame Law Review*, 81 (2006): 1793–1842.

41. "Common Sense about Original and Subsequent Understandings of the Religion Clauses,"*University of Pennsylvania Journal of Constitutional Law*, 8 (2006): 482–83, 485, 487, 495. Greenawalt gives several examples of early treaties that were used to protect freedom of religion in a territory. "Common Sense," 487, fn 18. He seems to think, however, that the Federalists were saying that Congress has absolutely no jurisdiction over religion, for he criticizes them for not paying attention to and oversimplifying the various ways that Congress could rightfully legislate on religion. "Common Sense," 495–96. What the preceding analysis shows, however, is that the Federalists were saying only that Congress has no power to *interfere* with religion, and, thus, they do not deserve such criticism.

42. Speech on 7/30/1788, in *Debate on Constitution*, 2: 906. Iredell's statement is used by Lash, "Power and Religion," 1081, 1085–86, to support the proposition that the Federalist position was "that the proposed Constitution granted no power to Congress *regarding the subject of religion*—express or implied." (emphasis added)

43. See *U. S. Constitution*, Art. IV, sec. 4 ("The United States shall guarantee to every State in this Union a Republican Form of Government. . . .")

44. Speech on 7/30/1788, in *Debate on the Constitution*, 2:906.

45. Speech on 7/30/1788, in *Debate on Constitution*, 2:904–05 (emphasis added). Rather surprisingly, Joseph Snee, one of the first scholars to contend that the establishment clause protects states' rights, concedes that the federal government's treaty-making power could be used to protect religious liberty and "to that extent interfere with state sovereignty and state establishments." Moreover, he points out that the 1803 treaty with France whereby the United States purchased the Louisiana Territory contains a guarantee of religious freedom for those living in that area and that "such agreements have frequently been made with foreign powers." "Religious Disestablishment and the Fourteenth Amendment,"*Washington University Law Quarterly*, (1954): 395–96. For examples of treaties that attempted to protect the religious freedom of American citizens in other countries, see Lash, "Power and Religion," 1138–43.

46. See Robert A. Destro, "The Structure of the Religious Liberty Guarantee,"*Journal of Law & Religion*, 11 (1994–95): 368, 371, 392, and Laycock, "'Non-preferential' Aid," 907–9.

47. *The Founding Fathers and the Place of Religion in America* (Princeton, N. J.: Princeton Univ. Press, 2003), 236–53.

48. *Founding Fathers*, 250–53. Agreeing with Lambert's explanation is Derek H. Davis, *Religion and the Continental Congress 1774–1789: Contributions to Original Intent* (New York: Oxford Univ. Press, 2000), 133.

49. Some Federalists who insisted that the national government had no power to legislate on religious issues did not explain why. See, e.g., James Wilson's speech in Philadelphia, 10/6/1787, in *DHRC*, XIII, *CC*, 1:339–40; A Freeman II [Tench Coxe], *Pennsylvania Gazette*

(Philadelphia), 1/30/1788, in *DHRC*, XV, *CC*, 3:508; An Independent Freeholder, *Virginia Gazette* (Winchester), 1/18/1788, in *DHRC*, VIII, *RCS: Virginia*, 311; and Cassius II, "To Richard Henry Lee, Esquire, II,"*Virginia Independent Chronicle*. 4/9/1788, in *DHRC*, IX, *RCS: Virginia*, 714–15.

50. Speech in the North Carolina Ratifying Convention, 7/30/1788, in *Debate on Constitution*, 2:904.

51. Speech in North Carolina Ratifying Convention, 7/30/1788, in *Debate on Constitution*, 2: 905.

52. "An American Citizen" I, *Independent Gazetteer* (Philadelphia), in *Debate on Constitution*, 1:22.

53. See James Madison's speech in the Virginia Ratifying Convention, 6/12/1788, *DHRC*, X, *RCS: Virginia*, 1223–24; and Edmund Randolph's speech in the Virginia Ratifying Convention, 6/10/1788, *DHRC*, IX, *RCS: Virginia*, 1100–1101.

54. "To the United Baptist Churches of Virginia," (May, 1789), in *The Papers of George Washington, Presidential Series*, ed. W. W. Abbot (Charlottesville, Va.: Univ. Press of Virginia, 1987), 2:423–24.

55. "To the Presbyterian Ministers of Massachusetts and New Hampshire" (11/21/1789), in *The Papers of George Washington, Presidential Series*, ed. W. W. Abbot and Dorothy Twohig (Charlottesville, Va.: Univ. Press of Virginia, 1993), 4: 274.

56. "Seditious Libel and the Lost Guarantee of a Freedom of Expression,"*Columbia Law Review*, 84 (Jan. 1984): 109, 108–19. Agreeing with Mayton are Milton M. Klein, "Liberty as Nature's Gift: The Colonial Origins of the Bill of Rights in New York," in *The Bill of Rights and the States: The Colonial and Revolutionary Origins of American Liberties*, ed. Patrick T. Conley & John P. Kaminski, (Madison, Wis.: Madison House, 1992), 227–33, and Anderson, "Origins of Press Clause," 486–93, 523–37. Cf. Leonard Levy, *Legacy of Suppression: Freedom of Speech and Press in Early American History* (Cambridge, Mass.: Harvard Univ. Press, 1960), which argues that the framers of the Constitution and First Amendment accepted the Blackstonian or common law interpretation of freedom of expression and, therefore, thought the federal government could pass laws against seditious libel. In his article, Mayton raises many challenges, too numerous to be summarized here, to Levy's argument. Also, see Anderson, "Origins of Press Clause," 494–515, for a thorough critique of Levy's argument.

57. Mayton, "Seditious Libel," 113–14, 128, 131–32.

58. There are also remarks from less prominent Federalists that agree with those of the more prominent ones. For example, "A Foreign Spectator" (Nicholas Collin) wrote that it would be "very unjust and pernicious to establish any religious system in the United States; but it is needless to guard against such a visionary evil. Congress cannot by any construction, claim such a power. . . . Partiality to any sect, or ill treatment of any, is neither in the least warranted by the Constitution, nor compatible with the general spirit of toleration; and equal security of civil and religious rights is therefore given to all denominations, without any formal stipulations; which, indeed, might suggest an idea, that such an equality was doubtful." Philadelphia *Federal Gazette*, (11/18/1788): 2. Also, see A Freeholder, Virginia *Independent Chronicle*, 4/9/1788, in *DHRC*, IX, *RCS:Virginia*, 725, and *Pennsylvania Gazette*, 7/16/1788, in *DHRC*, XVIII, *CC*, 6:269–70.

59. "The Jurisdictional Establishment Clause: A Reappraisal,"*Notre Dame Law Review*, 81 (2005–2006): 1849.

60. "Common Sense," 494.

61. In the Massachusetts ratifying convention, no one mentioned religious liberty explicitly as a right that might be denied by the new national government, and a provision protecting religious liberty was not included among the amendments asked for by the delegates. Although at one point in the convention's proceedings Samuel Adams moved that a declaration of rights (including a rights of conscience provision) be included among the proposed amendments to the Constitution, the reasons for his doing so are unclear, and because his motion upset the consensus that was developing among the delegates, he quickly withdrew it. Elliot, ed., *Debates in the State Conventions*, 2: 162. Also, see Gillespie, "Massachusetts," 156–67.

62. "The Ratifications of the New Foederal Constitution, Together with the Amendments, Proposed by the Several States," in *Contexts of Bill of Rights*, 135, 141. This language is taken directly and verbatim from the Virginia Declaration of Rights of 1776.

63. "Ratifications of New Constitution," 114.

64. "Ratifications of New Constitution," 127.

65. "The Address and Reasons of Dissent of the Minority of the Convention of the State of Pennsylvania to their Constituents,"*Pennsylvania Packet* (Philadelphia), 12/18/1787, in *Debate on Constitution*, 1:532.

66. Quoted in *Debate on Constitution*, 2:554.

67. Steven K. Green, "Federalism and the Establishment Clause: A Reassessment,"*Creighton Law Review*, 38 (2005): 784–85. Cf. Donald L. Drakeman, *Church-State Constitutional Issues: Making Sense of the Establishment Clause* (New York: Greenwood Press, 1991), 61, & Bradley, *Church-State Relationships*, 92, both of whom, for no apparent reason, say that the Pennsylvania Anti-federalists' proposal supports the thesis that Anti-federalists generally wanted a constitutional provision that would protect *all* existing state arrangements.

68. Quoted in *Debate on Constitution*, 2:554 (emphasis added).

69. See Hamburger, *Separation of Church and State*, 96 ("[M]any dissenters . . . described themselves as seeking religious liberty when they condemned the unequal privilege enjoyed by establishments. . . . [They] also enunciated their demands . . . in terms of some degree of equality. For example, many claimed equal liberty or an equality of religious liberty.")

70. On the connection between religious liberty and no religious establishments in the proposed amendments, see Noah Feldman, "The Intellectual Origins of the Establishment Clause,"*New York University Law Review*, 77 (May 2002): 400–401. Although Jay Bybee mistakenly (in my opinion) interprets the religion clauses as guarantees of states' rights, he does correctly describe the inverse relationship between the free exercise of religion and the establishment of a religion. He writes: "Religious establishment and religious free expression were inextricably connected in the states. Whatever freedom in religious practices the states guaranteed was subject to the state's decision to establish religion, in varying degrees. In other words, the free exercise of religion in the states was subject to whatever orthodoxy in religious practices the state prescribed." "Taking Liberties," 1565–66.

71. See above, p. 2.

72. Thomas J. Curry, *Farewell to Christendom: The Future of Church and State in America* (New York: Oxford Univ. Press, 2001), 14, 21-22, 44-45; Green, "Federalism and Establishment Clause," 783; and Feldman, "Intellectual Origins," 398–405.

73. Feldman, "Intellectual Origins," 398 ("In the time between the proposal of the Constitution and of the Bill of Rights, the predominant, not to say exclusive, argument against established churches was that they had the potential to violate liberty of conscience.").

74. John K. Alexander, "Pennsylvania, Pioneer in Safeguarding Personal Rights," in *The Bill of Rights and the States*, 327–28.

75. "Address and Reasons," 541.

76. See "Centinel II" [Samuel Bryan], Philadelphia *Freeman's Journal*, 10/24/1787, in *DHRC*, XIII, *CC*, 1:466; remarks by John Smilie at Pennsylvania Ratifying Convention, 12/12/1787, in *DHRC, Vol. II, RCS: Pennsylvania*, ed. Merrill Jensen (Madison, Wis.: State Historical Society of Wisconsin, 1976), 592; and Deliberator, Philadelphia *Freeman's Journal*, 2/20/1788, in *Complete Anti-Federalist*, 3:179. Also, see Feldman, "Intellectual Origins," 398 ("The logical connection between protection of liberty of conscience and establishment was clear in all of these Pennsylvania formulations.").

77. "An Old Whig V,"*Independent Gazetteer* (Philadelphia), 11/1/1787, in *DHRC*, XIII, *CC*, 1:539–41. Benjamin Workman also equated rights of conscience with the right of religious conscientious objectors not to bear arms. "Philadelphiensis II,"*Freeman's Journal* (Philadelphia), 11/28/1787, in *DHRC*, XIV, *CC*, 2:252–54. Although the ratifying conventions of Virginia, North Carolina, and Rhode Island proposed an amendment that would have, on certain terms, given religious pacifists the right not to bear arms, only the Pennsylvania Anti-federalists explicitly linked such a right to the principle of religious freedom. "Address and Reasons," 550–51.

78. Timothy Meanwell, Philadelphia *Independent Gazetteer*, 10/29/1787, in *DHRC*, XIV, *CC*, 2:512, and "Centinel II,"*DHRC*, XIII, *CC*, 1:466.

79. Article II of the Pennsylvania Declaration of Rights (1776) says: "That all men have a natural and unalienable right to worship Almighty God according to the dictates of their own consciences and understanding: And that no man ought or of right can be compelled to attend any religious worship, or erect or support any place of worship, or maintain any ministry, contrary to, or against, his own free will and consent: Nor can any man, who acknowledges the being of a God, be justly deprived or abridged of any civil right as a citizen, on account of his religious sentiments or peculiar mode of religious worship: And that no authority can or ought to be vested in, or assumed by any power whatever, that shall in any case interfere with, or in any manner controul, the right of conscience in the free exercise of religious worship." In *Sources of Our Liberties*, ed. Richard L. Perry (Chicago: American Bar Foundation, 1959), 329.

80. "An Old Whig V," 538 (emphasis in original). Also, see "An Old Whig IV,"*Independent Gazetteer* (Philadelphia), 10/27/1787, in *DHRC*, XIII, *CC*, 1:500–502. "The Address and Reasons of Dissent of the Minority of the Convention of Pennsylvania" made the same point: "The first consideration . . . is the omission of a BILL OF RIGHTS, ascertaining and fundamentally establishing those unalienable and personal rights of men without the full, free, and secure enjoyment of which there can be no liberty, and over which it is not necessary for a good government to have the control. The principal of which are the rights of conscience. . . ." In *Debate on Constitution*, 1: 541 (emphasis in original). According to Edward Dumbauld, *The Bill of Rights And What It Means Today* (Westport, Conn.: Greenwood Press, 1957), 11–14, the amendments proposed by the Pennsylvania Anti-federalists were very influential on public opinion and the framers of the First Amendment.

81. Hamburger, *Separation of Church and State*, 95–99.

82. Speech in Virginia Ratifying Convention, 6/12/1788, in *DHRC*, X, *RCS: Virginia*, 1213.

83. For examples, see Richard Henry Lee, Letter to Edmund Randolph, 10/16/1787, (which was latter published in Virginia newspapers and as a pamphlet), in *DHRC*, VIII, *RCS: Virginia*, 62, 65; Patrick Henry, Speeches in Virginia Ratifying Convention, 6-5,12,17-1788, in *DHRC*, IX, *RCS: Virginia*, 951, and *DHRC*, X, *RCS: Virginia*, 1213, 1347; and "Address of the Committee of the United Baptist Churches of Virginia . . .," in *The Writings of the Late Elder John Leland. . .* (New York: 1969), 53.

84. "The Society of Western Gentlemen Revise the Constitution,"*Virginia Independent Chronicle*, 4/30/1788, in *DHRC*, IX, *RCS: Va.*, 772 (". . . [T]he free exercise and enjoyment of religious profession, and worship without *preference*, shall forever hereafter be allowed within the United States.").

85. "Objections to the Foederal Constitution," in *DHRC*, XVI , *CC*, 4:254. Feldman, "Intellectual Origins," 400, says that Leland "made explicit the connection between liberty of conscience and the fear of establishment."

86. Whitman H. Ridgway, "Popular Sentiment and the Bill of Rights Controversy," in *The Bill of Rights*, 209, 222. See "Address [to George Washington] of the *General Committee*, representing United Baptist Churches in Virginia . . .," (May 1789), in *Papers of George Washington, Presidential Series*, 2:425 ("[W]e. . . had unusual strugglings of mind; fearing that the *liberty of conscience*, dearer to us than property or life, was not sufficiently secured. . . . fearing that we should be accessory to some religious oppression, should any one Society in the union preponderate over all the rest. . . .")

87. Letter to Edmund Randolph, pub. In Petersburg Virginia *Gazette*, 12/6/1787, in *DHRC*, XIV, *CC*, 2:370. Earlier in the same letter, Lee wrote, "Yet there is no restraint in form of a bill of rights, to secure . . . that residuum of human rights, which is not intended to be given up to society, and which indeed is not necessary to be given for any good social purpose. The rights of conscience, the freedom of the press, and the trial by jury are at mercy." At 368.

88. Thomas Jefferson, Letter to James Madison, 12/20/1787, in *Papers of James Madison*, 10:337. ("A Bill of Rights is what the people are entitled to against *every government on earth, general or particular*, and what no just government should refuse or rest on inference." [emphasis added]) He repeated the point in Letter to Alexander Donald, 2/7/1788, in *The Papers of Thomas Jefferson*, ed. Julian P. Boyd (Princeton, N. J.: Princeton Univ. Press, 1955), 12:571.

89. *Debate on Constitution*, 2: 558–59 ("That there be a Declaration or Bill of Rights asserting and securing from encroachment the essential and unalienable rights of the people in some such manner as the following: 1st. That there are certain natural rights of which men, when they form a social compact, cannot deprive or divest their posterity, ... 2d. That all power is naturally vested in, and consequently derived from, the people; that magistrates therefore are their trustees, and against, and at all times amendable to them. 3d. That government ought to be instituted for the common benefit, protection and security of the people; . . . .")

90. "Letter from a Countryman," New York *Journal*, 1/17/1788, in *Complete Anti-Federalist*, 6: 86–87. Also prior to the convention, the Albany Anti-Federal Committee condemned the absence of a provision "securing the rights of conscience in matters of religion" on the grounds that "the experience of all ages proves that the benevolence and humility inculcated in the gospel, are no restraint on the love of domination." "Address," 4/26/1788, in *Complete Anti-Federalist*, 6:124.

91. Delegate Treadwell, in Elliot, ed., *Debates in State Conventions*, 2:399. Also, see Cincinnatus, "Reply to Wilson's Speech, III," 125.

92. "Brutus II," New York *Journal*, 11/1/1787, in *DHRC*, XIII, *CC*, 1:524–26, and "Brutus IX," New York *Journal*, 1/17/1788, in *DHRC*, XV, *CC*, 3:393–94. The author of the "Brutus" essays is unknown. See *DHRC*, XIII, *CC*, 1:411.

93. *Debate on Constitution*, 2: 536–37.

94. Elliot, ed., *Debates in State Conventions*, 4: 200, 203. According to Henry Abbot, who actually voted for the Constitution, "some people" feared that the Roman Catholic religion could be established, "which would prevent the people from worshipping God according to their own consciences." Elliot, ed., *Debates in State Conventions*, 4: 191–92.

95. The preamble to North Carolina's proposed amendments stated: "*Resolved*, That a declaration of rights, asserting and securing from encroachment the great principles of civil and religious liberty, and the unalienable rights of the people . . . ought to be laid before Congress. . . . 1. That there are certain natural rights of which men, when they form a social compact, cannot deprive or divest their posterity. . . ." Elliot, ed., *Debates in State Conventions*, 4: 242–43.

96. Speech on 7/29/1788, in *Debate on Constitution*, 2: 888. Spencer added, "I still think that a bill of rights is necessary. This necessity arises from the nature of human societies. When individuals enter into society, they give up some rights to secure the rest. There are certain human rights that ought not to be given up, and which ought in some manner to be secured."*Debate on Constitution*, 2: 889.

97. According to one account, in Maryland "the question of religion was completely subordinated to political interests. . . ." Albert W. Werline, *Problems of Church and State in Maryland During the Seventeenth and Eighteenth Centuries* (South Lancaster, Mass.: College Press, 1948), 198 and 198–203. Cf. Lienesch, "Reinterpreting Rights," 260 (In Maryland, "antiaristocratic sentiments and a long tradition of toleration led to strong support for a bill of rights.")

98. Steiner, "Maryland's Adoption," 211–24.

99. "To the Citizens of Maryland, # II," 3/21/1788, in *DHRC*, XVI, *CC*, 4:456–57.

100. Herbert Storing, *Complete Anti-Federalist*, 5: 5.

101. "Essay by a Farmer," 2/15/1788, in *Complete Anti-Federalist*, 5: 11–15 (emphasis added).

102. For one particularly insightful analysis of Mercer's views, see Lienesch, "Reinterpreting Rights," 260–64.

103. The only concern over "religious rights" that was expressed, so far as we know, came from a delegate who argued, but without explanation, that "the security of our religious rights," including "the use of the holy scriptures," was threatened by the lack of a religious test in the proposed constitution. "New Hampshire State Convention,"*The American Herald*" (Boston), (March 3, 1788): 1. According to William G. McLoughlin, not even the Baptists of New Hampshire expressed concern about the federal government's threatening religious freedom. He speculates that they must have accepted the Federalists' argument that it had no power over religion and that their real fears concerned their own state government. *New England Dissent*,

1630–1883: The Baptists and the Separation of Church and State, 2 vols. (Cambridge, Mass.: Harvard Univ. Press, 1971), 2:780–83.

104. See Philip A. Hamburger, "Equality and Diversity: The Eighteenth-Century Debate about Equal Protection and Equal Civil Rights," in *The Supreme Court Review, 1992*, ed. Dennis J. Hutchinson et al. (Chicago: Univ. of Chicago Press, 1993), 336–43; Mark DeWolfe Howe, *The Garden and the Wilderness: Religion and Government in American Constitutional History* (Chicago: Univ. of Chicago Press, 1965), 18–19, 23–24; and Antieau et al., *Freedom from Establishment,* 120.

105. "Every individual has a natural and unalienable right to worship GOD according to the dictates of his own conscience, and reason; and no subject shall be hurt, molested, or restrained in his person, liberty or estate for worshipping GOD, in the manner and season most agreeable to the dictates of his own conscience, or for his religious profession, sentiments or persuasion; provided he doth not disturb the public peace, or disturb others, in their religious worship." Part I, sec. V, in *The Federal and State Constitutions, Colonial Charters, and Other Organic Laws of the States, Territories, and Colonies*, comp. and ed. Francis N. Thorpe (Washington, D. C.: Government Printing Office, 1909), 4: 2454.

106. *Constitution of New Hampshire* (1784), Part I, sec. VI, and Part II (in several places), in *Federal and State Constitutions*, 4:2454, 2460, 2463, 2467. Section VI also contained another provision that said, "And no portion of any one particular religious sect or denomination, shall ever be compelled to pay towards the support of the teacher or teachers of another persuasion, sect or denomination."*Federal and State Constitutions*, 4:2454.

107. This is the interpretation of the proposed amendment made by Yarbrough, "New Hampshire," 252; Bradley, *Church-State Relationships*, 76; and Rubenfeld, "Antidisestablishmentarianism," 2355. However, the source that Bradley cites to support this interpretation, a letter by the president of the convention, contains nothing that would support it. See John Sullivan, Letter to Jeremy Belknap, 2/26/1788, in Charles E. L. Wingate, *Life and Letters of Paine Wingate*, Vol. 1 (Medford, Mass.: Mercury Printing Co., 1930), 220–21. Rubenfeld simply cites Bradley and the same letter.

108. Green, "Federalism and Establishment Clause," 784. One of the first scholars to write that New Hampshire's proposed amendment reflected concern "for her own 'establishment'" was Edward S. Corwin, but he cited no evidence to support his contention. "The Supreme Court as National School Board,"*Law & Contemporary Problems*, 14 (1949): 3, 11.

109. *Constitution of New Hampshire* (1784), Part I, sec. VI, in *Federal and State Constitutions*, 4:2454 (emphasis added).

110. See *DHRC*, XVIII, *CC, 6:* 186–87, and Yarbrough, "New Hampshire," 250–55.

111. John Sullivan, Letter to Jeremy Belknap, 2/26/1788, in Wingate, *Life and Letters*, 1:220.

112. "New Hampshire State Convention," p. 1. Langdon's use of "free exercise of religion" again indicates that it was generally understood as a synonym for religious freedom. One scholar argues that because he said that the New Hampshire Constitution guaranteed the "free exercise of religion," even though it also authorized support for Protestant Christianity, he, too, had a conservative understanding of religious freedom. See Yarbrough, "New Hampshire," 245. Such a conclusion, however, flies in the face of Langdon's explicit condemnation of religious tests and government support of religion, quoted above. The more logical explanation of his remark is that it referred just to the religious liberty provision in the New Hampshire Constitution and not to the provisions requiring a religious test for office holders and authorizing aid for Protestant ministers.

113. This conclusion, however, is weakened by the fact that in 1791 at a New Hampshire constitutional convention at least nine Federalists who in 1788 had voted for the national Constitution, including its ban on religious tests, voted specifically for keeping a religious test in the New Hampshire Constitution. Morton Borden, "Federalists, Antifederalists, and Religious Freedom," 478.

114. Nicholas Collin, "Remarks on the Amendments to the Federal Constitution . . .," Philadelphia *Federal Gazette*, (11/18/1788): 2.

115. Curry, *Farewell to Christendom*, 37–38, and Ridgway, "Popular Sentiment," 209–25.

116. Green, "Federalism and Establishment Clause," 781–82, 785. Given the evidence presented above, it is astonishing and dismaying that so many scholars deny this conclusion. See,

for example, Kyle Duncan, "Subsidiarity and Religious Establishments in the United States Constitution,"*Villanova Law Review*, 52 (2007): 67, 115 ("These proposals . . . were meant to curtail federal power over a sensitive area of state competence. . . . [T]he pre-existing constituent states wanted to safeguard their own prerogatives. . . ."); Akhil R. Amar, "The Bill of Rights and the Fourteenth Amendment,"*Yale Law Journal*, 101 (April 1992): 1193, 1209 (The idea that the Bill of Rights "truly declared rights that . . . bound all governments . . . would have been deeply foreign to many of the men who had clamored for a Bill of Rights in the 1780s. The word 'right' had no talismanic natural law significance; after all, many sought a Bill to confer—or declare—*states'* rights. . . ."); Chris Bartolomucci, "Rethinking the Incorporation of the Establishment Clause: A Federalist View,"*Harvard Law Review*, 105 (May 1992): 1706 (". . . [The] concern [of many state delegates] was not so much that the federal government would establish a national religion, but that it would *interfere* with existing state establishments."); F. William O'Brien, *Justice Reed and the First Amendment: The Religion Clauses* (n.p.: Georgetown Univ. Press, 1958), 134 ("The reported debates in the various ratifying conventions . . . reveal that the delegates . . . wanted . . . a guarantee that the new national government would neither set up . . . a national church nor interfere with the various types of establishments, quasi-establishments and church-government arrangements existing in the several states."); James McClellan, "Hand's Writing on the Wall of Separation: The Significance of *Jaffree* in Future Cases on Religious Establishment," in *How Does the Constitution Protect Religious Freedom?* Ed. Robert A. Goldwin & Art Kaufman (Washington, D. C.: American Enterprise Institute, 1987), 46–47 ("During the ratification struggle Anti-federalists placed far greater emphasis on the federalism of the Bill of Rights than on the substantive content or meaning of the liberties themselves."); William K. Lietzau, "Rediscovering the Establishment Clause: Federalism and the Rollback of Incorporation,"*DePaul Law Review*, 39 (1989–90):1191, 1198 ("Recorded debates at the various ratifying conventions confirm the federalism based intent of state recommendations regarding religious liberty."); and Bradley, 92 (The final language of the religion clauses "tracked . . . the basic antifederalist endeavor to preserve existing state constitutional regimes from intermeddling federal legislation."). Given the evidence presented above, such assertions are simply not credible. Also, see Rubenfeld, 2354, fn 51, where he implies that amendments protecting state establishments of religion were proposed. ("The demand for amendments protecting freedom of conscience is well known. . . . Often overlooked, however, is that some states also sought to keep Congress from interfering with their pro-Protestant regimes.") To support this claim, Rubenfeld cites Thomas J. Curry, *The First Freedoms: Church and State in America to the Passage of the First Amendment* (New York: Oxford Univ. Press, 1986), 203, and Bradley, *Church-State Relationships. . .*, 76. Nothing, however, on p. 203 in Curry supports the claim, and the Bradley page refers only to New Hampshire's proposed religion amendment, which was discussed earlier. See above, pp. 72–73. Finally, Kent Greenawalt is contradictory on the issue. On the same page, he writes, "When state conventions considered the ratification of the original Constitution, Anti-Federalists complained that it failed to protect individual rights against abridgements by the federal government" and "The current version of the First Amendment was adopted in order to respond to the concern of the Anti-Federalists about impingements on state authority." "Common Sense," 494.

117. Letter IV from the "Federal Farmer" to "The Republican," New York, 10/12/1787, in *DHRC*, XIV, *CC*, 2:43–46 (emphasis added).

118. See, e.g., the speech by Patrick Dollard in the South Carolina Ratifying Convention, 5/22/1788, in *The Debate on the Constitution,* 2:592 ("The people of Prince Frederick's parish . . . are nearly to a man opposed to this new constitution, because, they say, they have omitted to insert a bill of rights therein, ascertaining and fundamentally establishing the unalienable rights of men, without a full, free and secure enjoyment of which there can be no liberty, and over which it is not necessary that a good government should have the controul."). For many other examples, see Hamburger, "Equality and Diversity," 299–313, 339–43.

119. For a clear and careful explanation of the Anti-federalist argument that a bill of rights was needed to protect the reserved natural rights of individuals because the movement to create a national government had put Americans back into a state of nature, see James H. Hutson, "The Bill of Rights and the American Revolutionary Experience," in *A Culture of Rights*, ed.

Michael J. Lacey & Knud Haakonssen (New York: Cambridge Univ. Press, 1991), 62, 80–83. For the historical and religious background of the understanding of the Constitution as a compact by the *people*, see Donald S. Lutz, "Religious Dimensions in the Development of American Constitutionalism,"*Emory Law Journal*, 39 (Winter 1990): 21–40. That the Anti-federalists would use such an argument to support their demand for a bill of rights is not only surprising, but ironic, for they were the ones who were most concerned to prevent the powers or rights of the states from being taken away by the central government. Logically, they should have argued that the states were the ones creating the national government, but in order to make their arguments for a bill of rights as persuasive as possible, they contended that the central government was being created by *individuals in a state of nature* and not by existing, sovereign *states*. Only a few years later, of course, in response to the Alien and Sedition Acts and in an attempt to preserve the states' powers and sovereignty, the political heirs of the Anti-federalists, led by Jefferson and Madison, would argue that the central government had been created by the states and not by the "people." See Saul Cornell, *The Other Founders: Anti-Federalism & the Dissenting Tradition in America, 1788–1828* (Chapel Hill, N. C.: Univ. of North Carolina Press, 1999), 237–45.

120. Hamburger, *Separation of Church and State,* 12 ("The dissenters or religious minorities whose views were reflected in the First Amendment assumed that legislation should not discriminate among religions and even that it should not take cognizance of religion.") Also, see other passages in Hamburger, *Separation of Church and State*, 12, 29, 94–95. This way of stating the basic principle reflected in the proposed amendment to the Constitution relating to religion leaves open the question of whether the proponents of religious liberty in early America favored government neutrality toward religion and non-religion or anti-religion. The evidence on this issue is divided and complicated, and, for that reason, will not be presented in this book. Whatever it might show, however, it would not change what the evidence presented thus far shows—that the proponents of adding a religious freedom amendment to the Constitution had normative, not federalist, reasons for doing so. See Steven K. Green, "Religion Clause Federalism: State Flexibility over Religious Matters and the 'One-Way Ratchet',"*Emory Law Journal*, 56 (2006): 115.

121. See below, p. 87–88.

122. Agreeing is Thomas Berg, "Religion Clause Anti-Theories,"*Notre Dame Law Review*, 72 (1996–97): 709–11. Also, see Paul Finkelman, "The Ten Amendments as a Declaration of Rights,"*Southern Illinois University Law Journal*, 16 (Winter 1992): 351–96 on all the rights and 382–88 on the rights of conscience.

Chapter Five

The Drafting of the Religion Clauses

After the Constitution was ratified and a new central government installed, it was unclear what would happen to the amendments to it that had been proposed by the various ratifying conventions and others. Many Federalist members of Congress were either apathetic about or opposed to their being considered by the First Congress,[1] but others felt duty-bound to draft some amendments. The person primarily responsible for introducing amendments and getting Congress to act on them was James Madison.

I. THE ROLE AND VIEWS OF JAMES MADISON

Although originally opposed to amending the Constitution, partially for fear that it would forestall its ratification, once it was ratified, Madison changed his mind, at least with respect to provisions protecting individual rights.[2] Madison changed his mind for three reasons. First, he sincerely wanted to protect "all essential rights, particularly the rights of conscience in the fullest latitude, the freedom of the press, trials by jury, security against general warrants, etc."[3] Second, he had promised both the members of the Virginia ratifying convention and the people who later elected him to Congress that he would work to add a number of rights provisions to the Constitution, and Madison was a man of his word.[4] Third, he was convinced that unless those rights provisions were promptly added to the Constitution, those who opposed it and the new government would soon replace them with another constitution and government.[5] Madison's fears were justified; even before the convening of the First Congress, the legislatures of two states, New York and Virginia, had petitioned it to call another constitutional convention.[6]

From the many amendments that had been proposed, therefore, Madison drew up his own list of nine, which he submitted to the House of Representatives on June 8, 1789.[7] Most of them were intended to protect individual rights. Two pertained to religious liberty: "The civil rights of none shall be abridged on account of religious belief or worship, nor shall any national religion be established, nor shall the full and equal rights of conscience be in any manner, or on any pretext infringed . . .," and "No state shall violate the equal rights of conscience. . . ."[8] Although the Anti-federalists had proposed several amendments that would have changed the structure of the federal government, Madison did not include most of them for fear that they would dangerously weaken the federal government.[9] For this reason, the amendments that Madison did present were criticized by some Anti-federalist members of the Congress for being weak and insignificant and were greeted apathetically by some Federalist members on the grounds that they were unnecessary and uncontroversial.[10]

Given Madison's role as "manager" of the bill to amend the Constitution, what he had to say by way of explaining and defending its provisions is absolutely crucial for anyone seeking to understand their meaning. Especially important in this respect is the speech he gave when he first submitted his nine amendments. In it, Madison emphasized that a declaration of rights was needed because many Americans were fearful that their individual liberties and rights would be encroached on by the new national government and because they desired "those safeguards which they have been long accustomed to have interposed between them and the magistrate who exercises the sovereign power . . .," i.e., state bills of rights. He conceded that because of the Necessary and Proper Clause, the central government "has certain discretionary powers with respect to the means [of attaining its delegated powers], which may admit of abuse to a certain extent, in the same manner as the powers of the State Governments under their constitutions may to an indefinite extent. . . ." Then, giving the example of a government's using general search warrants as a means of collecting its revenue, he argued, "If there was reason for restraining the State Governments from exercising this power, there is like reason for restraining the Federal Government."[11] In short, Madison considered the rights that he wanted to prevent the federal government from violating to be essential rights that *no* government, state or national, should violate.[12]

This is also the way that at least one unnamed observer outside Congress understood Madison's proposal pertaining to religion. In an article first published in New York, but then widely republished throughout the states, s/he wrote:

> The next article established religious liberty, and all of those political rights, which by various tricks of state have been wounded through its means, on the firmest

> ground. The tender, the almost sacred rights of conscience, says this inestimable article, shall by no means, on no account be abridged or interfered with. No self righteous or powerful church shall set up its impious domination over all of the rest. Every pious man may pay the Divine Author of his existence the tribute of thanksgiving and, adoration in the manner of his forefathers.[13] "A Pennsylvanian" 6/12/1789

Moreover, in Madison's opening speech there was no mention of a states' rights or a federalist justification for any of his proposed rights. Although he noted that "the State Legislatures will jealously and closely watch the operations of this Government, and be able to resist with more effect every assumption of power, than any other power on earth can do; and the greatest opponents to a Federal Government admit the State Legislatures to be sure guardians of the people's liberty,"[14] this is not an argument that the federal government should not be able to pass certain kinds of laws on the grounds that such laws fall under the jurisdiction of the states alone. It is, rather, an argument that the states will play a role in enforcing the provisions of a federal bill of rights.[15]

In fact, it is noteworthy that Madison said that the opponents of the federal government, *but not he himself*, thought the state legislatures were "sure guardians of the people's liberty." What *he* thought about the state legislatures was stated a few paragraphs later where he commented on the restrictions placed on them in Article I, section 10, e.g., they can pass no bills of attainder: "I think there is more danger of those powers being abused by the State Governments than by the Government of the United States. The same may be said of other powers which they possess, if not controlled by the general principle, that laws are unconstitutional which infringe the rights of the community." For this reason, Madison argued that the Constitution should be amended to prevent the state governments from violating "the equal rights of conscience, freedom of the press, or trial by jury in criminal cases; because it is proper that *every government* should be disarmed of powers which trench upon those particular rights."[16] Clearly, Madison did not have a federalist or states' rights understanding of the amendments that he wanted added to the Constitution.

Some scholars who oppose this conclusion cite the fact that in a letter to Jefferson, Madison wrote that in his list of proposed amendments "everything of a controvertible nature" that might imperil acceptance was "studiously avoided."[17] The only way this could have been accomplished, they argue, was by Madison's proposing religion clauses that had only federalist meaning.[18] This argument, however, can be challenged because of what Madison wrote in other letters. First, in October of 1788, he expressed reservations about adding a declaration of rights to the Constitution on the grounds that "the most essential rights," in particular the rights of conscience, "could not be obtained in the requisite latitude." Then, in January of

1789, Madison wrote that he favored amendments, provided they protected "all essential rights, particularly the rights of Conscience *in the fullest latitude*."[19] It is not surprising, therefore, that Madison proposed an amendment that would have protected religious liberty from *state* laws—an amendment that had not been suggested by any of the persons/groups who wanted a Bill of Rights added to the Constitution, and one that was controversial. [20] Moreover, even if his description of his amendments as non-controversial is correct, it does not follow that they had only or primarily federalist meaning. Rather, it suggests that there was a basic consensus among the framers on what the principle of religious liberty means or requires, and partially for that reason there was less interest in the amendments than there was in other issues.[21]

II. A SUMMARY OF WHAT HAPPENED IN THE FIRST CONGRESS

About a month after Madison submitted his proposed amendments, and after much prodding on his part, the House of Representatives created a select committee, including Madison, to review them, as well as other possible amendments, and to come up with a list to be submitted to the full House for its consideration.[22] A week later, on July 28, the committee made its report, which included the following two provisions: "No religion shall be established by law, nor shall the equal rights of conscience be infringed," and "No state shall infringe the equal rights of conscience."[23] Importantly, the first of these provisions was written in the passive voice and failed to identify which government it was intended to limit.

On August 15, the first provision was discussed on the floor of the House. Peter Silvester of New York expressed a fear that "it might be thought to have a tendency to abolish religion altogether." Elbridge Gerry, from Massachusetts, preferred that it read, "[N]o religious doctrine shall be established by law." Connecticut's Roger Sherman spoke against the provision on the grounds that it was unnecessary because no authority "to make religious establishments" had been delegated to Congress by the Constitution. Daniel Carroll of Maryland spoke in favor of the amendment because it would protect the "rights of conscience," which, he said, were "in their nature, of peculiar delicacy, and will little bear the gentlest touch of governmental hand." Madison then gave his interpretation of the provision: ". . . [C]ongress should not establish a religion, and enforce the legal observation of it by law, nor compel men to worship God in any manner contrary to their conscience." It was intended, he added, to prevent "laws of such a nature as might infringe the rights of conscience, or establish a national religion. . . ."[24]

Carroll's and Madison's comments, however, did not end the discussion. Benjamin Huntington, from Connecticut, repeated the concern that the amendment "might be taken in such a latitude as to be extremely hurtful to the cause of religion." Although he said he agreed with Madison's interpretation of the proposed amendment, he feared that "others might find it convenient to put another construction upon it." As an example of what might happen, he said that federal courts, when asked, might refuse to compel persons to pay their promised "contributions" to the churches to which they belonged—on the grounds that "a support of ministers, or buildings of places of worship might be construed into a religious establishment."[25] Then Huntington stated a second objection. He said he favored an amendment worded so as "to secure the rights of conscience, and a free exercise of the rights of religion, but not [worded] to patronize those who professed no religion at all," which he claimed had been done in Rhode Island, where, he said, mistakenly,[26] no religion could be established by law.[27] Presumably, he thought that a prohibition against establishing a religion would "patronize" atheists (perhaps by prohibiting laws requiring them to support some religion).[28]

As for his first objection, although the "contributions" that Huntington feared the federal courts would refuse to enforce might have referred to contributions voluntarily made, in that day the term was often used to refer to taxes levied to support a local church.[29] Because he was from Connecticut where inhabitants of towns were in fact taxed to support a minister of their choice (in theory, if not always in practice), most scholars assume that Huntington was concerned that federal courts might use the amendment, if ratified, to threaten the system established in that state.[30] Although he might not have considered the arrangement in Connecticut to be an "establishment of religion" (because, again, in theory, no one religion was officially established or supported by the state),[31] Huntington apparently thought that federal courts might interpret the proposed amendment (1) as applying to state laws and (2) as forbidding Connecticut's system of public support of religion on the grounds that it was an establishment of religion.[32]

Huntington's concern, of course, was misplaced because Madison's proposed provision was intended to limit the powers of the federal government, not those of states, townships, or churches.[33] On the other hand, given that Madison's proposed wording did not explicitly identify the federal or national government as the "target" of the amendment, it is perhaps understandable that Huntington thought it might be used to limit state and local governments.[34] In order to alleviate his concern, therefore, Madison proposed that the amendment be revised to read, "No *national* religion shall be established by law,"[35] but when this was objected to by Gerry on the grounds that it would imply that a consolidated, national government had been created, Madison withdrew his proposal. In the meantime, Samuel Livermore of New

Hampshire proposed language that apparently resolved the issue. He moved in favor of an amendment that had been proposed by his own state and that clearly indicated to whom it applied—"The *Congress* shall make no laws touching religion, or infringing the rights of conscience"—and his motion passed.[36]

Then on August 20, with no *recorded* debate and thus explanation, the House voted to replace what it had last agreed to on August 15 with a version submitted by Fisher Ames of Massachusetts: "Congress shall make no law establishing religion, or to prevent the free exercise thereof, or to infringe the rights of conscience."[37] The next day, it was slightly reworded to read: "Congress shall make no law establishing religion, or prohibiting the free exercise thereof; nor shall the rights of conscience be infringed."[38] It was this amendment that was sent to the Senate for its consideration. Importantly, Madison considered this final version to be essentially the same as the one contained in the report of the select committee.[39]

On September 3, the Senate got around to discussing the amendment proposed by the House. Although it considered a number of proposed changes in its wording, there is no record of the Senate's deliberations and thus of what individual senators thought about them. During the course of the day, one motion was made to delete the entire amendment, three motions were made to change its wording, and one motion was made to adopt the House's version, and all the motions failed.[40] At the end of the day, the Senate agreed to accept the House version, minus its last phrase, "nor shall the rights of conscience be infringed."[41] Then on September 9, the Senate made a final change in the wording of the amendment. It voted to replace the House's proposed amendment with the following: "Congress shall make no law establishing articles of faith or a mode of worship, or prohibiting the free exercise of religion," and it was this version that was sent back to the House for its consideration.[42]

On September 21, the House voted to reject the Senate's wording of the religious liberty and fifteen other provisions and asked the Senate for a conference committee to resolve their differences. The Senate agreed, and three days later, the committee (composed of Representatives James Madison, Roger Sherman, John Vining, and Senators Oliver Ellsworth, Charles Carroll, and William Paterson), reported to the Senate that the House would be willing to accept the Senate's wording of the other amendments at issue on condition that the Senate accept the committee's proposed wording of what is now the First and Sixth Amendments. Specifically, the committee proposed that the religion clauses read, "Congress shall make no law respecting an establishment of religion, or prohibiting the free exercise thereof." The next day the deal was approved by both houses of Congress, and all the amendments were submitted to the states for their approval.[43]

Finally, what about Madison's proposed amendment that would have prohibited the *states* from infringing "the equal rights of conscience" as well as the freedoms of speech, press, and the right to trial by jury? On August 17, two days after they had approved Livermore's version of the religion clauses to be applied to the national government, at least two-thirds of the House's members voted to adopt this amendment, albeit somewhat revised.[44] There was little recorded debate. One member objected that Congress ought "to leave the state governments to themselves, and not to interfere with them more than we already do; and that is thought by many to be rather too much." In reply, Madison said that it was "the most valuable amendment in the whole list" and added: "[I]f there was any reason to restrain the government of the United States from infringing upon these essential rights, it was equally necessary that they should be secured against the state governments. He . . . was satisfied that it would be equally grateful to the people."[45] Madison "carried the day." After the amendment went to the Senate, however, and for reasons not explained by the record, on September 7, it did not garner the two-thirds vote it needed to pass.[46]

III. THE MEANING OF THE DEBATE IN THE HOUSE ON AUGUST 15

In light of this record of events, it is clear that if one is trying to determine whether the religion clauses of the First Amendment originally had a normative or a federalist meaning, the most relevant information from its drafting is the debate that occurred in the House on August 15. What does it tell us? First, those, i.e., Madison and Carroll, who approved of the drafting committee's proposed amendment, did so for a normative or moral reason, i.e., because it protected the rights of conscience, which Carroll explicitly said should not be violated by *any* "governmental hand." Second, no one objected to such a goal (even Huntington professed a desire "to secure the rights of conscience"), and Livermore's motion adopted at the end of the day prohibited laws "infringing the rights of conscience." Third, Silvester and Huntington's objection to the wording of the proposed provision because it threatened "the cause of religion" and might "patronize those who professed no religion at all" clearly implies that they thought it had normative content. If they thought the law was federalist in content, they obviously would not have perceived it as a threat to religion or to state laws establishing one religion or supporting religion in general. Only a constitutional amendment with normative content, i.e., one that prohibited federal laws regulating religion on the grounds that they violate a natural right, had the potential to be used to threaten religion or state laws pertaining to religion.[47]

There is no evidence, moreover, that Silvester and Huntington sought or obtained an amendment with federalist meaning.[48] Although some persons argue otherwise, they do so primarily on the basis of one prominent scholar's misinterpretation of Huntington's remarks. In what is generally an excellent account of the adoption of the religion clauses, Thomas J. Curry writes that Huntington "feared the amendment might give *Congress* power to interfere with existing arrangements in the individual states. . . . he wanted to keep the *federal government* from any pronouncement that might tend to affect Connecticut's Church-State system."[49] Citing *only* this passage by Curry, Arlin Adams and Charles Emmerich write that "some Framers intended the establishment clause to prevent congressional interference with existing state establishments."[50] Jed Rubenfeld also relies on Curry to support the same conclusion.[51]

These scholars simply misconstrue what Huntington actually said, which was, as explained above, that he feared that a "*Federal Court*" would misinterpret the proposed amendment and use it to strike down Connecticut's system of supporting religion.[52] In other words, he favored an amendment with normative meaning but worded in such a way that it could not be used against a *state* law that supported religion.[53] *In fact, the issue of Congress' interfering with state establishments of religion never arose in the debate over the proposed religion clauses.*[54] Even if Huntington's expressed fears related to Congress as well as the federal courts, there is simply no evidence that his comments had any influence on the final drafting or wording of the religious clauses.[55]

Of course, Madison, by proposing to add the word "national" to the amendment, attempted to assuage Huntington's concern that the amendment posed a threat to state and local laws pertaining to religion. In other words, he attempted to make it clear that the amendment applied only to laws and policies of the national government and not to those of state and local governments.[56] Although he withdrew his proposal, even if it had been adopted, it would not have indicated that the reason for denying the national government jurisdiction over religion was simply or primarily to preserve the states' jurisdiction over it. There is a difference between an amendment having that purpose and one having the normative purpose of protecting religious freedom from federal laws (and only federal laws). Madison proposed the latter, not the former.[57]

In any case, the entire discussion in the House was predicated on the assumption that the proposed religion clauses had normative meaning and thus might be interpreted in such a way as to prevent both state as well as federal laws that in some way favored religion.[58]

IV. CHANGES IN THE WORDING OF THE CLAUSES

Based just on the record of the debate in the House on August 15, there is little or no evidence supporting a federalist interpretation of those clauses. Because we have no record of subsequent debates in the House or Senate, the only other evidence that might have a bearing on the issue at hand would be the changes that occurred in the wording of the proposed amendment. Were there changes that would indicate or imply a switch from a normative to a federalist understanding of the religion clauses or vice versa? There are four changes worth considering.

The first change in wording was made on August 15, but engendered no debate. Instead of the wording proposed by the select committee, Livermore proposed that "Congress shall make no laws touching religion, or infringing the rights of conscience," and at the end of the day it was adopted by the House. Mark DeWolfe Howe argues that it is significant for two reasons. First, by identifying Congress as the branch of government that was being restricted, it satisfied Huntingdon's desire that the amendment be phrased so as not to authorize the federal courts to refuse to enforce a state law "when it happened to sustain a religious enterprise."[59] Second, and more importantly, Howe suggests that Livermore's wording of the provision had more substance than did the provision that was initially worded by the select committee that reported the amendments to the floor of the House. In other words, "no laws touching religion" prohibits more than "no law establishing religion." Howe explains that even though no one thought that Congress had the power to establish a religion, there was concern that because of the Necessary and Proper Clause, "in exercising a granted power—most probably that of taxation—the Congress might . . . clumsily touch religious interests or institutions."[60] In short, although he cites no direct evidence, Howe sees Livermore's wording as reflecting a broad normative purpose.

Gary Glenn is another scholar who sees a normative reason for the adoption of Livermore's wording. Although he appears to agree with Howe's normative interpretation of Livermore's "no laws touching religion" phrase,[61] he emphasizes the switch from "*equal* rights of conscience" to "the right of conscience." According to Glenn, the issue that was being addressed by that change was whether the religious liberty provision should be worded in such a way as to protect atheists. He contends that Madison, and others, used the phrase "equal rights of conscience" in order to protect atheists from government discrimination. By adopting Livermore's proposal, which did not contain the word "equal," the House was signaling its desire to protect only the different religions—not anti-religion—and, thus, to address Silvester and Huntington's concern that the provision be worded so as "not to patronize those who professed no religion at all."[62] Although Glenn's interpretation of the change is plausible, again, there is no direct evidence to support it. If true, however, it would certainly indicate that normative issues were being addressed by the House.

In contrast to Howe and Glenn, Steven Smith, Gerard Bradley, and Jed Rubenfeld see Livermore's proposal as having purely federalist meaning, i.e., as expressing the point, agreed on by both Federalists and Anti-federalists, that only the states, not the national government, could legislate on the subject of religion. More specifically, its purpose was to protect the remnants of religious establishments that still existed in the states.[63] Given just the wording of the proposal, such an interpretation is plausible. Smith, however, presents no evidence, other than its wording, to support it. Bradley and Rubenfeld, on the other hand, stress the fact that the Livermore's language is almost identical to that of the amendment proposed by the New Hampshire ratifying convention, which they contend had been proposed to protect that state's religious establishment.[64]

There are, however, several weaknesses with this interpretation of Livermore's proposed amendment. First, it overlooks the part of the amendment that prohibits "infringing the rights of conscience." Surely Livermore, like all the others who spoke on August 15, believed in such rights and did not want the federal government, as a matter of principle, to violate them.[65] Second, as already explained,[66] the assumption that New Hampshire's proposed amendment was intended to protect state religious establishments from Congressional acts is very questionable. Third, it can be argued that Livermore's language was not broad or clear enough to protect states' rights or establishments of religion. Would a federal law that prohibited states laws that infringed on religious freedom be one "touching religion?"[67] Fourth, such an interpretation makes no sense in light of Livermore's acceptance of Madison's proposed amendment prohibiting the states from infringing "the equal rights of conscience." Although he proposed that it be changed from the active to the passive voice, Livermore stated that he "had no great objection to the sentiment."[68] If Livermore's proposal to prohibit Congress from passing laws "touching religion" was federalist in nature, i.e., was intended to protect states' rights and establishments of religion, then why would Livermore have supported Madison's amendment, which threatened both?[69]

In response to this last point, it could be argued that Livermore would not have thought that Madison's amendment prohibiting state laws infringing "the equal rights of conscience" threatened state laws that provided financial aid to religion because he did not believe that such laws violated "the equal rights of conscience." In his mind, an amendment protecting the rights of conscience and one prohibiting religious establishments were different. Moreover, that very point seemed to be implied by Madison's proposed amendments, for the one that he proposed to apply to the national government had both a rights of conscience clause and a no establishment clause whereas his amendment that applied to the states had only a rights of conscience clause. Perhaps, therefore, Livermore and others who may have favored laws providing financial aid to religion did not perceive the second of Madison's amendment as precluding such laws.[70]

The problem with this argument is that even if Livermore thought that religion could be established or aided in some way without violating the rights of conscience, surely he would have known that a very significant number of early Americans (Steven Green says "the vast majority" of them), including Madison, the residents of most states outside New England, and the dissenters in New England, "considered rights of conscience and religious disestablishment to be closely intertwined."[71] Surely he would have known that an amendment prohibiting states from infringing the equal rights of conscience might be used by courts to strike down the vestiges of religious establishments that existed in a few states, just as such a clause in Virginia's Declaration of Rights had been used to argue against such vestiges in that state.[72] The question, therefore, remains: if Livermore's proposed wording of the religion clauses ("Congress shall make no laws touching religion. . . .") was intended to protect state laws providing financial aid to religion, then why did he support Madison's proposed amendment that might have been used to strike down such laws?[73]

Even if Livermore's proposal expressed a purely federalist position, its relevance is undercut by the *second* change in wording that occurred four days after it was adopted. The House replaced Livermore's wording with the following: "Congress shall make no law establishing religion, or to prevent the free exercise thereof, or to infringe the rights of conscience."[74] If Livermore's proposal expressed a purely federalist position, then does not the fact that it was replaced by a more narrowly worded and clearly normative provision indicate conclusively that Congress rejected the idea that it had no jurisdiction whatever over religion or that it should protect state quasi-establishments of religion from federal legislation?[75] Does it not support what Kurt Lash calls the "residual implied power" theory, whereby "Congress retained some degree of implied power to regulate the subject of religion if (1) it was doing so incident to an enumerated end, and (2) the regulation did not exceed the (new) limitations of the First Amendment?"[76]

Essentially this is the interpretation advocated by Philip Hamburger. He suggests that Livermore's proposal was rejected because it would have disallowed all types of federal laws dealing with religion, including laws to "protect individuals in the free exercise of their religion." He shows, with considerable evidence, that early Americans generally believed that governments should pass such laws and, therefore, that the proponents of a religious liberty amendment would not have wanted to prohibit Congress from passing laws to *protect* religious freedom from both private and government actions.[77] If correct, Hamburger's explanation of why the Livermore proposal was replaced clearly suggests that members of the First House of Representatives were not necessarily opposed to Congress' passing laws protecting religious liberty from state laws.

Although Kurt Lash, to his credit, gives serious consideration to this interpretation of the religion clauses, he ultimately rejects it.[78] In doing so, however, he does not argue that the provision that replaced Livermore's was purely federalist in nature. In fact, he simply ignores it. Instead, what he does is compare Livermore's provision with the amendment that was ultimately and much later adopted by the conference committee and the Congress as a whole—the religion clauses as we know them today. Such a comparison, however, does not explain why the "no law touching religion" language was rejected. Although Lash speculates that it may have been rejected because it did not adequately prevent Congress from passing laws protecting religious freedom, including laws against state religious establishments,[79] that explanation makes no sense, because the provision that replaced it allowed such laws even more than it did. The best, therefore, that Lash can do is argue that "it is rather difficult to make an interpretative argument regarding the meaning of the First Amendment, based on the rejection of a draft, when there is no surviving record of why the draft was rejected."[80] While this may be true, it is also true with respect to all other actions of the First Congress, both its approvals and rejections of provisions, when there is no record of why it did what it did. This includes its decision to adopt the wording that we have today, about which we have no record. That, however, does not prevent Lash from asserting that the "no law respecting" language was adopted in order to protect state, as well as prohibit federal, establishments of religion.[81]

Like Lash, Steven Smith also has a difficult time explaining how the rejection of Livermore's wording is consistent with a federalist interpretation of the religion clauses. He speculates that the changes in wording that occurred during the process of drafting the religion clauses may not have reflected "deliberate alterations in substance so much as stylistic refinements or quirks or accidents in drafting. . . . Hence, arguments that place weight on proposals or drafts not finally adopted are tenuous. . . ." Smith also points out that there is no recorded explanation of the change and, thus, "no recorded statement by a member of Congress indicating dissatisfaction with a purely jurisdictional [federalist] measure and advocating a more substantive [normative] provision." For these reasons, he concludes that "the inference that Congress considered, initially accepted, and then later rejected a purely jurisdictional approach seems frail at best." [82]

The problem with this attempt to minimize the significance of Congress' replacing Livermore's broad language with narrower language is that it can be used against Smith—to challenge his federalist explanation of other provisions adopted at one point or another by the First Congress, including Livermore's "no touching" provision, as well as the provision ultimately adopted.

After all, Smith's argument boils down to this: changes in wording do not reflect changes in meaning, and even if they do, we cannot know the changed meaning unless there is a recorded explanation of that meaning. If this argument is valid, then how can Smith say, as he does, that Livermore's proposal or the provision finally adopted was "a purely jurisdictional [federalist] measure"? As explained earlier, the religion clauses first presented by Madison's committee were clearly normative in nature. If subsequent changes were primarily "stylistic" in nature or the result of "quirks or accidents," then on what grounds can Smith argue that Livermore was proposing a federalist provision? There is no recorded statement by a member of Congress indicating dissatisfaction with a purely normative measure or advocating a more federalist provision. Ultimately Smith uses a double standard: proposed provisions that on their face support a federalist interpretation of the religion clauses have meaning, whereas provisions that on their face support a normative interpretation do not have meaning.

That Smith is not really convinced of his own explanation of the rejection of the Livermore proposal is clearly indicated by the fact that he goes on to accept the position that there is a difference between the Livermore proposal (which, according to him, was a general disclaimer of jurisdiction over religion) and subsequent proposals that were approved, including today's religion clauses (which, according to him, were partial disclaimers of jurisdiction over religion).[83] Because what Smith means by "partial disclaimer of jurisdiction over religion" (which Lash calls the "residual implied power") was explained and criticized earlier in chapters two and three,[84] what was said there will not be repeated here.

The third change in the wording of the proposed religion clauses that is worth considering is the one made by the Senate in the version sent to it by the House, which read: "Congress shall make no law establishing religion, or prohibiting the free exercise thereof; nor shall the rights of conscience be infringed."[85] What is striking about the House's wording is that it mentions both the free exercise of religion and the rights of conscience. By including both, was the House simply being redundant, or did the two clauses have different meanings? In any case, the Senate dropped the reference to rights of conscience, and in all subsequent versions of the amendment of which we have a record, only the free exercise clause remains.

Although the most likely explanation for the Senate's action is that the two clauses were redundant and, thus, the rights clause was omitted for reasons of style,[86] Gary Glenn argues that the change made by the Senate reflected a normative move from a clause that could have been used to protect anti-religion to one that could not. More specifically, he contends that the "rights of conscience" language, even if it was not preceded by "equal," could be "construed as establishing constitutional equality between religious belief and nonbelief and providing grounds to argue that Congress had no right to support or protect religion." In contrast, the "free exercise of religion" language could not be so construed "since nonreligion (especially atheism) is rather obviously not religion. . . ." Glenn concludes, "Hence, forbidding Congress from prohibiting free exercise of religion would not forbid Congress from prohibiting nonreligion and *a fortiori* would permit Congress to protect, prefer or encourage religion as such as against nonreligion."[87]

Although Glenn's interpretation of this change supports the thesis of this book that the religion clauses have normative content, unfortunately it is not convincing because it is based on an assumption for which there is no evidence, namely, that the phrases, "rights of conscience" and "free exercise of religion," had different meanings in the minds of the framers and early Americans in general. To the contrary, most scholars who have studied the meaning of religious liberty in early America have concluded that the phrases were used interchangeably.[88] This was certainly true of those advocating the addition of a religious freedom amendment to the Constitution.[89] According to Michael McConnell, the drafters of the religion clauses also "alternated between the two formulations without apparent pattern, and participants in the debate later referred to the free exercise clause as a 'liberty of conscience' provision without apparent awareness of the difference in denotation." The most notable example of the latter is James Madison, who "used the terms 'free exercise of religion' and 'liberty of conscience' interchangeably when explaining the meaning of the first amendment."[90]

In addition to dropping the rights of conscience clause, the Senate also changed the House's wording of the amendment by substituting "articles of faith or a mode of worship" for "religion" as the object of "Congress shall make no law establishing. . . ."[91] This change (as well as the proposed changes that were considered but rejected) is relevant to the issue of whether the religion clauses have any normative content, for if it reflects a difference of opinion on what should not be "established" by Congress, this would be another indication that the framers were debating principle, not jurisdiction. On this issue, however, scholars are divided. Some, but especially Gerard Bradley, assume or argue that the Senate's language constricted what the House had said could not be established,[92] whereas others, but especially Thomas Curry, argue that the changes made or considered were merely stylistic in nature.[93] More specifically, Bradley says that the Senate was trying to prohibit only "a national church," whereas Curry says that both it and the House were trying to state "that the new government had no authority whatsoever in religious matters."[94] In either case, however, the changes made (or considered) by the Senate do not reflect an attempt on its part to make a federalist statement, and stylistic changes would not have transformed the House's normative statement on church-state relations into a federalist statement.[95]

Moreover, in this author's opinion, the evidence presented by Bradley to support the thesis that the Senate wanted to and did narrow the restrictions placed on Congress by the House's provision is more concrete and convincing than is the evidence presented by Curry in support of his contention that the changes were stylistic in nature. Without going into too much detail here, what Bradley does is to show that many Senators held somewhat conservative views on church-state relations, at least views more conservative that those of Madison, and that what the Senate did was understood *at that time* by various persons, including Madison, to have weakened the normative restrictions imposed on Congress by the House's provision.[96]

In contrast, the evidence presented by Curry is much more indirect and circumstantial. Although he concedes that "[o]n its face," the difference between the House and Senate versions represents "a clash between those who wanted a broad prohibition of government action with regard to religion and those who wanted a narrower restriction . . .," he rejects "a literal interpretation of the references to establishment in the Senate debate and in all the discussion dealing with the Bill of Rights" in favor of evidence on how Americans generally at that time understood an "establishment of religion."[97] Curry's "stylistic" interpretation of the Senate's wording, however, is undercut by the fact that he also says that Congregationalist writers in New England used the phrases "Articles of Faith" and "particular modes of worship" to refer to the establishment of Anglicanism in England, of which "they heartily disapproved," and to distinguish it from their own kind of "mild establishment."[98]

Even if Curry is right, however, it does not mean that his analysis supports a federalist or states' rights interpretation of the changes made or considered by the Senate. His point is simply that the House and Senate disagreed only over the best way to state the normative position they both shared.

VI. THE FINAL WORDING OF THE ESTABLISHMENT CLAUSE

The fourth, and final, change in wording—and one that might have been intended to give the amendment federalist content—was the one made by the conference committee, i.e., the change from no law "establishing religion" (proposed by House) or "establishing articles of faith or a mode of worship" (proposed by Senate) to no law "*respecting* an establishment of religion."[99] Although this final wording on its face is broad enough to make it consistent with a federalist interpretation of the religion clauses,[100] by itself that is insufficient to warrant the conclusion that the establishment clause "does not express a value of 'nonestablishment'"[101] or that its sole purpose was to prevent Congress from overturning state laws on religion.[102]

Instead, given its wording, the clause could have been intended to prohibit the federal government from passing laws that Americans would have associated with traditional establishments of religion. In other words, the word "respecting" may have been added to the proposed amendment in order to prohibit not just a law establishing a religion but any and all laws that were characteristic of such an establishment, including laws that discriminate in any way on the basis of religious belief, practice, or membership. According to one group of scholars, ". . . many [may have] feared that while Congress might not have the power to officially proclaim an established religion in one stroke of the legislative pen, the same undesired end might be reached by smaller steps by the quiet enactment of laws which in themselves would not amount to an establishment, but when added together might have the cumulative effect of totaling a *de facto* establishment."[103] Moreover, the reason for such a prohibition would have been normative—because such laws violate persons' natural rights or threaten the unity and stability of the nation.[104] In 1785 a perfect example of this fear came from the pen of John Carroll, a Catholic priest who later became the first Catholic bishop in the United States: "[Catholics] have all smarted heretofore under the lash of an established church and shall therefore to [sic—be?]*on our guard against every approach to it*."[105]

So which of these two readings—to protect state laws on religion or to protect religious liberty from anything like a national religious establishment—is the correct interpretation of the establishment clause?

Unfortunately we simply do not know for sure. There is nothing in the record of the First Congress or elsewhere that explains why the House/Senate committee worded the establishment clause the way it did. Specifically, there is no evidence showing that the clause was sought to protect state laws on religion, that persons who might have wanted to protect such laws were responsible for the final wording of the clause, or that *anyone* at the time of its drafting or ratification understood the establishment clause in this way.[106] Any explanation of the change, therefore, has to be based on circumstantial evidence.[107] This does not mean, however, that the circumstantial evidence supporting the competing interpretations of the establishment clause is equally strong and compelling.

What circumstantial evidence supports the federalist interpretation of the establishment clause? Those who contend that "respecting" was intended to protect (what they call) state establishments of religion cite, first, the fact that remnants of such establishments still existed in 1789 and that their defenders would not have wanted Congress to legislate against them.[108] By itself, of course, this fact counts for very little, as even some proponents of the federalist interpretation of the establishment clause concede.[109] They, therefore, contend that the final wording of the establishment clause ("no law respecting an establishment of religion") was novel, i.e., had not been used before in laws or public discourse to state what the relationship between government and religion should be, and, thus, must have had some new, special meaning, like protecting state laws promoting religion.[110]

What, however, about this language is novel? The phrase "respecting religion" had certainly been widely used "for some time at the state level to describe one of the most radical of the anti-establishment positions," so much so that Philip Hamburger says that it belies the states' rights interpretation of the establishment clause.[111] One example comes from Virginia, where in a memorial against a "general assessment" to support the teaching of religion, Hanover Presbyterians rejoiced that "all the oppressive Acts of Parliament *respecting* religion, which have been formerly enacted in the mother Country, shall henceforth be of no validity or force in this Common Wealth. . . ."[112] Synonyms of "respecting," such as "concerning" and "touching," had also been widely used in condemnations of certain relationships between religion and government. An example of the former word comes, again, from Virginia Presbyterians who argued that "it would be an unwarrantable stretch of prerogative in the legislature to make laws concerning it [religion], except for protection."[113] An example of the word "touching" comes from the First Congress where Representative Daniel Carroll, explaining the need for an amendment to protect religious freedom, said, ". . . [T]he rights of conscience are, in their nature, of peculiar delicacy, and will little bear the gentlest *touch* of governmental hand. . . ."[114] It is obviously only a short and natural step from "respecting religion" to "respecting an establishment of religion."

In this regard, Carroll's remark deserves additional comment. What he was saying is that even the "*gentlest* touch" of government, such as a law supporting religion, threatens the rights of conscience and, thus, should be avoided. Moreover, it could have been Carroll's sentiment that the conference committee had in mind when it drafted the establishment clause. After all, his cousin, Charles Carroll, was a memeber of the conference committe. Granted this is speculation, but the evidence cited above at least demonstrated that there was nothing novel about language that condemed laws "respecting," "concerning," or "touching" religion (and, by implication, establishments of religion) and, thus, no reason for concluding that such language could have been adopted only in order to protect the quasi-establishments that still existed in a few states.

What is not a matter of speculation is that Madison, another member of the conference committee, would most definitely have approved of a phrase that prohibited all kinds of laws associated with religious establishments. As noted earlier, all along he wanted to obtain a provision that would protect religious liberty "in the fullest latitude" and the amendment that he himself drafted had proscribed the infringement of "the *full* and equal rights of conscience. . . in *any manner, or on any pretext. . . .*"[115] In fact, Madison gave such an interpretation of the clause, albeit years later, when he stated that "the Constitution . . . forbids *everything like an establishment of a national religion.*"[116]

In summary, as one leading church-state scholar has said, the evidence for a federalist reading of the establishment clause is "very thin."[117] Not surprisingly, the main "evidence" cited by its proponents is simply other scholars' assertions that the clause was intended to protect state establishments of religion.[118] Essentially, the proponents of a federalist interpretation are asking others to believe that after the First Congress spent days debating what normative position to take on religious establishments and how to word it, then for some unknown reason the conference committee completely shifted the issue to whether and how to protect religious establishments in the states. This is simply too much to ask anyone to believe.[119]

On the other hand, there is significant indirect evidence that undercuts the states' right interpretation and supports an entirely normative interpretation of the "respecting" language. First, most New Englanders understood an establishment of religion in terms of the traditional Anglican establishment in England, i.e., state preference for one religion and the imposition of its articles of faith and modes of worship, and, therefore, did not consider their state's support of religion to be a religious "establishment."[120] Although Baptists accused the New England system of being an establishment of religion, this was denied by most of its proponents. They denied it because none of the states officially established a religion for the state (instead, each town decided for itself what church to support) and dissenters in each town (provided they were Protestant Christians!)[121] were allowed (in theory but not always in practice) to support their own church rather than being compelled to support the locally established church.[122]

If, therefore, most New Englanders did not think of their state's system of supporting religion as being an establishment of religion and if one of the objectives of the religion clauses was to protect such a system, it seems strange, to say the least, that the drafters of the religion clauses would have used the wording, "no laws respecting an establishment of religion," as the way to accomplish this objective. If they had wanted to protect the various systems of state aid to religion that existed in most of the New England states, it would have been more logical for them to have used wording that proponents of those systems would have understood and accepted, i.e., wording that did not refer to establishments of religion or that referred to state establishments of religion. The fact that the drafters did not use such wording, therefore, raises a serious question as to whether one of their objectives was to protect those systems.[123]

Supporting this argument is the fact that the two states that would have benefited the most from an amendment protecting so-called state establishments of religion, i.e., Massachusetts and Connecticut, failed not only to propose such an amendment, but to ratify the Bill of Rights.[124] If the establishment clause were generally understood as protecting the church-state arrangements that existed in those states and if their citizens really wanted to protect those arrangements from federal laws, then their failure to ratify it is especially puzzling. The fact that they did not logically suggests that the people of Massachusetts and Connecticut either were not all that interested in protecting their laws on religion from federal legislation or did not understand the establishment clause as designed to serve that purpose.[125]

A second piece of circumstantial evidence that undercuts the "states' rights" interpretation of the establishment clause is the fact that the "respecting" language was the product of the Conference Committee, not the Senate, which was the body most likely to have favored a provision to protect state laws pertaining to religion.[126] After all, the Senate represented states, and it had earlier voted down Madison's proposal that would have applied a religious liberty provision to the states. However, the religion clauses that the Senate finally adopted reflect an interest not in protecting states' rights, but rather in narrowing the *normative* limitation to be placed on the federal government. Specifically, the Senate replaced the House's prohibition against a "law establishing religion" with another normative, but narrower, prohibition against a law establishing "articles of faith or modes of worship."[127] According to some scholars, this language did not prevent government financial support of religion.[128] *It is only logical, therefore, to assume that the reason members of the House, especially Madison, objected to the Senate's wording was because it did not adequately restrict Congress' power to legislate on religious matters and thus provided too little protection to religious liberty.*[129]

If this is a correct assumption, then the most logical interpretation of the words "no laws respecting an establishment of religion" is that it was normative language proposed by the House members of the Committee as a replacement for the Senate's narrow, but normative prohibition. After all, there is no reason for thinking that the House, or its representatives on the Committee, especially Madison, suddenly became interested in protecting the quasi-establishments of religion that existed in a few of the states and proposed language to accomplish such an objective. To the contrary, the evidence suggests that their only interest was in making sure that religious freedom was protected as fully as possible from federal legislation. Thus, they secured language that prohibited not just laws establishing "articles of faith or modes or worship," but *all* laws "respecting an establishment of religion."[130] In short, the establishment clause had normative, not federalist, meaning.

There is, however, one problem with this explanation of the establishment clause—why would the Senate have agreed to a broad restriction on Congress' power to legislate with respect to religious establishments? Although admittedly speculative, there are three possible components to this question's answer.

First, even Senators with conservative positions on church and state might not have placed a very high priority on giving the national government some degree of power to legislate on matters of religion. After all, if they were in favor of protecting their states' quasi-establishments of religion, they would have been ambivalent about giving the federal government even limited power to promote religion. They may have anticipated conflicts between its policies regarding religion and their states' policies regarding religion, and it was the latter to which they were most committed.[131] On the other hand, because the religion clauses as finally worded did not apply to state laws or policies regarding religion, the Senators would not have perceived the clauses as threats to those state laws/policies.[132] In short, the more conservative Senators may have concluded that a provision worded so as to allow the national government to promote religion to some extent was just not all that important. Second, in return for agreeing to the final wording of the religion clauses (and what is now the Sixth Amendment), the Senate secured the House's acceptance of its wording on the fourteen other contested provisions. In short, the House may have offered the Senate a deal that was too good for it to turn down. Third, the House members of the conference committee, especially Madison, may have been very firm in demanding a broadly worded provision dealing with religion. Although they wanted a bill of rights, they may have been unwilling to compromise on religious liberty in order to get one.[133] Ultimately, it may have been a matter of which side "blinked first."

This last point relates to the final piece of evidence that is inconsistent with a states' rights interpretation of the establishment clause—the role of James Madison in the drafting of the religion clauses. Although one cannot legitimately claim that Madison alone drafted the clauses,[134] surely it cannot be denied that Madison was more "invested" in their drafting and adoption than anyone else in the First Congress.[135] Theodore Sky summarizes his importance as follows:

> . . . [I]t is fair to say that more than any other man in the first Congress James Madison was responsible for the first amendment. He introduced the initial version of the Bill of Rights; pestered the House into taking up the amendment; served on the House drafting committee; performed as a sort of floor manager during the House debate; and finally was active as one of the three House delegates on the conference committee.[136]

Also, as established earlier,[137] he clearly had a normative or principled understanding of the clauses that he originally introduced to Congress and wanted to protect the rights of conscience to the fullest extent possible. There is, moreover, some evidence that Madison was unhappy with the Senate's proposed amendment on religion.[138] If, therefore, the final version of the religion clauses had not reversed the Senate's action and protected religious liberty "in the fullest latitude," Madison surely would have vigorously protested against it—at least privately, if not publicly—but he did not. Several times during the fall of 1789 Madison referred in his letters to the amendments that Congress passed and sent to the states, and he not only did not express any reservations about them, but at one point said that they "correspond as far as they go with the proposition of the [Virginia] State Convention. . . ."[139] This indicates that he was mostly, if not entirely, satisfied with the final language of the clauses.[140]

Could Madison have accepted an amendment intended to protect state establishments of religion? Given the fact that he had previously attempted to secure the adoption of an amendment that had the potential to undermine such establishments and that he considered it the most valuable of all his proposed amendments, it is hard to imagine that he would have accepted an amendment to protect those establishments.[141] This can also be said of others in the First Congress who, like Madison, were from states that either had never had an establishment of religion or had essentially eliminated them prior to the meeting of the First Congress. As one scholar argues, "[i]t seems highly unlikely that representatives of these states . . . would have endorsed the [establishment clause] amendment merely to protect the religious establishments of those states that retained them."[142]

V. THE RELEVANCE OF MADISON'S AMENDMENT TO PROTECT RELIGIOUS LIBERTY IN THE STATES

Perhaps the most important piece of evidence from the record of the drafting of the religion clauses that supports a normative rather than a federalist interpretation of the religion clauses is the fact that two days after approving Livermore's language denying the federal government jurisdiction over religion, the House approved the second amendment that Madison had proposed to protect religious freedom, i.e., "No state shall infringe the equal rights of conscience."[143] Obviously, this provision could not have had any federalist or states' rights content because it was intended to restrict what the states could do. For this reason, it was objected to by one member of the House. In its defense, Madison said, "If there was any reason to restrain the Government of the United States from infringing upon these essential rights, it was equally necessary that they should be secured against the State Governments. He . . . was satisfied that it would be equally grateful to the people."[144]

In saying this, Madison made it as clear as he could have done that both amendments, the one applying to the federal government and the other to the state governments, had the same general meaning. That, of course, could not possibly have been the case if the purpose of the former amendment was to protect states' rights because clearly the purpose of the latter was to restrict, not protect, states' rights. The only way the two amendments could have had the same general purpose and justification was if they both had the normative objective of protecting, as Madison said, the essential rights of the people (not the states).[145]

The House was persuaded by Madison and voted for the amendment. Its doing so means either that the amendment it had earlier passed that applied to the federal government could not possibly have had federalist meaning or else that the House was being completely contradictory in its decision-making. It would have made no sense for it to pass an amendment that was intended to protect the states' power to legislate on religion and then immediately turn around and pass an amendment intended to reduce that power. Although the Senate, for reasons unknown, refused to approve of the amendment to be applied to the states,[146] that fact in no way undercuts the previous conclusion that the amendment to be applied to the federal government was understood by the House to have normative content.[147] Even if the Senate refused to approve the amendment that applied to the states because it wanted to protect states' rights, that would not count as evidence for a federalist interpretation of the amendment that applied to the federal government. The latter amendment could have had normative content, but yet the Senate might not have wanted, for reasons of states' rights, to apply it or a similar amendment to the states.[148]

VI. THE NUMBER OF CHANGES IN THE WORDING OF THE CLAUSES

A final piece of evidence that undercuts the states' rights explanation of the drafting and wording of the religion clauses is the large number of changes that were made in the wording of the proposed religion clauses during their drafting. Including the version proposed by Madison and the one ultimately accepted, the total number of drafts of the religion clauses considered by the First Congress was sixteen.[149] If the purpose of the religion clauses was simply to say that jurisdiction over the subject matter of religion is reserved to the states, why were there so many proposed changes in their wording?

Why, for example, did the House object so strongly to the Senate's version of the religion clauses that it was willing to accede to the Senate's wording of all the other amendments in order to get its version of the religion clauses accepted by the Senate?[150] Moreover, as David Steinberg argues, it would have been easy to make clear the federalist purpose of the religion clauses. The framers could and should have simply said, "All questions respecting religion are reserved to the states." Such wording would have been consistent with the wording of the other provision in the Bill of Rights that is clearly federalist in nature—the Tenth Amendment.[151] Because there were so many different wordings and because the final one is not what it should have been if its purpose were to protect states' rights, it seems only reasonable to conclude that some of the various changes, proposed and actual, represent attempts to state what the proper relationship between the federal government and religion should be.[152] In any case, the many changes do not support a federalist interpretation of the religion clauses.

VII. SUMMARY

Having looked in every "nook and cranny" of the First Congress for evidence relating to whether the religion clauses were intended to have normative or federalist meaning, I conclude the following. First, the advocates of a religious liberty amendment, Madison in particular, conceived of it in normative, not federalist, terms. Although Madison may have thought that theoretically such an amendment was not needed, he realized that as a practical matter it was needed to overcome the objections of many Anti-federalists to the Constitution and that what they wanted was a provision protecting what they considered to be a sacred, inalienable individual right.

Second, there is nothing explicit in the record of the discussion of the various earlier versions of the religion clauses to indicate that other members of Congress understood them differently from the way that Madison understood his proposed amendment. Other than the concern mistakenly expressed over the (normative!) clauses' being applied to the states, the only significant issues related not to states' rights or federalism, but to the scope of the protection that should be given to the right of conscience. Not a single person said anything to indicate that the religion clauses were meant to protect a states' right or state establishments of religion from federal laws.[153]

Third, except possibly for the final change to "respecting an establishment of religion," none of the changes in the wording of the proposed religious liberty amendment reflects an intention to move from a normative to a federalist understanding of the amendment. Moreover, although its final wording is consistent with a federalist interpretation of the establishment clause, there is no explicit evidence that the word "respecting" in that clause was adopted as a way of giving it federalist meaning and protecting the systems of public support of religion that existed in the New England states. Indeed, if the framers had such an objective in mind, one can only ask why they did not choose wording that would more clearly reflect such an intention.[154] Even if the "respecting an establishment of religion" language were intended to reflect a federalist point, that certainly proves nothing with respect to the meaning of the free exercise clause.

Finally, Madison proposed and the House adopted a provision that would have protected the equal rights of conscience from state laws, that was unquestionably normative in nature, and that was explained and discussed as if its meaning or content were analogous to that of the provision that was to be applied to the federal government. In short, members of the House understood the provision limiting the federal government in the same way that they understood the one limiting the state governments—as a guarantee of the liberty of conscience.

NOTES

1. For their reasons, see Charlene B. Bickford and Kenneth R. Bowling, *Birth of the Nation: The First Federal Congress 1789–1791* (Madison, Wis.: Madison House Pubs, 1989), 52–53.

2. See letters to Jefferson, 10/17/1788, Edmund Pendleton, 10/20/1788, George Eve, 1/2/1789, and Thomas Randolph, 1/13/1789, in *The Papers of James Madison* [hereafter cited as *PJM*], ed. Robert A. Rutland et al (Chicago: Univ. of Chicago Press, 1977), 11:297–300, 307, 404–5, 416. An excellent account of Madison's change of mind is found in Lance Banning, *The Sacred Fire of Liberty: James Madison and the Founding of the Federal Republic* (Ithaca, N. Y.: Cornell Univ. Press, 1995), 281–90. It gives special attention to the influence that Jefferson's letters had on his thinking.

3. See letters to George Eve, 1/2/1789, in *PJM*, 11:404–5, and to Richard Peters, 8/19/1789, in *PJM*, 12:353. Scholars who believe that Madison was motivated significantly, if not primarily, by a principled commitment to protecting essential rights include Ralph Ketcham, *James Madison: A Biography* (New York: 1971), 290–92, 303; Robert Rutland, "The Trivialization of the Bill of Rights,"*William and Mary Law Review*, 31 (1990): 290–91; Stuart Leibiger, "James Madison and Amendments to the Constitution, 1787–1789: 'Parchment Barriers',"*Journal of Southern History*, 59 (1993): 441–68; Douglas Laycock, "Individual Liberty and Constitutional Architecture: The Founders' Prompt Correction of Their Own Mistake,"*Harvard Journal of Law & Public Policy*, 16 (Winter 1993): 75–82; and Banning, *Sacred Fire of Liberty*, 265–90.

4. See "Letter to Richard Peters" (8/19/1789), in *PJM*, 12:353. Also, see Donald L. Drakeman, "Religion and the Republic: James Madison and the First Amendment,"*Journal of Church and State*, 25 (Autumn 1983): 428–29, and Thomas J. Curry, *The First Freedoms: Church and State in America to the Passage of the First Amendment* (New York: Oxford Univ. Press, 1986), 198–99.

5. See Madison's "Letter to Richard Peters" (8/19/1789), in *PJM*, 12:353; Donald S. Lutz, "The U. S. Bill of Rights in Historical Perspective," in *Contexts of the Bill of Rights*, ed. S. L. Schechter & R. B. Bernstein (Albany, N. Y.: New York State Commission on the Bicentennial of the U. S. Constitution, 1990), 13; and Bickford and Bowling, *Birth of a Nation*, 52. Scholars

who contend or imply that Madison acted primarily, if not entirely, from expediency include Kenneth R. Bowling, "'A Tub to the Whale': The Founding Fathers and the Adoption of the Federal Bill of Rights,"*Journal of the Early Republic*, 8 (1988): 223–51; Paul Finkelman, "James Madison and the Bill of Rights: A Reluctant Paternity,"*1990 Supreme Court Review* (1990): 301–47; Ralph A. Rossum, "*The Federalist's* Understanding of the Constitution as a Bill of Rights," in *Saving the Revolution: The Federalist Papers and the American Founding*, ed. Charles R. Kesler (New York: 1987), 219–33; and Jack Rakove, "The Madisonian Theory of Rights,"*William and Mary Law Review*, 31 (1990): 254.

6. John P. Kaminski, "The Making of the Bill of Rights: 1787–1792," in *Contexts of the Bill of Rights*, 45.

7. For the list, see *Documentary History of the First Federal Congress of the United States of America* (hereafter cited as *DH*), Vol. 4, *Legislative Histories*, ed. Charlene B. Bickford & Helen E. Veit (Baltimore, Md.: Johns Hopkins Univ. Press, 1986), 9–12. Regarding Madison's proposed amendments, Fisher Ames wrote, "They are the fruit of much labour and research. He has hunted up all the grievances and complaints of newspapers—all the articles of Conventions—and the small talk of their debates. . . . Upon the whole, it may do good towards quieting men who attend to sounds only, and may get the mover some popularity—which he wishes." "Letter to Thomas Dwight" (6/11/1789), in *DH*, Vol. 16, *Correspondence*, ed. Charlene B. Bickford et al. (Baltimore, Md.: Johns Hopkins Univ. Press, 2004), 748–49.

8. *DH*, Vol. 4, *Legislative Histories*, 10–11. For some inexplicable reason, Leonard Levy says that the word "national" in Madison's proposed amendment signified that "Congress had no power to enact an establishment of religion *or to interfere with state establishments*."*The Establishment Clause: Religion and the First Amendment* (Chapel Hill, N. C.: Univ. of North Carolina Press, 1994, 2d ed. rev.), 95 (emphasis added). There is, however, nothing in what Madison proposed to warrant the second part of this claim.

9. Madison himself said with respect to his proposed amendments, "The structure & stamina of the Govt. are as little touched as possible." "Letter to Edmund Randolph" (6/15/1789), in *PJM*, 12:219. Also, see his speech, 6/8/1789, to the First Congress in which he introduced his proposed amendments, in *DH*, Vol. 11, *Debates in the House of Representatives*, ed. Charlene B. Bickford et al. (Baltimore, Md.: Johns Hopkins Univ. Press, 1992), 818–21, 827. Also, see Donald S. Lutz, "The States and the United States Bill of Rights,"*Southern Illinois University Law Journal*, 16 (1992): 254–58, and Whitman H. Ridgway, "Popular Sentiment and the Bill of Rights Controversy," in *The Bill of Rights: Government Proscribed*, ed. Ronald Hoffman & Peter J. Albert (Charlottesville, Va.: Univ. Press of Virginia, 1997), 239.

10. For comments from both Federalists and Anti-federalists, see Gerard V. Bradley, *Church-State Relationships in America* (Westport, Conn.: Greenwood Press, 1987, 88–89.

11. Speech of 6/8/1789, in *DH*, Vol. 11, *Debates*, 821–24.

12. A little over two months later, on 8/19/1789, in a letter to Richard Peters, Madison wrote, "A constitutional provision in favor of essential rights is a thing not improper in itself and was always viewed in that light by myself. It may be less necessary in a republic than a monarchy and in a federal government than the former, *but it is in some degree rational in every government, since in every government power may oppress and declarations on paper, though not an effectual restraint, are not without some influence*."*PJM*, 12:353 (emphasis added).

13. "A Pennsylvanian,"*Federal Gazette*, 6/12/1789, quoted in Chester J. Antieau et al., *Freedom From Federal Establishment: Formation and Early History of the First Amendment Religion Clauses* (Milwaukee, Wisc.: Bruce Pub., 1964), 125.

14. *DH*, Vol. 11, *Debates*, 825.

15. The passage quoted above is in the same paragraph in which Madison said that "independent tribunals of justice will consider themselves in a peculiar manner the guardians of those rights. . . ."*DH*, Vol. 11, *Debates*, 825.

16. *DH*, Vol. 11, *Debates*, 826 (emphasis added). This was not the first time that Madison had expressed such views. He had done so earlier and most forcefully in essay # 10 of the *Federalist Papers*. There he explained why unjust factions were much more likely to control state governments than they were the national government, and he explicitly used religious

factions to illustrate his point. See James Madison et al., *The Federalist Papers*, ed. Isaac Kramnick (London: Penguin Books, 1987 ed. of 1788 ed.), Number X.

17. "Letter to Thomas Jefferson" (6/30/1789), in *PJM*, 12:272.

18. See Steven D. Smith, "The Religion Clauses in Constitutional Scholarship,"*Notre Dame Law Review*, 74 (March 1999): 1039–40, and Levy, *Establishment Clause*, 79.

19. "Letter to George Eve" (1/2/1789), in *PJM*, 11:404–5.

20. Even Steven Smith admits that Madison was not all that cautious in what he proposed and that his proposed amendments relating to religion were normative in content . He writes, "Even while insisting that he was doing nothing controversial, a politician would try to slip in something for his cause, wouldn't he? And in fact Madison did try to include in the Bill of Rights a provision dealing with religion and other subjects that would have gone beyond merely making explicit the jurisdictional division that all sides [according to Smith] had agreed on." "The Religion Clauses in Constitutional Scholarship," 1041.

21. For the existence and nature of such a consensus, see chapter six.

22. Curry, *First Freedoms*, 199–200.

23. *DH*, Vol. 4, *Legislative Histories*, 28–29.

24. *DH*, Vol. 11, *Debates*, 1260–61.

25. *DH*, Vol. 11, *Debates*, 1261–62.

26. Curry, *First Freedoms*, 203.

27. *DH*, Vol. 11, *Debates*, 1262.

28. Douglas Laycock, "'Non-preferential' Aid to Religion: A False Claim about Original Intent,"*William and Mary Law Review*, 27 (1986): 890–91, and Curry, *First Freedoms*, 203. Huntington was from Connecticut, which allowed persons to designate which church should receive their "church tax," but did not exempt nonbelievers from having to pay the tax. Laycock, "'Non-preferential' Aid," 891.

29. Levy, *Establishment Clause*, 100–101, including fn 8.

30. See, e.g., Mark DeWolfe Howe, *The Garden and the Wilderness: Religion and Government in American Constitutional History* (Chicago: Univ. of Chicago Press, 1965), 20–22; Noah Feldman, "The Intellectual Origins of the Establishment Clause,"*New York University Law Review*, 77 (May 2002): 409–10; Antieau et al., *Freedom From Establishment*, 140; Laycock, "'Non-preferential' Aid," 890; and Bradley, *Church-State Relationships*, 25.

31. Feldman, "Intellectual Origins," 409 ("Huntington did not wish to say that the New England arrangements were an establishment—establishment was a potentially derogatory term—but he was prepared to say that the New England Way might be construed into an establishment.") The problem with this speculation is that Huntington in his second objection to the proposed amendment implicitly defends religious establishments by explicitly condemning Rhode Island for not having one.

32. Some scholars say that the scenario Huntington feared was that the federal courts would refuse to enforce the "engagements" (contracts) not on the grounds that the Connecticut law itself was one establishing a religion and thus violating the Constitution but on the grounds that their enforcement of an "engagement" was the equivalent of establishing a religion and violating the Constitution. See, e.g., Howe, *Garden and Wilderness*, 22–23. Although plausible, this latter interpretation of Huntington's remarks is not as obvious or self-evident as the former interpretation is.

33. Huntington also failed to notice that Article III did not give federal courts jurisdiction over suits to collect state church taxes. Laycock, "'Non-preferential' Aid . . .," 908.

34. Theodore Sky, "The Establishment Clause, the Congress and the Schools: An Historical Perspective,"*Virginia Law Review*, 52 (Dec. 1966): 1418 (". . . [T]he committee's language itself was susceptible to the construction that it *automatically* prohibited state as well as federal 'establishments.'") (emphasis in original).

35. *DH*, Vol. 11, *Debates*, 1262 (emphasis added). This attempt on Madison's part to make it clear that the religion clauses limited only the *national* legislature did not constitute a compromise on Madison's part because at this time his proposed amendment to prohibit the *states* from infringing the rights of conscience was still "alive and well."

36. *DH*, Vol. 11, *Debates*, 1262 (emphasis added).

37. *DH*, Vol. 4, *Legislative Histories*, 28, fn 9.

38. *DH*, Vol. 3, *House of Representatives Journal*, ed. Linda G. De Pauw et al (Baltimore, Md.: Johns Hopkins Univ. Press, 1977), 159.

39. "Letter to Alexander White" (8/24/1789), in *PJM*, 12:352–53.

40. The first change that was considered but defeated would have replaced "religion or prohibiting the free exercise thereof" with "One Religious Sect or Society in preference to others." The next two proposals would have replaced the entire article with the following: "Congress shall not make any law, infringing the rights of conscience, or establishing any Religious Sect or Society" and "Congress shall make no law establishing any particular denomination of religion in preference to another, or prohibiting the free exercise thereof, nor shall the rights of conscience be infringed."*DH*, Vol. 1, *Senate Legislative Journal*, ed. Linda G. De Pauw et al. (Baltimore, Md.: Johns Hopkins Univ. Press, 1972), 151.

41. *DH*, Vol. 1, *Senate Legislative Journal*, 151.

42. *DH*, Vol. 1, *Senate Legislative Journal*, 166, 168, and Vol. 4, *Legislative Histories*, 36, fns 6, 8.

43. *DH*, Vol. 1, *Senate Legislative Journal*, 181–82, 189, 192; Vol. 3, *House of Representatives Journal*, 199, 217–18, 228; and Vol. 4, *Legislative Histories*, 47. Also, see Levy, *Establishment Clause*, 103–4, and Antieau et al., *Freedom From Establishment*, 130–31, 236, fns 48 & 50.

44. At the suggestion of Livermore, it was changed from the active to the passive voice. *DH*, Vol. 4, *Legislative Histories*, 29, fn 23, & 39, and Vol. 11, *Debates*, 1292.

45. *DH*, Vol. 11, *Debates*, 1292.

46. *DH*, Vol. 1, *Senate Legislative Journal*, 158.

47. See Howe, *Garden and Wilderness*, 20–23. Gary Glenn argues that what Silvester and Huntington most objected to was the "*equal* rights of conscience" language, which, according to Glen, was intended to protect atheists and atheism and, thus, manifested an indifference, if not hostility, to religion. "Forgotten Purposes of the First Amendment Religion Clauses,"*Review of Politics*, 49 (Summer 1987): 346–51.

48. Laycock, "'Non-preferential' Aid," 889–91.

49. *The First Freedoms*, 203 (emphasis added). Leonard Levy makes the same mistake. *Establishment Clause*, 100–101 ("Huntington . . . probably expressed a fear that state establishments might be interfered with by *Congress*.") (emphasis added). Both scholars may have been misled by Joseph M. Snee, who in a much earlier work made the same mistake. See "Religious Disestablishment and the Fourteenth Amendment,"*Washington University Law Quarterly*, 1954 (Dec. 1954): 371, 385.

50. *A Nation Dedicated to Religious Liberty: The Constitutional Heritage of the Religion Clauses* (Philadelphia, Penn.: Univ. of Pennsylvania Press, 1990), 46. The use of the word "intended" in the above quote is also misleading, for it implies that what Huntington may have "wanted" became part of what the First Congress "intended" when it drafted the First Amendment. In fact, however, except for the final wording of the Establishment Clause (no law *respecting* an establishment of religion), there is no evidence to show that that happened.

51. Jed Rubenfeld, "Antidisestablishmentarianism: Why RFRA Really Was Unconstitutional,"*Michigan Law Review*, 95 (Aug. 1997): 2355–56.

52. See Feldman, "Intellectual Origins," at 409–10, for an elaboration of this criticism.

53. See Howe, *Garden and Wilderness*, 23.

54. Steven K. Green, "Federalism and the Establishment Clause: A Reassessment,"*Creighton Law Review*, 38 (2004–2005): 788–89, and Feldman, "Intellectual Origins," 409–11.

55. Laycock, "'Nonpreferential' Aid," 889–91. Cf. Kurt T. Lash, "The Second Adoption of the Establishment Clause: The Rise of the Nonestablishment Principle,"*Arizona State Law Journal*, 27 (1995): 1085, 1090–91.

56. Kurt T. Lash, "Power and the Subject of Religion,"*Ohio State Law Journal*, 59 (1998): 1098, fn 105 and Levy, *Establishment Clause*, 76, 97, 101.

57. Feldman, "Intellectual Origins," 410–11. Even Rubenfeld, one of the leading advocates of the federalist interpretation of the religion clauses, concedes that "Madison's proposed wording of the religion clauses was antiestablishment . . . but in no way antidisestablishment." "Antidisestablishmentarianism," 2355.

58. Given the evidence presented above, there is no basis for Daniel O. Conkle's claim that the debate in the First Congress over the wording of the establishment clause was "primarily" over the "issue concerning the appropriate *means* for effecting a policy of federalism on questions of church and state." "Toward a General Theory of the Establishment Clause,"*Northwestern University Law Review*, 82 (1988): 1113, 1133–34.

59. Howe, *Garden and Wilderness*, 20–23. Feldman, "Intellectual Origins," at 410–11, agrees. Also, see Jay S. Bybee, "Taking Liberties with the First Amendment: Congress, Section 5, and the Religious Freedom Restoration Act,"*Vanderbilt Law Review*, 48 (Nov. 1995): 1560–62, and Lash, "Power and Religion," 1098, fn. 105.

60. Howe, *Garden and Wilderness*, 21–22.

61. Glenn says that it was "a defeat" for those "who wished to permit some sort of Congressional support for religion" because it "seems even less open to such support than either the Madison or the committee language." "Forgotten Purposes," 351.

62. Glenn, "Forgotten Purposes," 346–51.

63. Smith, *Foreordained Failure*, 31–33; Bradley, *Church-State Relationships*, 92; and Rubenfeld, "Antidisestablishmentarianism," 2355–56.

64. Bradley, *Church-State Relationships*, 76, 92; Rubenfeld, "Antidisestablishmentarianism," 2354–55.

65. Feldman, "Intellectual Origins," 407–12.

66. See above, pp. 72–73.

67. Lash, "Power and Religion," 1090. On this issue, Glenn, "Forgotten Purposes," appears to contradict himself. At 352, he says that "prohibiting *any* laws touching religion, *a fortiori* prohibits any laws about religious establishments" (emphasis in original). Then, at 354, he says that Livermore's proposal "still arguably permitted federal legislation to *protect* or *support* the rights of conscience" (emphasis in original).

68. *DH,* Vol. 11, *Debates*, 1292.

69. Drakeman, "Religion and Republic," 432, fn 27 ("A restriction applicable to the states . . . could have the effect of disestablishing churches in several states and would have made major changes in the relationship of church and state in virtually all of the states.").

70. See Snee, "Religious Disestablishment," 379–82.

71. Green, "Federalism and Establishment Clause," 787, and also 767, 775–80. Also, see Laycock, "'Nonpreferential' Aid," 917, and Curry, *First Freedoms*, 217, 222.

72. Curry, *First Freedoms*, 137–38, 143–46.

73. After considering three different interpretations of Livermore's proposed amendment, Donald Drakeman concludes, ". . . [W]e have no idea what Samuel Livermore or, more broadly, the New Hampshire ratifying convention sought to achieve with the 'no touching' proposal."*Church, State, and Original Intent* (New York: Cambridge Univ. Press, 2010), 234.

74. *DH,* Vol. 4, *Legislative Histories*, 28, fn 9.

75. See Bradley, *Church-State Relationships*, 96.

76. "Power and Religion," 1089–90.

77. *Separation of Church and State* (Cambridge, Mass.: Harvard Univ. Press, 2002), 101–7, and "Equality and Diversity: The Eighteenth-Century Debate about Equal Protection and Equal Civil Rights,"*1992 Supreme Court Review* (1993): 343–45. Also, see Douglas Laycock, "Regulatory Exemptions of Religious Behavior and the Original Understanding of the Establishment Clause."*Notre Dame Law Review*, 81 (2006): 1793–1842.

78. "Power and Religion," 1090–93.

79. "Power and Religion," 1090.

80. "Power and Religion," 1090.

81. "Power and Religion," 1090.

82. *Foreordained Failure*, 32.

83. *Foreordained Failure*, 32–34.

84. See above, pp. 29–33, 48–49.

85. *DH,* 3:159.

86. On this point, Thomas Curry writes, ". . . [T]he Senate debate can be seen as a discussion about style, not substance. By omitting the redundant phrase 'nor shall the rights of conscience be infringed' from the House version, and by combining the sections dealing with

freedom of religion, press, and assembly, the Senate manifested its concern for form."*The First Freedoms*, 213.

87. "Forgotten Purposes," 354.

88. See, e.g., Michael McConnell, "The Origins and Historical Understanding of Free Exercise of Religion,"*Harvard Law Review*, 103 (May 1990): 1410, 1482–83, 1488, 1493–94; and Feldman, "Intellectual Origins," 381, 404–5.

89. See above, pp. 65–73.

90. "Origins and Historical Understanding," 1494. For an example of Madison's doing this, see his "Report of 1800" (1/7/1800), in *PJM*, 339, 346–47.

91. See above, p. 92.

92. See, e.g., Bradley, *Church-State Relationships*, 93–94, and Green, "Federalism and Establishment Clause," 792.

93. See, e.g., Curry, *First Freedoms*, 213–15, and Levy, *The Establishment Clause*, 103.

94. Bradley, *Church-State Relationships*, 94, and Curry, *First Freedoms*, 215.

95. Green, "Federalism and Establishment Clause," 792.

96. Bradley, *Church-State Relationships*, 89–90, 93–94. Agreeing with Bradley that the Senate was trying to narrow the scope of the establishment clause ban are Sky, "Establishment Clause," 1415–17, and Green, "Federalism and Establishment Clause," 792–94.

97. *First Freedoms*, 207–8, 209–15.

98. *First Freedoms*, 116, 210.

99. See above, p. 92.

100. See Chris Bartolomucci, "Rethinking the Incorporation of the Establishment Clause,"*Harvard Law Review*, 105 (1992): 1706–7; Bradley, *Church-State Relationships*, 94–95; Rubenfeld, "Antidisestablishmentarianism," 2356; and Bybee, "Taking Liberties," 1560.

101. As asserted by Lash, "Second Adoption," 1111.

102. Howe, *Garden and Wilderness*, 23 ("Grammatically persuasive as that interpretation of the amendment may be, I find it historically unconvincing.") Among the scholars who have misinterpreted or misstated Howe's position on this issue are Smith, *Foreordained Failure*, at 18, and Bybee, "Taking Liberties," at 1564–65.

103. Antieau et al., *Freedom From Establishment*, 136. Also, see *Lemon v. Kurtzman*, 403 U.S. 602, 612 (1971) ("A given law might not *establish* a state religion but might nevertheless be one 'respecting' that end in the sense of being a step that could lead to such an establishment. . . .") (emphasis in original).

104. See Hamburger, *Separation of Church and State*, 89–107; Antieau et al., *Freedom From Establishment*, 136–37; and Adams and Emmerich, *Nation Dedicated*, 45, 47.

105. "Letter to Charles Plowden" (2/27/1785), in *The John Carroll Papers*, 3 vols, ed. Thomas O. Hanley (Notre Dame, Ind.: Univ. of Notre Dame Press, 1976), 1:168.

106. Drakeman, *Church, State*, 241–42, and Bartolomucci, "Rethinking Incorporation," 1706–7. Kurt Lash, in "Power and Religion," 1099–1105, relies on the following statement made by James Iredell *one year before* the religion clauses were discussed in the First Congress: "Had Congress undertaken to guarantee *religious freedom*, or any particular species of it, they would then have had a pretence to interfere in a subject they have nothing to do with. Each state, so far as the clause in question [the clause guaranteeing to every state a republican form of government] does not interfere, must be left to the operation of its own principles." Speech in North Carolina Ratifying Convention, 7/30/1788, in *The Founders' Constitution*, ed. Philip B. Kurland & Ralph Lerner (Chicago: Univ. of Chicago Press, 1987), 5:90 (emphasis in original). This quote, however, provides little support for Lash's explanation of the "respecting" wording of the establishment clause. Although Iredell's comment clearly reflects *his* view that the original Constitution did not give the national Congress the power to guarantee religious freedom in the states, it obviously says nothing about whether the establishment clause, proposed a year later, was intended to express Iredell's view. After all, not being a member of the First Congress, neither Iredell nor anyone from North Carolina (which was not yet represented in Congress) had anything to do with the drafting of the religion clauses.

107. Michael S. Ariens & Robert A. Destro, *Religious Liberty in a Pluralistic Society* (Durham, N. C.: Carolina Academic Press,1996), 88, and Antieau et al., *Freedom From Establishment*, 142.

108. See, e.g., *Elk Grove Unified School District v. Newdow*, 542 U.S. 1, 50 (2004) (J. Thomas, concurring).

109. Vincent P. Munoz, "The Original Meaning of the Establishment Clause and the Impossibility of Its Incorporation,"*University of Pennsylvania Journal of Constitutional Law*, 8 (2006): 601–2.

110. See, e.g., Lash, "Power and Religion," 1105; Lash, "Second Adoption," 1111; and Glenn, "Forgotten Purposes," 358.

111. Hamburger, "Equality and Diversity . . .," 345, fn 122, and 310–11, 339–44.

112. "Memorial of the Presbytery of Hanover to the General Assembly of Virginia Presented to the House June 3, 1777," in *American State Papers and Related Documents on Freedom in Religion*, ed. William A. Blakely (Washington, DC: Religious Liberty Association, 1949, 4[th]ed.), 106 (emphasis added).

113. "Memorial of the Presbyterians of Virginia to the Virginia General Assembly" (8/13/1785), in *American State Papers Bearing on Sunday Legislation*, ed. William A. Blakely and Willard A. Colcord (New York: Da Capo Press, 1970 rep. of 1911 ed.), 114. A dissenting township in Massachusetts explained its opposition to Article III of the Constitution of 1780 on the grounds that "all that is Necessary in the Form of Civil Government respecting Religion is fully and happily exprest in the Second Article [guaranteeing liberty of conscience]." "The Return of the Town of Needham on the Constitution of 1780," quoted in Ronald M. Peters, *The Massachusetts Constitution of 1780* (Amherst, Mass.: Univ. of Massachusetts Press, 1978), 82.

114. *DH*, Vol. 11, *Debates*, 1261 (emphasis added).

115. See above, pp. 88–89. Also, see Antieau et al., *Freedom From Establishment*, 138–39. Cf. Clifton Kruse, "The Historical Meaning and Judicial Construction of the Establishment of Religion Clause of the First Amendment,"*Washburn Law Journal*, 2 (Winter 1962): 65 ("Madison was not the author of the first amendment, nor does the amendment reflect his attitude toward the role of government in religion.").

116. "Detached Memoranda," ca. 1817, in *Founders' Constitution*, 5:104 (emphasis added)

117. John Witte, Jr., "Facts and Fiction About the History of Separation of Church and State,"*Journal of Church and State*, 48 (Winter 2006): 33.

118. For examples, see Michael A. Paulsen, "Religion, Equality, and the Constitution: An Equal Protection Approach to Establishment Clause Adjudication,"*Notre Dame Law Review*, 61 (1986): 311, 321–22; Akhil Amar, *The Bill of Rights: Creation and Reconstruction* (New Haven, Conn.: Yale Univ. Press, 1998), 32–33; Bybee, "Taking Liberties," 1560; Rubenfeld, "Disestablishmentarianism," 2351–57.

119. See Drakeman, *Church, State*, 236, 240 ("While it may be possible, there is not enough affirmative evidence to convert 'possible' even into 'plausible.'"), and Feldman, "Intellectual Origins," 407.

120. Thomas J. Curry, *Farewell to Christendom: The Future of Church and State in America* (New York: Oxford Univ. Press, 2001), 31–32, 38–39, 41, 128, n. 25; Curry, *The First Freedoms*, 172–75, 191–92, 212–13; Charles H. Lippy, "The 1780 Massachusetts Constitution: Religious Establishment or Civil Religion,"*Journal of Church and State*, 20 (Autumn 1978): 533–49; Green, "Federalism and Establishment Clause," 777–80; Levy, *Establishment Clause*, 32–33, 76–78; and Feldman, "Intellectual Origins," 407–8. Even though he contends that the establishment clause was intended to prevent Congress from interfering with New England's laws, Rubenfeld concedes that the supporters of such laws "overwhelmingly denied" that they amounted to an establishment of religion. "Disestablishmentarianism," 2361–62. Cf. Lash, "Second Adoption," 1111.

121. In Massachusetts, although Roman Catholics, Jews, and Muslims possessed, at least in principle, the right to worship as they chose, the law did not exempt them from paying taxes for the support of a town's established Protestant church. Feldman, 385, fn 218.

122. Green, "Federalism and Establishment Clause," 780; Curry, *The First Freedoms*, 172–75, 189, 191; Rubenfeld, "Disestablishmentarianism," 2361–62, 2371. Citizens of Connecticut were more likely than other New Englanders were to admit that their state's system of

support for Protestant Christianity constituted an establishment of religion. Curry, *The First Freedoms,* 178–84, 210.

123. Curry makes the point this way: "The First Amendment was not intended to protect the establishments in the states because in the understanding of Americans at the time, there were no state establishments to protect."*Farewell to Christendom*, 41. See also 41–42, and accompanying endnotes. Also, see Feldman, "Intellectual Origins," at 407–8.

124. *Farewell to Christendom*, 42.

125. *Farewell to Christendom*, 129, note 28. Curry adds, "The 'federalism' argument belongs entirely to the world of logical distinctions and has no connection with the world of history."

126. Bradley, *Church-State Relationships,* 89–90, 93.

127. See above, p. 92.

128. See, e.g., Edmond Cahn, "The 'Establishment of Religion" Puzzle, *New York University Law Review*, 36 (Nov. 1961): 1280.

129. Sky, "Establishment Clause," 1415–17. Sky also makes the important point that if the scope of the protection afforded by the religion clauses was too narrow, it would imply that the federal government had the power to either control or promote religion in ways that had never been contemplated under the un-amended Constitution. "Establishment Clause," 1417.

130. Drakeman, *Church, State*, 240, and Laycock, "'Nonpreferential Aid," 880–81.

131. Ira C. Lupu and Robert W. Tuttle, "Federalism and Faith,"*Emory Law Journal*, 56 (2006): 44, fn 135 ("[A]ny effort to establish a governmentally approved 'national church' would create a potential and powerful rival to state-established churches. . . ."). The mere fact, however, that *some* members of the Senate *may* have approved of the final language of the religion clauses because they feared that a national religious establishment would threaten their state's limited religious establishment does not mean that the religion clauses are federalist in content. Clearly the final version of the religion clauses was pushed by members of the House, who had a broad normative understanding of those clauses, and the issue is why the Senate would have been willing to accept their proposal. There is no record of any member of Congress giving a federalist interpretation of the clauses.

132. Drakeman, *Church, State*, 241 (". . . [T]here is no reason to believe that anyone imagined that the final version of the clause would ever affect church-state relations in the various states.").

133. Sky, "Establishment Clause," 1416 ("The House was clearly insisting on its version of the clause.").

134. Sky, "Establishment Clause," 1423, fn 135. Cf. Bernard Schwartz, *The Great Rights of Mankind: A History of the American Bill of Rights* (New York: Oxford Univ. Press, 1977), 185.

135. For some inexplicable reason, James Hitchcock attributes the final wording of the religion clauses primarily to Fisher Ames. *The Supreme Court and Religion in American Life*, 2 vol's (Princeton, N.J.: Princeton Univ. Press, 2004), 2:29. To support his contention, he cites Winfred E. A. Bernhard, *Fisher Ames, Federalist and Statesman, 1758–1809* (Chapel Hill, N. C.: Univ. of North Carolina Press, 1965), 330–31, but there is nothing on those pages relating to the religion clauses of the First Amendment.

136. "Establishment Clause," 1423, fn 135. Also see, Drakeman, "Religion and the Republic," 431–34.

137. See above, pp. 87–89.

138. Sky, "Establishment Clause," 1415, writes that Madison was "appalled" over what the Senate had done to the religion clauses, and Bradley, *Church-State Relationships*, 94, says that he was "exasperated." The only direct evidence supporting their claims, however, is his statement in a letter to Edmund Pendleton on 9/14/1789 that "[t]he Senate have sent back the plan of amendments with some alterations which strike in my opinion at the most salutary articles." Although Madison goes on to give examples of the changes to which he objects, he does not mention the changes made by the Senate in the religion clauses. *PJM*, 12:402. On the other hand, a member of the Senate, Paine Wingate, wrote that "Madison says he had rather have none than those agreed to by the Senate," quoted in Bradley, *Church-State Relationships,* 94, including presumably the Senate's version of the religion clauses.

139. "Letter to George Washington," 11/20/1789, in *PJM*, 12:453.

140. An argument made by McConnell, "Origins and Historical Understanding," 1487; Drakeman, "Religion and Republic," 431–33; Sky, "Establishment Clause," 1423, fn 135; and Green, "Federalism and Establishment Clause," 793. As explained earlier, Madison could have been entirely satisfied with the final ("respecting") wording of the establishment clause because it comes close to expressing his position that government should have no authority over religion. If Madison's understanding of the amendments was generally shared by others, then clearly the religion clauses were normative and not federalist in nature.

141. See Sherryl E. Michaelson, "Religion and Morality Legislation: A Reexamination of Establishment Clause Analysis,"*New York University Law* Review, 59 (May 1984): 362, fn 258. A final piece of evidence against the states' right interpretation of the word "respecting" in the establishment clause is Madison's interpretation of the word. Because, however, he did not state this interpretation until several years after the drafting of the religion clauses, it is presented later in chapter seven, which discusses how the clauses were understood after they were ratified.

142. Michaelson, "Religion and Morality Legislation," 362, fn 258. In agreement is Drakeman, *Church, State*, 236–41.

143. *DH*, Vol. 4, *Legislative Histories*, 29, fn 23, & 39.

144. *DH*, Vol. 11, *Debates. . .*, 1292.

145. See Glenn, "Forgotten Purposes," 355–56.

146. *DH*, Vol. 1, *Senate Legislative Journal*, 158.

147. Mark P. Denbeaux, "The First Word of the First Amendment,"*Northwestern University Law Review*, 80 (Spring 1986): 1166 ("The House clearly was committed to making a strong and complete statement in favor of the rights of citizens. . . ."). Cf. Kyle Duncan, who in "Subsidiarity and Religious Establishments in the United States Constitution,"*Villanova Law Review*, 52 (2007): 67, 116, inexplicably says that Madison's "interest in amending the Constitution to extend guarantees . . . in the area of religion to the states . . . was not widely held and was not influential in the drafting debates."

148. Cf. Adams and Emmerich, *Nation Dedicated*, at 44, 143, fn 8, who assume that objections to Madison's proposed amendment that would have restricted the states reflect a federalist understanding of the religion clauses, i.e., "that authority over religion, to the extent it could be exercised, was a state matter."

149. John Witte, Jr., *Religion and the American Constitutional Experiment* (Boulder, Col.: Westview Press, 2005, 2nd ed.), 89.

150. See above, p. 92.

151. "Gardening at Night," 987, 997.

152. Green, "Federalism and Establishment Clause," 790–94. Of course, some of the changes were simply stylistic changes. See Curry, *The First Freedoms*, 213–15.

153. Green, "Federalism and Establishment Clause," 790–94. Again, inexplicably, Kyle Duncan writes that "the debates strongly suggest a shared anxiety about reserving state management over a sensitive area of social policy. . . . this was a debate over subsidiarity, and not one over substantive church-state matters." "Subsidiarity and Establishments," 118–19.

154. Steinberg, "Gardening at Night," 997.

Chapter Six

Were the Framers Hopelessly Divided over the Issue of Government and Religion?

Is there no evidence, then, from the record of the drafting of the religion clauses of the First Amendment that supports a federalist interpretation of those clauses? The best evidence that Steven Smith, the leading proponent of such an interpretation, can adduce is the "fact" that the debate in the First Congress over the wording of the religion clauses to be added to the Constitution was "desultory," "listless," and "superficial." He notes that "there was virtually no discussion at all of what we now call the free exercise clause." If one assumes, Smith says, that the law-makers were trying to express a normative position on the very important issue of the national government's policy toward religion, then their apparent "apathy," "complacency," and "carelessness" are truly puzzling, for in the states the discussion of this issue had been energetic. "Conversely, if the enactors believed that they were not answering the difficult questions at all but were merely deferring those questions to someone else—the states—then the complacent and lackluster character of the discussion is entirely understandable."[1]

This argument, meager as it is, simply does not "hold water"—for several reasons. First, it assumes that the *record* of the debate is an accurate and complete account of what actually transpired, but we know that this is not the case.[2] It is certainly possible, therefore, that the debate was extensive and energetic, for we simply do not have a decent record of what was said.

Second, even if the record were a good indicator of the debate's quantity and quality, it was not just the debate pertaining to the religion clauses, but the debate pertaining to *all* of the select committee's proposed amendments, that was brief and lackluster.[3] Those other amendments, moreover, were discussed even less than were the religion clauses.[4] This indicates that whatever accounted for the nature of the discussion, it was not the result of issues pertaining to the relationship between religion and government.

Third, there are other explanations for the character of the debate besides the one posited by Smith. One obvious explanation is that most members of Congress were not interested in the proposed amendments. After all, many Federalists did not believe they were necessary, and they had what they thought was more important business to take care of, such as the organizing and financing of the new government.[5] More importantly, *in contrast to amendments sought by Anti-federalists that would have changed the structure and powers of the national government*, the amendments proposed by Madison were considered "innocent," "inoffensive," "harmless," "milk and water," "water gruel," and above all "a tub to the whale"—on the belief that they were designed to placate the opponents of the Constitution.[6]

On the other hand, some Anti-federalists in Congress had lost interest in the proposed amendments, if indeed they had ever had a genuine desire to see them adopted. According to certain scholars, they believed that passage of the amendments proposed by Madison would "pull the rug out from under" the effort to add amendments that would radically reduce the powers of the central government.[7] Given the lack of interest on both sides, "it is not difficult to understand why there was so little discussion of the substance of the Bill of Rights. . . ."[8]

A second obvious explanation for the lack of debate, if it occurred, is that even if the proposed religion clauses were entirely normative in content, the great majority of Congressmen would not have objected to them or considered them to be very controversial.[9] In other words, it is possible that by the time of the First Congress there was a broad consensus among Americans on the policy the national government should have toward religion and on the meaning of the other rights included in the Bill of Rights. Thus, one scholar writes: "It seems much more likely that the relative lack of debate on the merits of the bill of rights reflected the extent to which both Federalists and Antifederalists agreed about the fundamental meaning and importance of its contents. It was not necessary to debate these guarantees because their protection from government attack formed the core of the Radical Whig ideology so broadly accepted in the colonies."[10] According to this interpretation, the primary issue at the First Congress was one of style—how best to state the consensus—not substance.[11]

I. THE CASE FOR LACK OF CONSENSUS

Of course, this last explanation for the "desultory and superficial" quality of the debate in the First Congress over the religion clauses is one that Smith and other federalist interpreters of the religion clauses reject out of hand, for their thesis is predicated on the assumption that there was no such consensus. Thus, Smith writes, "The founders *did not* answer the religion question because they *could not* have done so."[12] He believes that early Americans generally, and the framers of the religion clauses specifically, were so divided in their views on what the principle of religious freedom means or prohibits that the framers could not have agreed and did not even attempt to agree on its meaning, but passed the religion clauses, nevertheless, as an indication that they wanted the states, not the national constitution, government, or courts, to be the ones to settle the issue of what religious freedom means or prohibits.[13]

Over what were early Americans, and the framers, so divided? As previously explained,[14] Smith argues that in late eighteenth century America there were two competing views on the proper relationship between government and religion. The "traditional" view held that because religion is essential to a stable social and political order, the government should support religion, through "monetary subsidies, laws prohibiting blasphemy and Sabbath-breaking, exclusion of the religiously heterodox from public office."[15] This view, according to Smith, prevailed in New England, except for Rhode Island. The "voluntarist" view, although agreeing on the social usefulness of religion, opposed government's supporting religion because such support is not essential for but rather harmful to the growth of authentic religion. This view prevailed in states like Virginia and Pennsylvania. Smith assumes that the difference between these two positions was so fundamental and that the proponents of each so nearly equal in number that the framers of any religious liberty amendment to the Constitution could not possibly have agreed on its normative or principled meaning.[16]

According to Smith, the issues over which there were fundamental differences of opinion related to the free exercise as well as the establishment of religion. Although most Americans believed in and most state constitutions protected "freedom of conscience" or the "free exercise of religion," they disagreed over whether these principles/provisions prohibited religious tests for public office, Sabbath-observance laws, and the punishment of blasphemy.[17] Smith concludes, "These divergent views [on these issues] suggest that just as it would have been impossible for the founders to reach any consensus on the issue of 'establishment,' they likewise could not have achieved any general agreement on the issue of 'free exercise'. . . . Once again, the natural course for the First Congress was not to attempt any substantive answer to such questions but rather to leave such controversies to the state. . . ."[18]

II. AN ASSESSMENT OF THE CASE FOR LACK OF CONSENSUS

This analysis of the situation in early America, however, is very questionable and misleading. Its basic weakness is that it overstates the differences of opinion and understates the consensus that existed at that time on the meaning of religious freedom. Americans, of course, did not *entirely* agree on *all* the issues relating to government treatment of religion, just as they did not entirely agree on all issues that were raised by other provisions in the proposed Bill of Rights, but that is no reason to assume that there was not a significant degree of agreement. As Steven K. Green says, the framers could have "agreed on broad principles while leaving their disagreements over specific issues for another day." They could have agreed that establishments of religion are oppressive without agreeing on exactly what constitutes an establishment or a "law respecting an establishment of religion."[19] This means that the case made by Smith and others for a states' rights interpretation of the religion clauses is superficial and incomplete. It fails to address specific, but important questions: On any given issue how divided were early Americans? Were they divided over "kind" or "degree"? Was the extent of the division *changing*? If so, what was the direction of the change? To what extent were the laws supporting religion actually enforced?[20]

Take, for example, the issue of government aid to religion. Smith gives a simplistic explanation of the issue (persons were either for or against it) and implies that the split was about fifty/fifty. The fact is that with the possible exception of a few radical thinkers, e.g., Jefferson, most Americans, including most members of the dissenting sects who sought a religious liberty amendment to the Constitution, were not opposed to *all* government aid to religion.[21] They favored in particular laws that protected the free exercise of religion.[22] In New England even the dissenting Baptists were not advocates of complete separation of religion and government but favored laws protecting Sunday as a day for worship and prohibiting public expressions of blasphemy.[23] Even the "extremists"—Jefferson, Madison, and the citizens of Rhode Island—condoned, if not favored, some laws and government actions that aided religion.[24]

On the other hand, those more inclined to defend government support of religion were generally very careful to place restraints on the kind of support that government could give. They all condemned the kind of establishment of religion that existed in England, other European countries, and the American colonies. They thus usually insisted that government could not punish or discriminate against persons because of their religious beliefs and practices and could not favor one sect or religion over others. For this reason, most defenders of the New England system of public support for religion denied that it amounted to an establishment of religion, and those persons who did concede that it was a type of religious establishment insisted that it was barely such.[25] John Adams, for example, said that the "laws of Massachusetts were the most mild and equitable establishment of religion that was known in the world, if indeed they could be called an establishment."[26]

Smith also fails to present convincing evidence that the New England system of church-state relations was anywhere near as popular as the more liberal system that existed in all the other states. For example, to support the claim that "it enjoyed widespread support in this country," he cites two scholarly sources that present information about the situation in *colonial*, not late eighteenth century, America.[27] This will not do because a significant change in church-state relations and thinking occurred during and after the struggle for independence.[28] Smith also cites Article Three of the Massachusetts Constitution of 1780, which authorized laws providing for mandatory church attendance and compelling all persons to support financially either the church to which they belonged or the church favored by a majority of the voters in the town where they resided,[29] but he fails to note that public support of ministers was the "most vitriolic political issue in Massachusetts" during the colonial and revolutionary periods and "the subject of vigorous political debate in the newspapers."[30] He also fails to note that Article III itself was very controversial and actually failed to be approved by the required two-thirds of the voters.[31] Finally, he quotes *one* person who favored such a policy.[32] This is simply not enough evidence to support the claim that the New England system of church-state relations was widely approved in early America. In fact, what the evidence indicates is that if there was a lack of consensus on the appropriate relationship between government and religion, it existed in New England, but not necessarily in the rest of the country.

Moreover, Smith overlooks the fact that by the time of the First Congress, the trend in America was clearly away from the New England system of direct government support of religion and toward the voluntary system. By then, as Thomas Curry points out, "all the states," except for some in New England, had come "to the same conclusion as Virginia, that religion had to be supported voluntarily."[33] One particularly compelling piece of evidence that supports Curry's point is that in 1776, in its instructions to a group of delegates who went to Canada to ask it to join the colonists' war of independence, the Continental Congress promised the Canadians (mostly Catholics) "the free and undisturbed exercise of their religion," provided that "all other denominations of Christians be equally entitled to hold offices and enjoy civil privilege and the free exercise of their religion and *be totally exempt from the payment of any tythes or taxes for the support of any religion.*"[34]

On this point, David Steinberg writes: ". . . [B]y 1789 a clear trend toward the abolition of religious assessments had developed in the United States. As of 1758, nine of the original states collected taxes that supported ministries, with only four states declining to collect assessments. Between 1758 and 1789, five states that had collected religious assessments repudiated the practice. In 1789, nine states proscribed religious assessments. Such taxes were collected in only four states, located primarily in New England."[35] Even in New England, as a result of court decisions, "[d]issenters who were duly organized in congregations and who supported a full-time minister were . . . placed nearly on a par with Congregationalists. Although dissenters were required to pay taxes, their taxes, like the taxes of Congregationalists, were used only to support their own sect."[36]

After the adoption of the First Amendment, the trend continued and culminated in the elimination of Vermont's quasi-establishment of religion in 1807, Massachusetts' in 1811,[37] Connecticut's in 1818, and New Hampshire's in 1819.[38] The "spirit of the times," however, was ahead of these laws, in that "state persecution for religious conscience's sake had ceased to plague New England long before the enactment of these formal liberalizing statutes."[39] In New Hampshire, the change in its constitution reflected beliefs and practices that existed as early as 1783. For that reason, in 1789 the legislators of that state "had no qualms" about the proposed religious freedom amendments to the Constitution.[40] Similarly, in Massachusetts by the mid-1780s, prosecutions for religious offenses had also begun to decline and by the 1810s seldom occurred.[41]

Because the trend was so clearly and predominantly away from religious establishments toward a system of volunteerism, a good case can be made for the proposition that very few persons would have been interested in defending a "lost cause." As Steven Green puts it, it would have been a "waste [of] political capital."[42] Any potential defenders would have known that the attempt to maintain even the "mild establishments" in Massachusetts and Connecticut had generated a strong and growing opposition. They would also have known that any attempt to draft an amendment that had as its purpose the protection and preservation of those establishments would have been very controversial and unpopular, and had no chance of being ratified. They would have been more than satisfied with an amendment protecting religious liberty that applied only to the federal government and not to the states, which, of course, is what they got.

What about the laws that discriminated against persons for religious reasons and that still existed in some states in 1789? Were they sufficiently controversial and widespread that the framers of the First Amendment would have had them in mind when trying to write the religion clauses? One kind of discriminatory law that Smith emphasizes to make his case that framers were so divided in their views that they could not have written religion clauses with any normative content is a law imposing a religious test as a condition for holding public office. Although most states still had such laws as of 1789,[43] in some states the laws were not enforced.[44] Even if they had been, this issue would not have been on the minds of the framers of the religion clauses for the simple reason that the Constitution itself had already eliminated the use of religious tests by the federal government (and for normative reasons).[45] More importantly, the fact that the ban on religious tests was widely understood as a partial, if not complete, ban on a national establishment of religion, that the framers of the Constitution had no trouble agreeing on it, and that it was ratified in spite of some objections to it indicates clearly that there was an emerging consensus against the use of religious tests.[46]

Certainly those Americans who favored the Article VI ban on religious tests for public office-holding thought that there was an emerging consensus against such tests and that it was based on normative considerations. In fact, when what came to be the Article VI ban was discussed at the Constitutional Convention of 1787, the only delegate who spoke against it, Roger Sherman, did so not because he opposed the ban in principle, but because he thought it was "unnecessary, the prevailing liberality being a sufficient security agst. such tests."[47] Even more supportive of this point is what James Iredell said at the North Carolina Ratifying Convention in defense of the ban:

> I did not expect any objection to this particular regulation, which in my opinion, is calculated to prevent evils of the most pernicious consequences to society. . . . Under the colour of religious tests the utmost cruelties have been exercised. . . . America has set an example to mankind to think more modestly and reasonably; that a man may be of different religious sentiments from our own, without being a bad member of society. . . . I consider the clause under consideration as one of the strongest proofs that could be adduced, that it was the intention of those who formed this system, to establish a general religious liberty in America.[48]

Not surprisingly, "[t]he federal test oath clause apparently had a liberalizing effect on the states," for shortly after its ratification four states removed religious tests from their constitutions, and one significantly weakened its test.[49]

What about laws against blasphemy and breaking the Sabbath? Were they likely to have been on the minds of the framers of the religion clauses? Although the federal government was not explicitly prohibited from passing such laws, as it was in the case of religious tests, because these laws were already on the books in all the states,[50] there surely would have been no reason for the federal government to pass such laws and thus very little likelihood that the framers of the religion clauses would have thought about them as issues that the clauses would have to settle. Another reason that very few persons would have wanted Congress to pass laws against blasphemy was because even at the state level, they may not have been very popular.[51]

As for the Sabbath laws, as Thomas Curry has argued, they must be understood within the cultural and social context of the time—a context in which Protestant Christianity and American culture were often indistinguishable. This meant that "a contemporary would in many instances have been hard put to define where Protestantism ended and secular life began." As a result, "[c]ustoms like days of prayer and thanksgiving appeared not so much matters of religion as part of the common coin of civilized living." More importantly, contrary to what Smith contends, such laws were not controversial. For example, "Sabbath laws," according to Curry, "enjoyed widespread support and were so little the subject of dissent that citizens never even felt challenged to think how those laws might impose a particular religious viewpoint."[52] It is difficult to believe, therefore, that the framers of the religions clauses would have had such laws on their minds or, if they did, would have considered them as raising issues "too hot for them to handle."

A careful reading of Smith also reveals that he is inconsistent on the issue of whether there was a "free exercise consensus." In responding to Michael McConnell's contention that early American may have thought that religious liberty gives persons/groups a right to be exempt from obeying valid, secular laws that their religion tells them not to obey,[53] Smith says that "if there was a consensus at all, it was *opposed* to the 'free exercise of religion' *in anything like the contemporary sense of that term,*"[54] i.e., it did not include the idea of a right to religion-based exemptions from valid, secular laws. He then proceeds to present several pieces of evidence that indicate, contrary to McConnell's claim, that early Americans did not subscribe to such a right. He then concludes:

> Virtually all Americans of the time also agreed that freedom of conscience or of religion did not include any right to disturb the public peace, and state constitutions sometimes made this limitation explicit. The qualifier had an elastic quality. For example, punishment of blasphemy was not an infringement of religious freedom, the orthodox maintained, because blasphemy disturbed the public peace by upsetting majoritarian religious sensibilities.
>
> In short, while Americans may have concurred in endorsing the slogan 'freedom of conscience,' the agreement was largely verbal. There clearly was *not* agreement about the substantive content or meaning to be given to that slogan.[55]

It is difficult, however, to see how this conclusion follows from what Smith writes just before it. What he actually shows, and correctly,[56] is that "[v]irtually all Americans of the time"did not believe that religious freedom entails the right to religion-based exemptions from valid, secular laws. The fact that this early consensus might not hold in America today obviously does not refute the fact that it existed then. Also, the fact that early Americans may have disagreed over what kinds of actions disturbed the public peace does not mean that they disagreed fundamentally on the meaning of religious liberty.

III. THE CASE FOR THE EXISTENCE OF CONSENSUS

Contrary to what Steven Smith contends, what the historical evidence suggests is that on the issue of how government should treat religion, early Americans agreed much more than they disagreed—that there was a moderate or centrist position to which most of them subscribed. This position was that in order to protect liberty of conscience, government should not establish, prefer, or aid one church or one religion over all others and should not punish persons because of their religious beliefs and practices (unless they violated a secular law designed to protect or promote persons' lives, liberties, and property).[57] On this point, Noah Feldman writes, "By the late eighteenth century, some version of Locke's basic view of the nature of the liberty of conscience had been formally embraced by nearly every politically active American writing on the subject of religion and the state. . . . There also was agreement that establishment of religion, in the sense at least of a single establishment of a preferential system, violated liberty of conscience because it led to compelled actions against conscience."[58] In a similar vein, Steven K. Green says that the framers of the First Amendment "shared common, broad ideals" that were incorporated into the religion clauses: "freedom of conscience; no compelled support of religion; no delegation of government authority to religious institutions; and equal treatment of all sects."[59]

This consensus was based on and reflected what had happened in the states during and after the Revolutionary War, prior to which most of them had had an established church and sometimes engaged in religious discrimination, if not persecution. During and after the War, however, most of them abolished most elements of those establishments. Even the New England states changed from a system that unofficially established Congregationalism to one that not only allowed each locality to select which church to support with taxpayer funds, but allowed other churches in a town to receive public financing if their members were willing to go through certain administrative hurdles.[60] By 1780, at least in Massachusetts, there was a very strong minority, if not majority, that opposed public financing of the clergy on the grounds that it violated "the right of conscience" guaranteed in Article III of the state's constitution.[61] By 1790, popular sentiment in New England may have shifted to such an extent that it favored the separationist position associated with Jefferson and Madison.[62]

One well known scholar, Carl Esbeck, describes the extent of the shift in church-state relations, what he calls the "American settlement," in these terms:

> All the early European models . . . assumed that the ultimate unity of the nationstate, hence its survival, required a union of its subjects or citizens around one religion. . . . During the War of Independence, the ensuing Confederation, and then early republic . . ., relations between church and state underwent a marked shift toward a new and decidedly non-European approach. *In decline was the conventional argument that material government support for religion and religious institutions was necessary to ensure religion's salutary effect on public morality and civic virtue*. . . . [T]he church and its ecclesiastical affairs were deregulated. Henceforth, the civil state had no legal authority, and its courts thus had no subject matter jurisdiction over those topics that were inherently religious and thus within the sole province of the church. Faith, if it was to be genuine, was acquired as a voluntary act, without Caesar's aid . . . The momentousness of this paradigm shift cannot be over emphasized.[63]

Moreover, Esbeck contends that the shift occurred first and foremost at the state level of politics. It was reflected in, but not caused by the First Amendment.[64] In short, by 1789 the traditional position on relations between government and religion had been abandoned by most Americans.

Not surprisingly, therefore, most Americans insisted, *even before the adoption of the Bill of Rights*, that they possessed religious freedom. For example, in a sermon delivered in London, in 1788, Elhanan Winchester, a distinguished Baptist minister in Philadelphia, declared that in America "religious liberty is in the highest perfection." He explained, "All stand there on equal ground. There are no religious establishments, no preference of one denomination of Christians above another. The constitution knows no difference between one good man, and another. A man may be chosen there to the highest civil offices, without being obliged to give any account of his faith, subscribe [to] any religious test, or go to the communion table of any church."[65] Consequently, for most Americans the proposed religious liberty amendment was not controversial because it affirmed principles already adhered to by most, if not all, of the states.[66] On this point, Gerard V. Bradley writes, ". . . [T]he religious liberty endangered [by the federal government], and for which protection was sought, was that liberty the people had long enjoyed, which was currently enshrined in all state constitutions and accorded with contemporary popular views on the subject."[67] Thomas Curry agrees: ". . . [T]hey [persons wanting an amendment protecting religious freedom] wanted to be sure that the new government would not assume powers they had never given to—or had already taken from—the states."[68]

This fact then leads Curry to make a rather sharp, but cogent criticism of the federalist or states' rights interpretation of the religion clauses. He writes:

> [I]t depreciates the extraordinary American achievement of religious liberty by focusing on what the states did not do rather than on what they did. Adherents of this point of view focus not on the revolution that America brought about in Church and State but on the remnants of Christendom that perdured. . . . The great majority of states . . . had either never set up any establishment of religion or had dismantled the establishments they had inherited from pre-Revolutionary times. In the estimation of their citizens, they had abandoned Christendom and inaugurated complete religious liberty. While they did not implement that principle in every aspect of Church and State, their accomplishments on its behalf were enormous, fundamental, and enduring. . . . The pity of the [federalist] argument is that it obscures one of the great advances in Western civilization. . . . A majority of Americans came to believe that for government to withdraw from religious affairs would be good for both Church and State. To reduce this movement, one that broke with the practice of a millennium-and-a-half of Christendom, to a scheme to protect the dying remnants of the petty tyrannical New England Church-State systems represents a lamentable loss of historical wisdom.[69]

In fairness to Steven Smith, it should be noted that in responding to one review of his book, he admits that by 1789 Americans were committed to one basic, but narrow principle of religious liberty—"that people should not be punished merely for holding unpopular or heretical religious beliefs, or for acting on those beliefs in private." However, he contends that this principle had never been "seriously contested" and was "taken for granted" since the beginning of the country. For this reason, he argues, that it could not have been the purpose of the religion clauses to state this principle. Since no one had ever doubted it, there would have been "no reason to engraft it onto the Constitution."[70] In effect, Smith goes from one extreme to the other. He argues either that there was no consensus on church-state policy or if there was, it was extremely well established. Either situation, he argues, would have prevented the framers of the religion clauses from encasing a normative principle/policy in those clauses. He refuses to acknowledge the possibility of a third or middle situation, i.e., there was a consensus, but one that had only recently been obtained and that was still not solidified and overwhelming and thus needed to be reinforced by the addition of the religion clauses to the Constitution.[71]

In addition to the consensus that the religion clauses were needed to protect religious liberty, another kind of normative consensus may also have existed and been reflected in those clauses, namely, a consensus that because of the religious pluralism in the new nation as a whole, it would have been destabilizing, if not dangerous, for the federal government to legislate directly on religious matters. The leaders of America at this time were well aware of the likelihood that government favoritism toward particular religions would lead to political disunity and conflict.[72] Even those who may have in principle favored a significant degree of government intervention into religious matters most likely realized that in a religiously heterogeneous society such intervention would cause more problems than it solved.[73] Even Congressmen from New England who wanted to preserve the church-state system that existed there could have voted for a reasonably stringent provision against government involvement with religion at the federal level because they knew that such involvement would have been divisive.[74]

It might be argued in reply that such a reason for voting for the religion clauses is not a normative reason, but that is not so. Obviously it is not a reason that would prevent *all* governments from legislating with respect to religion, but as explained in chapter two,[75] reasons can be normative without being ones that apply universally. For sure, when one argues that a particular government should not adopt an otherwise desirable policy because under the circumstances it will not work or will cause more harm than good, s/he is not making a federalist or states' right argument. Rather s/he is making a normative argument based on the particular situation or circumstances. In the case of the religion clauses, if they were adopted for this kind of reason, it would mean that they stand for the principle that in a religiously pluralistic society the government should not legislate directly on religious matters for fear that such legislation will engender religious division and strife.

Although John Courtney Murray, some years ago, argued that the religion clauses were entirely "articles of peace" and not "articles of faith,"[76] there is little, if any, evidence to support that claim. Rather, what the evidence presented thus far shows is that one normative reason (to protect religious liberty) was primary and the other (to maintain social harmony) was secondary.[77] In any case, regardless of their relative importance, both normative reasons for the religion clauses support the same understanding of those clauses: government should not legislate or take a position on essentially religious issues.

More importantly, the preceding analysis makes it clear that enough drafters and ratifiers of the religion clauses could have agreed on their normative content or meaning to have gotten the clauses written and adopted. If the debate in the First Congress was languid, therefore, it does not follow that the reason for such was, as Smith claims, that the framers/legislators could not agree on a normative principle to guide the federal government's policy toward religion. It is more likely that the debate was as it was for the opposite reason—because there was a consensus among the framers/legislators on what the government's policy should be.

This is not to say, of course, that all significant issues pertaining to the relationship between religion and government had been resolved,[78] but, on the other hand, surely it is unrealistic to think, as Smith seems to, that the framers of the Bill of Rights would not have adopted any provision unless they thought it addressed and resolved all issues related to it. To the contrary, it makes more sense to assume, as most scholars do, that they agreed on and stated basic general principles whose applications and implications they knew would have to be worked out by later generations of citizens or judges.[79]

Finally, there are two other pieces of evidence from the First Congress that undercut Smith's assumption that the framers of the religion clauses could not have agreed on any substantive principles to encase in those clauses. The first is the fact that the House of Representatives voted, by at least a two to one margin, in favor of a provision prohibiting the states from infringing the equal rights of conscience[80]—a provision whose content was necessarily normative and not federalist in nature. If Smith's thesis (that the framers were so conflicted over the meaning of religious liberty that they could not have agreed on any normative principles) is correct, then how could members of the House have agreed on a provision intended to protect the rights of conscience from state laws? In his book, *Foreordained Failure*, Smith ignores this action on the part of the House.

In a later article responding to a critical review of his book, however, Smith not only acknowledges the House's action but admits that it had normative meaning. He does not, however, seem to see that such an admission is extremely damaging to his argument. All that he says is that "in the Senate . . . the proposal was deleted from the Bill of Rights, never to be revived. We cannot know exactly why this more-than-Federalist measure was defeated . . . but the decision was at least entirely consistent with a jurisdictional [federalist] interpretation of the First Amendment."[81] Well, yes, what the Senate did is consistent with a federalist interpretation of the First Amendment, but this is beside the point. What *is not* consistent with such an interpretation is the fact that the *House*, the most representative of the two bodies, was able to agree on the normative meaning of "equal rights of conscience," which, according to Smith's thesis, would have been "impossible" for it to do.[82]

The other action taken at the First Congress that does not square with Smith's argument that its members could not possibly have adopted a normative right or principle is the fact that it reenacted the Northwest Ordinance, including the following provision: "No person demeaning himself in a peaceable and orderly manner shall ever be molested on account of his mode of worship or religious sentiments."[83] Smith concedes that this provision expresses a normative right or principle, and then rightly asks, "And if Congress was capable of adopting a substantive [normative] right of religious freedom for a territory, might it not have done the same for the nation as a whole—subject, of course, to a federalist side constraint?"[84] He then, however, gives two reasons for answering the question, No. First, because the "source" of the provision appears to be the Massachusetts Constitution (itself a vague and speculative assertion), New Englanders, Smith says, could accept it on the grounds that it had a conservative meaning.[85] That, however, will not work to support the argument that the framers of the religion clauses could not possibly have agreed on a normative religious liberty provision. To the contrary, it indicates that they could have agreed on one if it had been worded like the one in the Northwest Ordinance.

The second reason that Smith gives for answering his rhetorical question with a, No, is that the framers of the Northwest Ordinance had a practical, not principled, reason for including a religious liberty provision in it, namely, they were anxious to encourage, not discourage, migration into the area. He explains that by 1789 the Northwest Territory was characterized by such religious pluralism that no denomination could have achieved dominance in it. Even the New England Congregationalists came to accept the religious heterogeneity that existed and changed their attitudes toward church-state relations. Remarkably, Smith then writes, "In this respect, the Northwest Territory reflects the American experience generally, in which a commitment to broader religious freedom has evolved of necessity out of the fact of religious pluralism."[86]

This is remarkable, of course, because Smith, perhaps unintentionally, is himself explaining how and why the religion clauses could have had normative meaning—even in 1789. Just as the Northwest Territory was religiously pluralistic as of 1789, so was the nation as a whole. If it made sense to guarantee religious freedom in that Territory in order to attract immigrants to it and preserve harmony among them, so would it not have made sense to guarantee religious freedom in the nation as a whole for the same reasons? Smith might reply that such a reason is only a practical one, but, as explained earlier,[87] a practical reason of this sort is still a normative, not a federalist, reason. In short, because it clearly indicates that the First Congress could agree on a normative religious liberty principle, the passage of the Northwest Ordinance undercuts Smith's federalist interpretation of the religion clauses.

IV. CONCLUSION

In summary, although the debate over the religion clauses may have been desultory, listless, and superficial, it does not follow that the reason for that fact was that the members of Congress were so hopelessly divided over the meaning of religious liberty that they did not try to come to an agreement on that issue. It does not follow because there are other more plausible explanations for the quality of the debate, the most likely being that they *did* agree on the basic core principles of religious liberty and therefore did not need to take time to clarify them.[88]

Most likely, they agreed that the federal government should not establish a religion or pass any laws of the sort associated with traditional establishments of religion, i.e., laws that discriminated for or against religions, religious doctrines/practices, or persons because of their religion. Even if they might not have agreed that such laws were universally wrong, they would have certainly agreed that they were impractical and dangerous for a nation as religiously pluralistic as America was at that time. Finally, the assumption that members of the First Congress would not have been able to agree on the normative meaning of religious liberty is undercut by the fact that the House passed a provision prohibiting the states from violating the equal rights of conscience and the entire Congress reenacted the Northwest Ordinance that contained a religious liberty provision, and both pieces of legislation were normative in nature.

In short, there is an abundance of evidence from the First Congress supporting a normative interpretation of the religion clauses and very little, if any, supporting a federalist interpretation. The case for the latter is almost entirely circumstantial and speculative in nature. Unless there is substantial evidence supporting it from the period immediately after the framing of the religion clauses, it should be rejected.

NOTES

1. *Foreordained Failure: The Quest for a Constitutional Principle of Religious Freedom* (New York: Oxford Univ. Press, 1995), 26–27, 39.

2. The notes of the discussion in the House were taken by a man with a drinking problem and were condemned at the time by Madison and other Congressmen, as well as more recently by impartial investigators, as being incomplete and full of errors. Marion Tinling, "Thomas Lloyd's Reports of the First Federal Congress."*William and Mary Quarterly*, 3rdser., 18 (Oct. 1961): 519–45, and James H. Hutson, "The Creation of the Constitution: The Integrity of the Documentary Record," in *Interpreting the Constitution: The Debate over Original Intent*, ed. Jack N. Rakove (Boston, Mass.: Northeastern Univ. Press, 1990), 168–69.

3. Leonard Levy, *Emergence of a Free Press* (New York: Oxford Univ. Press, 1985), 266–68. Even Smith notes this. *Foreordained Failure*, 29.

4. Levy, *Emergence of Free Press*, 266–67.

5. Again, Smith himself notes this as a possible reason. *Foreordained Failure*, 29.

6. Kenneth R. Bowling, "'A Tub to the Whale': The Founding Fathers and Adoption of the Federal Bill of Rights."*Journal of the Early Republic*, 8 (Autumn 1988): 236–46.

7. Saul Cornell, *The Other Founders: Anti-federalism and the Dissenting Tradition in America, 1788–1828* (Chapel Hill, N.C.: Univ. of North Carolina Press, 1999), 158–63; Bowling, "'Tub to the Whale'," 241; and Levy, *Emergence of a Free Press*, 261–62.

8. Mark P. Denbeaux, "The First Word of the First Amendment,"*Northwestern University Law Review*, 80 (Spring 1986): 1164.

9. Madison wrote Edmund Randolph (6/15/1789) that he had tried to limit his amendments "to points which are important in the eyes of many and can be objectionable in those of none."*The Papers of James Madison* [hereafter cited as *PJM*], ed. Robert A. Rutland et al (Chicago: Univ. of Chicago Press, 1977), 12:219. See Gerard V. Bradley, *Church-State Relationships in America* (Westport, Conn.: Greenwood Press, 1987), 88 ("To . . . [his] congressional colleagues, Madison's amendments were more than inoffensive; they were restatements of such obvious, taken-for-granted essentials that only the belabored discussion of them was offensive.")

10. David M. Rabban, "The Ahistorical Historian: Leonard Levy on Freedom of Expression in Early American History,"*Stanford Law Review*, 37 (Feb. 1985): 831. For the argument that such a consensus existed on the proper relationship between religion and government, see below, pp. 127–32.

11. Thomas J. Curry, *The First Freedoms: Church and State in America to the Passage of the First Amendment* (New York: Oxford Univ. Press, 1986), 193–94, 213–15.

12. Smith, *Foreordained Failure*, 26 (emphasis in original).

13. Agreeing with Smith are Kurt T. Lash, "Power and the Subject of Religion,"*Ohio State Law Journal*, 59 (1998): 1117; Daniel O. Conkle, "Toward a General Theory of the Establishment Clause,"*Northwestern University Law Review*, 82 (1988): 1133; William K. Lietzau, "Rediscovering the Establishment Clause: Federalism and the Rollback of Incorporation,"*DePaul Law Review*, 39 (1989–1990): 1200; and Chris Bartolomucci, "Rethinking the Incorporation of the Establishment Clause,"*Harvard Law Review*, 105 (1992): 1705.

14. See above, p. 41.

15. "The Religion Clauses in Constitutional Scholarship,"*Notre Dame Law Review*, 74 (March 1999): 1046.

16. *Foreordained Failure*, 19–21, 26 (". . . Americans in the late eighteenth century held *contradictory* positions at a *basic* level regarding the religion question.")(emphasis added).

17. *Foreordained Failure*, 37–41.

18. *Foreordained Failure*, 38–39.

19. "Federalism and the Establishment Clause: A Reassessment,"*Creighton Law Review*, 38 (2005): 794, 797. Kent Greenawalt agrees. "Common Sense about Original and Subsequent Understandings of the Religion Clauses,"*University of Pennsylvania Journal of Constitutional Law*, 8 (2006): 492 ("We are familiar with legislators enacting a principle into law even when they disagree about its scope.")

20. For evidence on the decline in prosecutions for religious offenses in Massachusetts after the mid-1780s, see William E. Nelson, *Americanization of the Common Law: The Impact of Legal Change on Massachusetts Society, 1760–1830* (Cambridge, Mass.: Harvard Univ. Press, 1975), 110–11.

21. For examples, see Chester J. Antieau et al, *Freedom from Federal Establishment: Formation and Early History of the First Amendment Religion Clauses* (Milwaukee, Wisc.: Bruce Pub. , 1964), 62–91; Curry, *First Freedoms*, 217–18; and Bradley, *Church-State Relationships*, 89–91.

22. Philip Hamburger, *Separation of Church and State* (Cambridge, Mass.: Harvard Univ. Press, 2002), 101–7.

23. Curry, *First Freedoms*, 168–77.

24. For Jefferson, see Daniel Dreisbach, *Thomas Jefferson and the Wall of Separation between Church and State* (New York: Oxford Univ. Press, 2002), 57–59; for Madison, see Bradley, *Church-State Relationships*, 86–87; for Rhode Island laws supporting religion, see Antieau et al., *Freedom from Federal Establishment*, 69, 74–75, 135, 165, 172, 176.

25. See Curry, *First Freedoms*, 133, 172–74; Bradley, *Church-State Relationships*, 89; and Nelson, *Americanization of the Common Law*, 104. Also, see Noah Feldman, "The Intellectual Origins of the Establishment Clause,"*New York University Law Review*, 77 (May 2002): 386.

26. Quoted in Curry, *First Freedoms*, 131. Isaac Backus, the leader of New England Baptists, remembered Adams as saying that "there is indeed an ecclesiastical establishment in our province, but a very slender one, hardly to be called an establishment." Quoted in Curry, *First Freedoms*, 131.

27. *Foreordained Failure*, at 19 & 134, fn 8.

28. On the extent of the change, see Jon Butler, "Why Revolutionary America Wasn't a 'Christian Nation'," in *Religion and the New Republic*, ed. James H. Hutson (Lanham, Md.: Rowman & Littlefield, 2000), pp. 192–96; Mark Tushnet, "The Origins of the Establishment Clause,"*Georgetown Law Journal*, 75 (April 1987): 1511–12; and Antieau et al., *Freedom from Federal Establishment*, 1–61.

29. Smith, *Foreordained Failure*, 19–20. For the practical meaning of Article III, see Philip A. Hamburger, "Equality and Diversity: The Eighteenth-Century Debate about Equal Protection and Equal Civil Rights," in *The Supreme Court Review, 1992*, ed. Dennis J. Hutchinson et

al. (Chicago: Univ. of Chicago Press, 1993), 331–35, and Nelson, *Americanization of the Common Law*, 104–9.

30. Ronald M. Peters, *The Massachusetts Constitution of 1780* (Amherst, Mass.: Univ. of Massachusetts Press, 1978), 31, 33.

31. Even so, Article III was treated as ratified. See John Witte, Jr., "'A Most Mild and Equitable Establishment of Religion': John Adams and the Massachusetts Experiment," *Journal of Church and State*, 41 (Spring 1999): 219–32, 242–50, and Curry, *First Freedoms*, 167. Because many of the towns that voted against Article III did so because they wanted it amended, Curry writes, ". . . [T]he vast majority of the people of the state did accept its principle of a publicly supported ministry." *First Freedoms*, 167. This claim seems questionable because one of the towns that voted for the article, Boston, the largest town in the state, supported its churches through a system of voluntary contributions and was careful to specify that Article III would not affect that system. *First Freedoms*, 167.

32. Smith, *Foreordained Failure*, 20.

33. "Church and State in Seventeenth and Eighteenth Century America," *Journal of Law and Religion*, 7 (1989): 268. Also, see Tushnet, "Origins of the Establishment Clause," 1511–12.

34. Quoted in John Witte, Jr., *Religion and the American Constitutional Experiment*, 2d ed. (Boulder, Col.: Westview Press, 2005), 74 (emphasis added). This provision may have been included because Americans had complained so vehemently about the Quebec Act of Parliament (1773), which created an establishment of Catholicism in Canada similar to the one in Massachusetts and Connecticut, and also because at the First Continental Congress (1774) Baptists and Quakers had complained so bitterly about their treatment in New England. See Curry, 131, 133.

35. "Gardening at Night: Religion and Choice," *Notre Dame Law Review*, 74 (March 1998): 999–1000. Steven Smith's response to Steinberg's point is puzzling, to say the least: "[W]hy these facts counts as an argument about what nearly all Americans ostensibly agreed to (or could have agreed to) in 1789 remains a bit mysterious." "Religion Clauses," 1048.

36. Nelson, *Americanization of the Common Law*, 108.

37. Nelson, *Americanization of the Common Law*, 108 ("Although the religious establishment officially lingered on until 1833, the Religious Freedom Act of 1811 in effect destroyed it. The act . . . constituted a complete victory for the dissenters. . . .").

38. Arlin M. Adams and Charles J. Emmerich, *A Nation Dedicated to Religious Liberty: The Constitutional Heritage of the Religion Clauses* (Philadelphia, Penn.: Univ. of Pennsylvania Press, 1990), 20.

39. Robert T. Miller, "Religious Conscience in Colonial New England," *Journal of Church and State*, 50 (Autumn 2008): 675.

40. Frank C. Myers, "New Hampshire Accepts the Bill of Rights," in *The Bill of Rights and the State: The Colonial and Revolutionary Origins of American Liberties*, ed. Patrick T. Conley and John P. Kaminski (Madison, Wisc.: Madison House, 1992), 174–76.

41. Nelson, *Americanization of the Common Law*, 110. Cf. John T. Noonan, Jr., "'Quota of Imps'," in *The Virginia Statute for Religious Freedom: Its Evolution and Consequences in American History*, ed. Merrill D. Peterson & Robert C. Vaughan (New York: Cambridge Univ. Press, 1988), 171–99.

42. "Religion Clause Federalism: State Flexibility over Religious Matters and the 'One-Way Ratchet'," *Emory Law Journal*, 56 (2006): 114.

43. See Ellis M. West, "Religious Tests for Office-holding (Article 6, Cl. 3)," in *Encyclopedia of American Civil Liberties*, ed. Paul Finkelman, 3 vols (New York: Routledge, 2006), 3:1314–15.

44. In North Carolina, for example, almost from its inception in 1776, a constitutional provision limiting office holders to Protestants was not enforced. Antieau et al., *Freedom from Federal Establishment*, 109.

45. U. S. Constitution, art. VI, cl. 3 (". . . [N]o religious Test shall ever be required as a Qualification to any Office or public Trust under the United States.").

46. See Antieau et al, *Freedom from Federal Establishment*, chap. 4.

47. Debate on 8/30/1787, in *Founders' Constitution*, ed. P. B. Kurland & Ralph Lerner (Chicago: Univ. of Chicago Press, 1987), 4:638.

48. Speech in North Carolina Ratifying Convention, 7/30/1788, in *Founders' Constitution*, 5:89.

49. Adams & Emmerich, *Nation Dedicated*, 16.

50. Christopher T. Anglim, *Encyclopedia of Religion and the Law in America*, 2d ed. (Amenia, N. Y.: Grey House Pub., 2009), 49.

51. Anglim says that in the entire eighteenth century there were only ten prosecutions for blasphemy in the whole country and that in the nineteenth century, such prosecutions became even rarer. *Encyclopedia of Religion and Law*, 49. Of course, the small number of such prosecutions could also have been the result of there being very few blasphemers.

52. *The First Freedoms*, 218.

53. See "The Origins and Historical Understanding of the Free Exercise of Religion,"*Harvard Law Review*, 103 (1990): 1409–1517.

54. *Foreordained Failure*, 39 (second emphasis added).

55. *Foreordained Failure*, 40.

56. See Ellis M. West, "The Case Against a Right to Religion-Based Exemptions,"*Notre Dame Journal of Law, Ethics & Public Policy*, 4 (1990): 623–33, and "The Right to Religion-Based Exemptions in Early America: The Case of Conscientious Objectors to Conscription,"*Journal of Law and Religion*, 10 (1993–94): 367–401; Gerard V. Bradley, "Beguiled: Free Exercise Exemptions and the Siren Song of Liberalism,"*Hofstra Law Review*, 20 (1991): 245–319; and Philip Hamburger, "A Constitutional Right of Religious Exemption: An Historical Perspective,"*George Washington Law Review*, 60 (1992): 915–48.

57. Curry, "Church and State," 269, and *First Freedoms*, 222.

58. "Intellectual Origins," 378, 405, 411.

59. "Federalism and the Establishment Clause," 767, 775. Other scholars who have concluded that a consensus along these lines existed and that the religion clauses were intended to express it include Mark D. McGarvie, *One Nation Under Law: America's Early National Struggles to Separate Church and State* (Dekalb, Ill.: Northern Illinois Univ. Press, 2004), 47–60; Barbara A. McGraw, *Re-Discovering America's Sacred Ground: Public Religion and the Pursuit of the Good in a Pluralistic Society* (Albany, N. Y.: SUNY Press, 2003), Part I, pp. 23–106; James H. Smylie, "Protestant Clergy, the First Amendment and Beginnings of a Constitutional Debate, 1781–91," in *The Religion of the Republic*, ed. Elwyn A. Smith (Philadelphia, Penn.: Fortress Press, 1971), pp. 151–53; Bradley, *Church-State Relationships*, 69–81, 88–89; and Antieau et al, *Freedom from Federal Establishment.*

60. Curry, *First Freedoms*, 105–21, 162–92; McGarvie, *One Nation Under Law*, 21–46; Antieau, et al., *Freedom from Federal Establishment*, 1–61; and Butler, *Why Revolutionary America*, 192–96.

61. Curry, *First Freedoms*, 192 and Peters, *Massachusetts Constitution*, 79–86.

62. In 1801, when President Jefferson wrote his now famous letter to the Baptists of Danbury, Connecticut, in which he said that the religion clauses created a "wall of separation" between church and state, his Postmaster General and political adviser, Gideon Granger, who was from Connecticut, said that the letter "*is but a declaration of Truths which are in fact felt by a great Majority of New England, & Publicly acknowledged by near half of the People of Connecticut. . . .*" Quoted in Dreisbach, *Jefferson and the Wall*, 147 (emphasis added). Of course, this was said ten years after the ratification of the Bill of Rights. For an analysis of Jefferson's letter, see below, pp. 157–64.

63. "Dissent and Disestablishment: The Church-State Settlement in the Early Republic,"*Brigham Young Univ. Law Review*, (2004): 1385, 1395–97 (emphasis added).

64. Esbeck, "Dissent and Disestablishment," 1393, 1398.

65. "A Century Sermon" (Nov. 16, 1788), in *Political Sermons of the American Founding Era, 1730–1805*, ed. Ellis Sandoz (Indianapolis, Ind.: Liberty Press, 1991), 988–89.

66. The citizens of New York, for example, considered the religion clauses to be "merely a confirmation of beliefs long held and habitually proclaimed." Milton M. Klein, "Liberty as Nature's Gift: The Colonial Origins of the Bill of Rights in New York," in *The Bill of Rights and the States: The Colonial and Revolutionary Origins of American Liberties*, ed. Patrick T. Conley & John P. Kaminski (Madison, Wisc.: Madison House, 1992), 227.

67. *Church-State Relationships*, 78. Also, see Antieau et al., *Freedom from Federal Establishment*, 158, 207.

68. *Farewell to Christendom: The Future of Church and State in America* (New York: Oxford Univ. Press, 2001), 42.

69. Curry, *Farewell to Christendom*, 43–44.

70. "The Religion Clauses," 1049–51.

71. In addition to those already cited, other scholars who believe that a basic consensus existed on the proper relationship between religion and government and was reflected in the religion clauses include Walter Berns, *The First Amendment and the Future of American Democracy* (New York: Basic Books, 1976), 30; Morton Borden, *Jews, Turks and Infidels* (Chapel Hill, N. C.: Univ. of North Carolina Press, 1984), 5; and Steinberg, "Gardening at Night," 1015–23.

72. Donald Drakeman writes, ". . . [T]he reason . . . to restrict the federal government might not have been philosophical aversion to the concept of a state-supported church but rather fear that a national government would favor the *wrong* church."*Church-State Constitutional Issues: Making Sense of the Establishment Clause* (New York: Greenwood Press, 1991), 70. For an especially sophisticated analysis of the different opinions about how to overcome the discord associated with religious diversity, see Hamburger, "Equality and Diversity," 295, 355–67.

73. See Frank Lambert, *The Founding Fathers and the Place of Religion in America* (Princeton, N. J.: Princeton Univ. Press, 2003), 237–38; Derek H. Davis, *Religion and the Continental Congress 1774–1789: Contributions to Original Intent* (New York: Oxford Univ. Press, 2000), 134–35; and Butler, *Why Revolutionary America*, 192–97.

74. This possibility is suggested, e.g., by one of the reasons Oliver Ellsworth, of Connecticut, gave for not having a religious test for holding office in the federal government: "A test in favor of any one denomination of Christians would be to the last degree absurd in the United States. If it were in favor of either congregationalists, presbyterians, episcopalians, baptists, or quakers, it would incapacitate more than three-fourths of the American citizens for any public office." "Landholder, No. 7,"*Connecticut Courant*, 12/17/1787, in *The Founders' Constitution*, 4:640.

75. See above, p. 18.

76. *We Hold These Truths: Catholic Reflections on the American Proposition* (Garden City, N. Y.: Doubleday & Co., 1964), 65. Murray adds, "Like the rest of the Constitution these provisions are the work of lawyers, not of theologians or even of political theorists. They are not true dogma but only good law. . . . If history makes one thing clear it is that these clauses were the twin children of social necessity, the necessity of creating a social environment, protected by law, in which men of differing religious faiths might live together in peace."*We Hold These Truths*, 65–66. For compelling criticisms of the pragmatic explanation of the religion clauses, see Leo Pfeffer, "The Case for Separation," in *Religion in America: Original Essays on Religion in a Free Society*, ed. John Cogley (New York: Meridian Books, 1958), 59–77; McGarvie, *One Nation Under Law*, 54–58; and Smylie, "Protestant Clergy," 151–53.

77. For a perfect example of an influential early American (St. George Tucker) who gave both kinds of normative reasons for the religion clauses, but gave priority to the protection of religious liberty, see below, p. 144.

78. Feldman, "Intellectual Origins," 353–54, 379. One issue that had probably not been resolved was whether the equality that is required by the principle of religious liberty is not only among different churches or religions, but between religion and irreligion or anti-religion. "Intellectual Origins," 376–78. At the time, however, that was not a pressing issue.

79. See, e.g., Thomas C. Berg, "Religion Clause Anti-Theories,"*Notre Dame Law Review*, 72 (1997): 711, fn 80; Green, "Federalism and the Establishment Clause," 794, 797; and Feldman, "Intellectual Origins," 404–5.

80. See above, p. 92.

81. "The Religion Clauses," 1041–42.

82. *Foreordained Failure*, 38–39.

83. Quoted in Smith, *Foreordained Failure*, 41.

84. *Foreordained Failure*, 41.

85. *Foreordained Failure*, 41.

86. *Foreordained Failure*, 42.
87. See above, pp. 18, 130.
88. Rabban, "Ahistorical Historian," 831.

Chapter Seven

The Early American Understanding of the Religion Clauses

I. COMMENTS ON THE CLAUSES DURING THEIR RATIFICATION

Although ratification of the Bill of Rights took twenty-six months, the record of its discussion in the state legislatures and elsewhere during this time is very limited.[1] The most extensive discussion of the religion clauses occurred in the Virginia Senate, where a number of its members objected to them on the grounds that they did not protect the rights of conscience. In particular, they thought that the federal government, although precluded from establishing a national religion, could still and might indirectly favor and support one particular denomination over others. These objections, however, were probably feigned and simply part of an Anti-federalist effort to derail the new government and secure a new constitutional convention, and the Senate eventually gave in to the Virginia House of Delegates and ratified all the proposed amendments, including the religion clauses.[2] Nevertheless, whether the objections of the Virginia senators were genuine or not, it is noteworthy that they were normative, not federalist, in nature. The senators' concerns were that the rights of conscience and religious equality, not the rights of states, might still be violated by the national government.

In Rhode Island, in 1790, a convention met to consider ratifying both the Constitution and the Bill of Rights, and there is a sketchy account of a debate relating to the religion clauses. According to it, one Anti-federalist delegate said "that every State ought to [be] precluded from making any law respecting Religion or abridging the Rights of Consci[ence]." Another agreed: "If it is right that Congress should not make any Laws respecting it, no State ought to have the Right."[3] These remarks support a normative interpretation of the religion clauses, for the two delegates were contending that the same principles that control the federal government's policies on religion should also control the states' policies. If they had understood the religion clauses as federalist in nature, i.e., as having no normative meaning, it would have made no sense for them to have suggested that the states should be limited in the same way that the central government is limited by the religion clauses. This is true, even though the two delegates also appear to have understood the First Amendment as prohibiting laws respecting religion, and not just establishments of religion.

The response to the suggestion that the states should be limited in the same way that the federal government was limited is also noteworthy. It came from Benjamin Bourne, the chief spokesman for the Federalists and a soon-to-be U. S. Senator from Rhode Island. Rather than saying that the religion clauses could not be applied to the states because they had no normative meaning, he insisted that the states did not need to be limited because given "the highest practice and the present General Sentiment of the World on this Subject," there was no likelihood that the states would establish a religion or infringe the rights of conscience.[4] This remark is important because it is yet additional evidence that among early Americans there was enough consensus on the normative meaning of religious liberty to have enabled the framers and ratifiers to agree on a constitutional amendment that would protect it.

In other state legislatures, unfortunately, we have no record of the discussions, if any, that occurred of the proposed religion clauses. Some scholars, however, make a good case for the fact that the normative and liberal changes that occurred around 1790 in the religion clauses in some of the state constitutions were influenced by the drafting and ratification of the religion clauses of the First Amendment. In other words, the state constitutional provisions relating to religion were brought into line with those applying to the federal government.[5] Obviously, if this occurred, it would have meant that the states that made changes in their own constitutions must have understood the religion clauses of the First Amendment to be normative, and not federalist, in nature.

Finally, it is worth noting that the two states that had the most to gain from the proposed religion clauses *if they had been federalist in nature*, Massachusetts and Connecticut, failed to ratify the Bill of Rights.[6] Although their failure to ratify is surely not enough to warrant the conclusion that the religion clauses were not federalist in nature, it is, however, another piece of evidence that tends to support such a conclusion. Moreover, even if their failure to ratify had nothing to do with the religion clauses and most persons in those two states favored the religion clauses because they understood them as guarantees of states' rights, how much weight should be given to their understanding? As Douglas Laycock says, ". . . the understanding of religious liberty in states that ratified the religion clauses is more important than the understanding of religious liberty in states that did not."[7]

II. INTERPRETATIONS OF THE CLAUSES BY THE CLERGY

Were the persons and groups who demanded that the Constitution be amended so as to protect religious liberty satisfied with the religion clauses of the First Amendment? What about the Baptists? One of their "principal leaders" told James Madison that "the amendments had entirely satisfied the disaffected of his Sect. . . ."[8] John Leland (the person who had extracted from Madison a promise to add religion clauses to the Constitution) certainly appeared to be. In a sermon delivered in 1791, he described the clauses as forbidding the federal government from making "any laws establishing any kind of religion." This was praiseworthy in his opinion, not because it upheld states' rights, but because it avoided the numerous "evils" of religious establishments, which he presented in great detail and the most egregious of which was the harm they caused to the flourishing of true religion. "And did not religion receive a deadly wound by being fostered in the arms of civil power and regulated by law?" Leland also contrasted the "religious liberty" that existed as a result of the Constitution's ban on religious establishments with the lack thereof that existed in the state of Connecticut where he had just moved.[9] Later, in 1802, he wrote that the religion clauses were based on "republican principles" and expressed "the principles of religious liberty" to which he subscribed.[10] Clearly Leland had a normative understanding of the religion clauses.

So did other Baptists. For example, in an 1803 petition to the Connecticut legislature, three associations of Baptists compared the laws pertaining to religion in that state to the guarantees of religious freedom in the U. S. and other state constitutions. The former, they said, compel persons to worship in a prescribed mode, time, and place, and to pay taxes and in other ways support religious teachers, and subordinate one or more denominations of Christians to another. Such laws are "unjust and oppressive, . . . productive of evil, both to the sect exalted, and to those who are depressed," and violate the *rights of conscience*. In contrast, under the Constitution, "the Christian religion is not an object of civil government, not any ways under its controul," but "left on the same footing where the Lord Jesus himself placed it . . . *distinct from the laws of state*." Why? Because "the interference of Magistrates to befriend it, has never done it any good, but much harm. . . ."[11]

There are other examples. In 1795, and again in 1804, Isaac Backus, the leader of Baptists in Massachusetts, wrote that Massachusetts and Connecticut "act contrary to it [First Amendment] to this day." He, of course, would not have said this if the religion clauses had been intended to protect state laws pertaining to religion. Later, in 18ll, another spokesman of Massachusetts Baptists said that the religion clauses provided "that no law enacting a religious establishment shall ever be made" and that their language should be included in a revised Massachusetts constitution.[12]

What about the leaders of other churches? They, too, believed that the Constitution called for religious equality. In 1793, a prominent and influential Congregationalist minister said that because of the Constitution (but no mention of the religion clauses per se):

> no man is abridged of the liberty of enquiry—no religious test is required—no bait is thrown out by government to encourage hypocrisy, or exclude the honest and deserving. . . . The importance of religion to the peace and order of society, is unspeakably great. . . . But as to all decent modes and outward expression of it, the rights of conscience remain untouched. Here all religious opinions are equally harmless, and render men who hold different opinions equally good subjects, be-cause there are no laws to oppose them, no force to compel them.

This was a blessing, he said, because it prevented "bigotry, superstition and nonsense." He expressed hope that the arrangement in the United States would "become in an eminent degree the model of that glorious temple of universal liberty which is about to be established over the civilized world."[13] Similarly, in 1793, the leaders of the Dutch Reformed Church contrasted the American government, "where full freedom of conscience and worship is equally protected and insured to all men, and where truth is left to vindicate her own sovereign authority and influence," with one "where men in power promote their favorite denominations by temporal amendment and partial discriminations. . . ."[14] Clearly, nothing in the preceding quotations suggests that the religion clauses in the Constitution were understood as guarantees of states' rights.

III. INTERPRETATIONS OF THE CLAUSES BY OTHER PUBLIC FIGURES

In 1798, Congress passed the Alien and Sedition Acts, the second of which essentially made it illegal to criticize the federal government, its laws, and officials.[15] During the course of the debate over the act, many of its opponents argued that it violated the First Amendment. A few of them argued that the Sedition Act violated the free press clause in the same way and to the same extent that a law establishing a religion would violate the religion clauses, and one of them, Edward Livingston, Republican Congressman from

New York, gave an interpretation of those clauses. He said they protected a "dear and valuable privilege—the liberty of conscience," an individual right not a states' right. He then asked, "What is liberty of conscience?" He answered his question by explaining what it prevented the federal government from doing; it could not "establish a national religion . . . on the ground of an uniformity of worship being more consistent with public happiness than a diversity of worship."[16] Here, again, an early American expressed a normative understanding of the religion clauses that equated liberty of conscience with the absence of laws establishing a religion.

A similar argument was made a year later by George Hay, a critic of the Alien and Sedition Acts, who, in order to show that the First Amendment guaranteed a normative and "absolute" freedom of the press, contended that it protected freedom of the press to the same extent and for the same reason that it protected freedom of religion. He wrote:

> In the United States . . ., religious freedom is completely understood to mean the power uncontrolled by law of professing and publishing any opinions on religious topics, which any individual may choose to profess or publish, and of supporting those opinions by any statements he may think proper to make. . . . [H]e may announce if he pleases his atheism to the world. He may endeavor to corrupt mankind, not only by opinions that are erroneous, but by facts which are false. Still however he will be safe, because he lives in a country where religious freedom is established.[17]

Moreover, Hay said that both religion and press were protected, not because of states' rights, but because of "the *sublime precept* inculcated by the act establishing religious freedom [in Virginia], that 'where discussion is free, error ceases to be dangerous'. . . ."[18]

Two years later, Tunis Wortman, a New York City lawyer and one of the most influential spokesmen for the Jeffersonian Republicans, declared that "our present constitution" prevents the government, "as a body corporate and politic, as an organized artificial systematized corps" (as distinguished from the individuals in the government), from having "any religion" and from interfering with the "exercise of conscience . . . unless social law, and order, and morals become invaded. . . ." He added that "if a contrary doctrine should ever prevail, every fibre of my heart would bleed for the misery of my country."[19] These are not the words of someone concerned about states' rights.

IV. COMMENTARIES ON THE CONSTITUTION

From 1800 to 1835, at least twelve commentaries were written on the Constitution.[20] Of these, five discussed the meaning of the religion clauses of the First Amendment. The first of these commentaries was published in 1803 by St. George Tucker, a Virginian, professor of law at the College of William and Mary, and a leading spokesperson for the Democratic Republicans. During the first part of the nineteenth century, his commentary, *View of the Constitution of the United States*,[21] was an important reference for American lawyers, judges, and statesmen.[22] It contained several pages explaining the rights guaranteed by the First Amendment.

That Tucker understood the religion clauses as having normative meaning is clear from the beginning of his comments on them, where he says they express an "axiom, concerning the human mind" that is contained in the Virginia Bill of Rights, namely, that "religion, or the duty we owe to our Creator, and the manner of discharging it, can be dictated only by reason and conviction, not by force or violence." He adds that the violation of that axiom, i.e., the blending together of civil and religious institutions, has produced "numberless martyrdoms and massacres which have drenched the whole earth with blood. . . ." The purpose of the religion clauses, therefore, is "[t]o separate them by mounds which can never be overleaped," which "is the only means by which our duty to God, the peace of mankind, and the genuine fruits of charity and fraternal love, can be preserved or properly discharged."[23] It is obvious that Tucker thinks the religion clauses express a principle applicable to all governments and laws.

In a later section, Tucker defines "[l]iberty of conscience in matters of religion" as "the absolute and unrestrained exercise of our religious opinions, and duties, in that mode which our own reason and conviction dictate, without the control or intervention of any human power or authority whatsoever." He says that "[t]his inestimable and imprescriptible right is guaranteed to the citizens of the United States" by both the U. S. and Virginia constitutions (including the religion clauses of the First Amendment). Tucker contrasts this liberty or right with "toleration," which he says exists, e.g., in England, "where there is a civil establishment of a particular mode of religion; that is, where a predominant sect enjoys exclusive advantages, and makes the encouragement of it's [sic] own mode of faith and worship a part of the constitution of the state; but at the same time thinks fit to suffer the exercise of other modes of faith and worship." True liberty of conscience, which exists in America, means that "[n]ot only all Christians, but all men of all religions, ought to be considered by a state as equally entitled to it's [sic] protection, as far as they demean themselves honestly and peaceably." Why is liberty of conscience to be preferred to toleration? Because religious establishments "engender strife . . . turn religion into a trade . . . shore up error . . . produce hypocrisy and prevarication . . . lay an undue bias on the human mind in its inquiries, and obstruct the progress of truth . . . genuine religion is incapable of receiving any aid from human laws. It is contaminated as soon as worldly motives and sanctions mix their influence with it."[24] Clearly Tucker has a normative or libertarian interpretation of the religion clauses.

Equally important, nowhere does Tucker mention the protection of states' rights or state establishments of religion as the reason for the religion clauses. Indeed, he writes that "the new American states are at present strangers to such establishments. In this respect . . . they have shewn in framing their constitutions, a degree of wisdom and liberality which is above all praise."[25] His failure to mention states' rights as a reason for the religion clauses is made even more significant by the fact that in other parts of his commentary on the Constitution he defends states' rights, warns against consolidation, and advocates strict construction of the limited powers granted to the national government.[26] If anyone might be expected to have a federalist interpretation of the religion clauses, it would be Tucker. He, however, not only fails to explain the religion clauses in those terms, but ironically praises them for their ability to unite the country. He contends that because of the normative axiom it expresses, "[t]his prohibition . . . may be regarded as the most powerful cement of the federal government, or rather, the violation of it will prove the most powerful engine of separation. Those who prize the union of the states will never think of touching this article with unhallowed hands."[27]

A second early commentary on the Constitution that discussed the religion clauses was written by William Rawle, a resident of Philadelphia, and published in 1825. Entitled *A View of the Constitution of the United States of America*, it "achieved broad and lasting appeal throughout the country." Although a Federalist and ardent Unionist, Rawle could be said to be an advocate of states' rights, in that he took the position that the Constitution allows states to secede from the Union.[28] He did not, however, interpret the religion clauses as a guarantee of states' rights. To the contrary, he writes that the clauses reflect the principle of "the equality of all our citizens"—a basic principle reflected in the Constitution as a whole. The clauses were intended to prevent the arrangement, common in Europe, where "some one religious system enjoys a preference, enforced with more or less severity, according to circumstances . . . [and] a human government interposes between the Creator and his creature, intercepts the devotion of the latter, or condescends to permit it only under political regulations." Calling such an arrangement a "gross injustice" and "manifest impiety," Rawle contrasts it with the situation in America where "[n]o predominant religion overpowers another . . . ; no lordly hierarchy excites odium or terror; legal persecution is unknown, and freedom of discussion, while it tends to promote the knowledge, contributes to increase the fervour of piety." The religion clauses, he says, express "[j]ust and liberal principles" that "throw a luster round the Constitution . . . dignify the nation, promote its internal peace and harmony."[29] One could hardly find a more normative interpretation of the religion clauses than this.

A third commentary on the Constitution was included in James Kent's *Commentaries on American Law*, which was first published in 1826 and soon became the "standard treatise for general American law."[30] Although Kent has little to say about the meaning of the religion clauses of the First Amendment, what he does say is significant. After quoting the clauses, he writes, "[A]nd the same *principle* appears in all the state constitutions," and goes on to illustrate his point by quoting several provisions in colonial charters that guaranteed "the full and perfect enjoyment of religious liberty."[31] Obviously, Kent believed that the religious clauses had normative, not federalist, meaning, for he says they expressed a principle that was also expressed in state constitutions, and a principle limiting what the states can do cannot possibly be a federalist or states' right principle.

In 1833, James Bayard, a Delaware lawyer who became a U. S. Senator in 1851, published *A Brief Exposition of the Constitution of the United States*. His explanation of the religion clauses is as follows:

> The imposition of any "religious test" had already been prohibited by the Constitution, and nothing in it could be construed to invest the government with a right to interfere in matters of religion. But such was the solicitude of the people on this point; such was their sense of the evils of a national religious establishment, and their determination to preserve the utmost freedom of conscience; that, it was deemed proper, thus to deprive Congress of all pretense for ever attempting to legislate upon this subject.[32]

Although he says that the religion clauses were intended to deprive Congress of all power to legislate upon the subject of religion, Bayard does not say that this was because the "people" thought the states should have exclusive jurisdiction over religion. To the contrary, he says the establishment clause resulted from "their sense of the evils of a national religious establishment" and the free exercise clause from "their determination to preserve the utmost freedom of conscience"—both normative, principled reasons.

The last-to-be-discussed, but most influential of the early nineteenth commentaries on the Constitution was written by Justice Joseph Story and first published in 1833. Although his interpretation of the religion clauses is rather lengthy, it is ambiguous. At the beginning of his comments, Story writes that when the First Amendment was adopted, "the general, if not universal, sentiment in America was, that Christianity ought to receive encouragement from the state, so far as it is not incompatible with the private rights of conscience and the freedom of religious worship."[33] This language suggests that the religion clauses do not forbid the national government from aiding Christianity in general.[34] Consistent with this interpretation, Story goes on to say, "The real object of the amendment was . . . to prevent any national ecclesiastical establishment, which should give to an hierarchy the exclusive patronage of the national government." To prevent such an establishment, he says that "all power to act upon the subject" was excluded from the national government. What subject? A few lines later, he refers to "the subject of ecclesiastical ascendancy" and says, "The only security was in extirpating the power ["to create a religious establishment"]." [35] At the end of his comments, however, Story writes: "Thus, the whole power *over the subject of religion* is left exclusively to the state governments, to be acted upon according to their own sense of justice, and the state constitutions. . . ."[36] In short, it is simply not clear from what Story wrote whether the power denied the federal government by the religion clauses was just the power to create a religious establishment or was the more inclusive power to legislate in any way on the subject of religion. If it were the former, then the clauses do not prevent the federal government from legislating in favor of Christianity in general or against state laws that threaten religious freedom, but if it were the latter, they do prevent such legislation.[37]

Regardless of his understanding of the kind of federal law prohibited by the religion clauses, it is abundantly clear that Story views the clauses as having normative content. Even if he believes that "the whole power over the subject of religion is left exclusively to the state governments," he never says that the reason for that is to protect states' rights or state establishments of religion. To the contrary, he explicitly states that the religion clauses "sought to cut off the means of religious persecution, (the vice and pest of former ages), and the power of subverting the rights of conscience in matters of religion, which had been trampled upon almost from the days of the Apostles to the present age." Even more to the point, he writes,

> It was under a solemn consciousness of the dangers from ecclesiastical ambition, the bigotry of spiritual pride, and the intolerance of sects . . . that it was deemed advisable to exclude from the national government all power to act upon the subject. . . . It was impossible, that there should not arise perpetual strife and perpetual jealousy on the subject of ecclesiastical ascendance, if the national government were left free to create a religious establishment. The only security was in extirpating the power. But this alone would have been an imperfect security, if it had not been followed up by a declaration of the right of the free exercise of religion.[38]

Clearly, Story believed that *both* the establishment clause and the free exercise clause have normative meaning and were intended to prevent the same evil—religious strife and persecution. Moreover, given the strong feelings he expressed against this evil, it is equally clear that he thought the states should be limited by their constitutions in the same way that the federal government is limited by the religion clauses.[39] Although his understanding of religious freedom may not have been as radical as that of Jefferson and Madison, Story emphatically believed in it and believed that no government should deny it.

V. THE WIDESPREAD BELIEF THAT THE BILL OF RIGHTS APPLIED TO THE STATES

Given the widespread normative understanding of the religion clauses and Bill of Rights generally that existed at the time of their adoption, it was only natural that in the years after its adoption, the Bill of Rights was often said to apply to the states. Although the Supreme Court said otherwise,[40] a "considerable number" of lawyers, scholars, and, most importantly, state court judges "implied in passing or stated explicitly that various provisions in the Bill did limit states."[41] In his recently published work on the Bill of Rights, Akhil Amar explains why they took such a position. Lawyers and judges in the early nineteenth centuries were trained in the common law and accepted its premise that the people possessed certain fundamental, natural rights declared in authoritative legal sources, such as the Magna Charta, and that judges' decisions should be informed and guided by these basic rights. Given this way of thinking, it was natural for them to construe the Bill of Rights, although technically not binding on the states, as a declaration by the American "people" of their basic, natural rights that state as well as federal judges should uphold. Amar correctly writes:

> To a nineteenth-century believer in natural rights, the Bill was not simply an enactment of We the People as the Sovereign Legislature bringing new legal rights into existence, but a declaratory judgment by We the People as the Sovereign High Court that certain natural or fundamental rights already existed. Under this view, the First Amendment was not merely an interpretation of the positive law code of the original Constitution, declaring that Congress lacked Article I, Section 8 enumerated power to regulate religion or suppress speech; the Amendment was also a declaration that certain fundamental "rights" and "freedoms" . . . preexisted the Constitution.[42]

These rights bound, both morally and legally, all governments. Moreover, Amar cites a large number of state court decisions in which judges, some of whom were very distinguished, used various provisions in the Bill of Rights to strike down state laws.[43]

Unfortunately, Amar's account of how the Bill of Rights was understood after its adoption does not stop here. He makes two additional comments that are not supported with evidence. First, he writes: "This way of thinking would have been deeply foreign to many of the men who had clamored for a Bill of Rights in the 1780's. The word 'right' had no talismanic natural law significance; after all, many sought a Bill to confer—or declare—*states'* rights, once again revealing the original intertwining of rights and structure."[44] Such a claim ignores or distorts the arguments that were actually made (and summarized earlier) by those persons who sought a bill of rights, including especially a guarantee of religious freedom. Clearly they believed that what they demanded were natural rights that no government should violate.[45] Their understanding of the Bill of the Rights, therefore, is not only consistent with but most likely the source of the later understanding that Amar describes.

Secondly, and more specifically, Amar asserts that the establishment clause has no normative meaning, but was intended solely to prevent the federal government from interfering with the religious establishments that existed in some states.[46] The assertion, however, is not supported by any direct evidence.[47] It is also inconsistent with the considerable evidence, discussed earlier, that advocates of amendments to the Constitution wanted a ban on anything like an establishment of religion and wanted it in order to protect religious liberty, not states' rights.

These two mistakes aside, Amar's overall point is correct. In the early years of the nineteenth century, Americans did believe that the religion clauses, including the establishment clause, express basic, natural rights that no government, national or state, should violate. A perfect illustration of this belief is contained in one of the most eloquent addresses on religious freedom ever delivered in America. In January, 1819, the Maryland legislature debated a bill that if adopted (which it was) would have repealed a law that prohibited Jews from holding office in that state. One legislator, H. M. Brackenridge, in a lengthy speech, argued for the law's repeal on the grounds that it discriminated against persons on the basis of their religion and thus violated the principle of religious liberty. More importantly, he contended that in making such an argument, he was doing "nothing more than repeat what has already been so often and so much better expressed, by the enlightened statesmen of our country. There is hardly a distinguished American who has not in some mode or other, given to these ideas a decided approbation. They are deeply engraven on the tablets of those political doctrines which are considered as eternal and immutable."[48] Specifically, Brackenridge said:

> . . . [T]he right which this bill professes to give, is already *secured* by our national compact. . . . If we cannot find it in the express letter of the instrument, can we hesitate for a moment, in believing, that it has at least virtually abrogated every part of state laws or constitutions, whose tendency is to infringe the RIGHTS OF CONSCIENCE? . . . Let us now turn to the first amendment of the constitution of the United States; we find that congress is expressly forbidden, *to pass any law respecting an establishment of religion*. Does not this speak volumes?[49]

In short, Brackenridge believed that the religion clauses, including the establishment clause, have normative or principled meaning, protect the rights of conscience, and should be adhered to by state governments. He also believed that his understanding of the clauses was the original understanding.

VI. JEFFERSON AND MADISON'S INTERPRETATION OF THE CLAUSES

So far, all the explicit evidence presented supports the thesis that after the ratification of the Bill of Rights, Americans understood the religion clauses as guarantees of individual rights. Surely, the reader might be thinking, there must be some explicit evidence that supports the claim that early Americans understood the clauses as guarantees of states' rights. Ironically, some of the scholars who make the claim cite certain writings of Thomas Jefferson and James Madison to support it. This is ironic, of course, because the two early Americans most identified with a normative or principled position on the relationship between religion and government are Jefferson and Madison. To see why this is so, one need only to read the former's "Bill for Establishing Religious Freedom" and the latter's "Memorial and Remonstrance," both of which give practical, philosophical, and religious arguments against *any* government's attempting to influence what persons believe to be their religious duty.[50] In short, to most minds, Jefferson and Madison would be the last persons one would go to for evidence to support a states' rights interpretation of the religion clauses, yet it is precisely to them that some scholars go for such evidence.[51]

A. Jefferson and Madison's Criticism of the Alien and Sedition Act of 1798

After Congress passed the Alien and Sedition Acts in 1798, the Kentucky and Virginia legislatures responded to the Acts by passing resolutions, drafted by Jefferson and Madison respectively, condemning the laws as unconstitutional and asking other states to do likewise. In addition, a year later and in reply to the responses of other states to the Virginia Resolution, Madison authored a lengthy committee report that explained and elaborated on the points made in that resolution.[52] The Kentucky and Virginia Resolutions gave *two* reasons why the Sedition Act was unconstitutional. The first reason was that the national government had never been delegated any power to regulate speech or press. This meant that to the extent that any government had such a power, it was the state governments who possessed it. Thus, the Sedition Act violated the Tenth Amendment because in passing it, the federal government exercised a power reserved to the states. Moreover, in making this first argument, the resolutions linked "press" and "religion" together, thereby implying that the states, but not the federal government, could legislate on matters of religion, at least to the extent to which their own constitutions allowed them to do so.

A perfect example of this point is contained in Jefferson's draft of the Kentucky Resolutions of Nov. 10, 1798:

> ". . . [T]he powers not delegated to the U.S. by the constitution, nor prohibited by it to the states, are reserved to the states respectively or to the people"; [Tenth Amendment] and . . . no power over the freedom of religion, freedom of speech, or freedom of the press being delegated to the U. S. by the constitution, nor prohibited by it to the states, all lawful powers respecting the same did of right remain, & were reserved, to the states or the people.[53]

Jefferson added that by not delegating such powers to the federal government, the states "manifested their determination to retain to themselves the right of judging how far the licentiousness of speech and of the press may be abridged without lessening their useful freedom." They also "guarded against all abridgment by the U. S. of the freedom of religious opinions and exercises, & retained to themselves the right of protecting the same, as this state, by a law . . . had already protected them from all human restraint or interference. . . ."[54]

Madison's Report of 1800 contained similar language. He said that the federal government had "usurped the authorities, rights and liberties appertaining to the states, as parties to the constitution." How so? Because "no powers were given beyond those enumerated in the Constitution, and such as were fairly incident to them; . . . the power over the rights in questions [including rights of conscience], and particularly over the press, was neither among the enumerated powers, nor incident to any of them; and consequently . . . an exercise of any such power, would be a manifest usurpation." Most importantly, Madison added that the First Amendment was adopted to make it absolutely clear that no power over the press or other rights had been granted to Congress.[55]

On the basis of these and other similar passages, some scholars conclude that Jefferson, Madison, and other critics of the Sedition Act must have had a federalist or states' rights understanding of the First Amendment, including the religion clauses. Leonard Levy, for example, writes,

> It now appears that the [First Amendment] prohibition on Congress was motivated far less by a desire to give immunity to political expression than by a solicitude for states' rights and the federal principle. *The primary purpose of the First Amendment was to reserve to the states an exclusive legislative authority in the field of speech and press [and religion?]. This . . . is explicit in the Republican arguments during the controversy over the Sedition Act.*[56]

Similarly, Kurt Lash argues,

> To our ears, the Bill of Rights in general, and the First Amendment in particular, sound in terms of libertarianism—the protection of individual rights against unwarranted intrusion by the government. However, as the Virginia and Kentucky Resolutions make clear, the First Amendment was originally understood to protect the rights of popular majorities [in the states] against a possible unrepresentative and self-interested Congress.[57]

One final example, from Jay Bybee:

> The legacy of the Sedition Act is a modest, but perceptible, shift from viewing the First Amendment as confirming the total absence of congressional power over religion, speech, and press, to assuming that . . . [it] conferred a personal privilege whose substantive [normative] content could be defined. . . . a shift from . . . affirming an exclusive power in the states to stating a personal privilege.[58]

The problems with such a conclusion are twofold. First, the conclusion does not logically follow from its premises (that no power over religion, speech, and press was given to the federal government, that the First Amendment was intended to make that clear, and that the states retained their authority to legislate with respect to such subjects). Given these premises, it does follow, of course, that federal laws dealing with religion, speech, and press violate states' rights, but it does not follow that the sole or even partial purpose of the First Amendment was to protect states' rights. In other words, a federal law respecting an establishment of religion (or freedom of the press) could violate both an individual right and a states' right—but in different ways. It could violate the former because the power to pass such a law had been explicitly withheld by the First Amendment in order to protect a natural right, and it could violate a states' right because the power to pass such a law had not been delegated to the national government and, thus, according to the Tenth Amendment, was reserved to the states. In short, the fact that Jefferson and Madison thought the Sedition Act violated states' rights does not, by itself, show that they thought the First Amendment was intended to protect states' rights.

Secondly, the conclusion is based on only one of the arguments made by Jefferson and Madison against the Sedition Act, i.e., the argument that no power over religion, speech, and press had ever been delegated to Congress. It ignores the second argument they made, which was that the Act violated a basic, individual right, which was guaranteed and protected by the First Amendment. It overlooks the fact that the Virginia Resolution condemned the Act because it exercised a power not only not delegated to Congress, but one "*expressly and positively forbidden by one of the amendments thereto; a power which more than any other ought to produce universal alarm, because it is levelled against that right of freely examining public characters and measures, and of free communication among the people thereon, which has ever been justly deemed, the only effectual guardian of every other right.*" It overlooks the fact that the Resolution noted that the Virginia ratifying convention, *because of "its extreme anxiety to guard these rights from every possible attack of sophistry or ambition*," had "expressly declared, 'that among other essential rights, the liberty of conscience and of the press cannot be cancelled, abridged, restrained or modified by any authority of the United States'. . . ."[59]

The conclusion that Jefferson and Madison thought the First Amendment guarantees states' rights and not individual rights also ignores the fact that Madison's Report devotes several pages to arguing that the Sedition Act violates the "idea" or "principle" of freedom of the press as it was understood in America, as opposed to Great Britain. That idea was that ". . . the right of electing the members of the government . . . depends on freedom of the press," which also enables the people to freely examine, discuss, and, when called for, condemn public policies and officials. [60] It overlooks the praise that Madison gives to the more radical American idea of liberty of press on the grounds "that to the press alone, chequered as it is with abuses, the world is indebted for all the triumphs which have been gained by reason and humanity, over error and oppression; . . . [and] the United States owe much of the lights which conducted them to the rank of a free and independent nation; and which have improved their political system, into a shape so auspicious to their happiness."[61]

Yes, Madison says that the First Amendment "was meant as a positive denial to Congress, of any power whatever on the subject [of the press]," but *why* was it so meant? His answer is that the various state ratifying conventions had proposed amendments to the Constitution for the purpose of rendering it "more explicit, and more safe to the rights, not meant to be delegated by it" and that it was "[i]n pursuance of the wishes thus expressed" that the first Congress "proposed certain amendments. . . ." The result was that ". . . the liberty of conscience and the freedom of the press, were *equally* and *completely* exempted from all authority whatever of the United States."[62]

Finally, the states' rights interpretation of Madison overlooks the fact that he said that "[a]ny construction or argument . . . which would turn the amendment into a grant or acknowledgment of power with respect to the press, might be equally applied to the freedom of religion." Thus, he contends that the Sedition Act, which limits freedom of the press, establishes "a precedent that may be fatal to the liberty of conscience and it will be the duty of all, in proportion as they value the security of the latter, to take the alarm at every encroachment on the former."[63] In short, in criticizing the Act, Madison expresses as much concern for individual rights as he expresses for states' rights.[64]

Admittedly, Jefferson's Kentucky Resolutions are not as explicit or emphatic as the Virginia Resolution is in condemning the Sedition Act on the grounds that it violates individual rights. It does, however, quote the First Amendment and say that it was intended to guard "the freedom of religion, of speech, and of the press" by withholding "libels, falsehoods, and defamation, equally with heresy and false religion . . . from the cognizance of federal tribunals." Later, in enumerating the consequences of upholding the legitimacy of the Sedition Act, the Resolutions emphasize that "a very numerous and valuable description of the inhabitants of these States" will be "reduced, as outlaws, to the absolute dominion of one man"—persons "who for other causes, good or bad, may be obnoxious to the views or marked by the suspicions of the President, or be thought dangerous to his or their elections or other interests public or personal. . . ."[65] This passage clearly reflects a concern for individuals and their rights.[66]

What Madison said in his Report of 1800 is also important because it undercuts the states' rights or federalist interpretation of the establishment clause that is based on the word "respecting" in the clause. Madison essentially said that the word "respecting" applies not just to the establishment clause but to all the other provisions in the First Amendment, i.e., the free exercise and free speech/press clauses. To understand his interpretation of the word "respecting," one must first understand the defense of the Sedition Act that was made by various Federalists. They contended that the speech and press clauses did not deprive Congress of *all* power to legislate on the subjects of speech and press, but only the power to *abridge* the *freedom of speech and press*. To establish this point, they argued that because the word "respecting" appears only in the establishment clause, the restraint imposed by that clause is broader than that imposed by the other clauses of the First Amendment.[67] Specifically, John Marshall, defending the Sedition Act in the Virginia General Assembly, made the following argument:

> Congress is prohibited from making any law RESPECTING a religious establishment, but not from making any law RESPECTING the press. When the power of Congress relative to the press is to be limited, the word RESPECTING is dropt, and Congress is only restrained from the passing any law ABRIDGING its liberty. This difference of expression to religion and the press, manifests a difference of intention with respect to the power of the national legislature over those subjects, both in the person who drew, and in those who adopted this amendment.[68]

Madison, however, would have none of Marshall's argument. He rejected the idea that "the words and phrases in the amendment" were "chosen with a studied discrimination, which yields an argument for a power over the press, under the limitation that its freedom be not abridged. . . ." He argued that if Congress may regulate freedom of the press "because it is said only, 'they shall not abridge it,' and is not said, 'they shall make no law respecting it,'" then it logically follows that "Congress may *regulate* and even *abridge* the free exercise of religion, provided they do not *prohibit* it, because it is said only 'they shall not prohibit it,' and is *not* said 'they shall make no law *respecting* or no law *abridging* it."[69] To Madison, this was an absurd conclusion. In short, he thought the words "prohibiting" and "abridging" meant "respecting." Congress was forbidden to pass laws respecting the free exercise of religion and respecting the freedoms of speech and press as well as laws respecting an establishment of religion.[70] To drive his point home, he said that "the liberty of conscience and the freedom of the press, were *equally* and *completely* exempted from all authority whatever of the United States." He also said, "Any construction or argument . . . which would turn the amendment into a grant or acknowledgment of power with respect to the press, might be equally applied to the freedom of religion,"[71] and there was no doubt in his mind that the First Amendment was intended to deprive Congress of *all* power over religious freedom.[72] This position, of course, was consistent with what he had said all along (and was to say later) about the power of the federal government to legislate on religious matters.[73]

The main point, however, is that Madison did not see the establishment clause, with its word "respecting," as playing any special role in depriving Congress of all power over religious freedom. Even if the word had not been used, as it was not used in the free speech and press clauses, and perhaps even if there had not been an establishment clause, the First Amendment, according to Madison, would still have meant that the federal government can not legislate with respect to religion, at least when such legislation threatens religious freedom.[74] It would have meant that, moreover, because the purpose of the First Amendment was to protect individual rights, not states' rights.

This, however, is not meant to deny that Madison, Jefferson, and other Republicans argued that the Sedition Act was unconstitutional on the grounds that it violated states' rights. Clearly they did so argue, *but the reason they thought the Act violated states' rights (and was unconstitutional) was not because it violated the First Amendment, but because it was an exercise of power never granted to Congress.* As such, the Act violated the Tenth Amendment and the general principle that Congress could exercise only those powers granted to it by the Constitution. *They also argued, however, that it violated the First Amendment, and they did so because they believed it violated the freedom of the press—an individual right.*

Of course, Madison's interpretation of the First Amendment, as stated in his 1800 Report—that it deprived Congress of all power respecting the freedoms of religion/speech/press—is not inconsistent with a federalist interpretation of the religion clauses, and indeed it might even support such an interpretation, *but* only if Madison had also said that the reason for the Amendment was to protect a states' right, i.e., the right of states to legislate as they pleased with respect to religion and press. As we have seen, however, this was not his explanation for the Amendment; rather, he clearly stated that it was added to protect the individual rights of freedom of religion, speech, and press.

This, moreover, was also the view of other Republicans who spoke against the Sedition Act. Although they, like Madison and Jefferson, objected to the Act on states' rights grounds, they also objected to it on the additional ground that it violated individual rights guaranteed by the First Amendment. During the debates in the House of Representatives over the Sedition Act, John Nicholas argued that a constitutional guarantee of freedom of the press was needed because a free government depended on the existence of a free press: "To restrict the press, would be to destroy the elective principle, by taking away the information necessary to election, and there would be no difference between it and a total denial of the right of election, but in the degree of usurpation."[75] Albert Gallatin condemned the Act on the grounds that such laws "had uniformly been one of the most powerful engines used by tyrants to prevent the diffusion of knowledge, to throw a veil on their folly or their crimes, to satisfy those mean passions which always denote little minds, and to perpetuate their own tyranny."[76] Congressman John Dawson condemned the Act solely on the grounds that "it will have a tendency to curtail one of the first and dearest privileges which we enjoy; that of freely expressing our sentiments on all public men and measures."[77] These are clearly normative arguments.

One final point on the debate over the Sedition Act—even if what Jefferson and Madison wrote could be construed as being a states' rights interpretation of the First Amendment, including the religion clauses, obviously the Federalists, who controlled Congress and passed the Act, did not accept their interpretation. They did not believe that the First Amendment deprived Congress of all power over religion or press, but rather believed that it "was an independent disability, and one that protected individuals, not states."[78] For them, the issue was the scope of the freedoms of speech, press, and religion or how much protection the provisions of the First Amendment gave to those freedoms. In addition, even if the Kentucky and Virginia Resolutions were meant to express a federalist interpretation of the First Amendment, the fact that no other state legislature expressed agreement with those Resolutions indicates[79] that a majority of the people at that time did not subscribe to such an interpretation.

Of course, if Jefferson, Madison, and the Republicans did not subscribe to such an interpretation, as the preceding pages have hopefully shown, then it would mean that at the end of the eighteenth century just about all Americans had a normative understanding of the First Amendment and that the Federalists and Republicans disagreed only over the extent of the protection afforded by the Amendment.

B. Jefferson's Letter to the Baptists of Danbury, Connecticut, and Other Writings

Perhaps the most well-known and influential post-ratification interpretation of the religion clauses is that contained in Thomas Jefferson's letter of January 1, 1802, to the Danbury Baptist Association of Connecticut.[80] Moreover, what Jefferson said in the letter has traditionally, if not universally, been taken as a normative or principled interpretation of the religion clauses. The Supreme Court, in particular, has assumed that Jefferson was presenting a normative interpretation of the clauses[81]—and for good reasons. On its face, the letter clearly appears to equate the religion clauses with the policy that Jefferson believes *all* governments should have with respect to religion.

To see this, one must first understand what the Danbury Baptists had said in an earlier letter to Jefferson, to which he was responding. After expressing satisfaction in his having been elected President, the Baptists affirm their understanding of religious liberty: "That Religion is at all times and places a Matter between God and Individuals—That no man ought to suffer in Name, person or effects on account of his religious Opinions—That the legitimate Power of civil Government extends no further than to punish the man who *works ill to his neighbour*." Clearly the Baptists are espousing a policy that they think should be universally practiced. They go on to complain that such a policy is not being practiced in their state of Connecticut; in contrast, they praise Jefferson because he "will not, dares not assume the prerogative of Jehovah and Make Laws to govern the Kingdom of Christ." Finally, the Baptists say that although they realize that "the national government cannot destroy the Laws of each State," they strongly hope "that the sentiments of our beloved President, which have had such genial Effect already, like the radiant beams of the Sun, will shine & prevail through all these States and all the world till Hierarchy and tyranny be destroyed from the Earth."[82] In short, the Danbury Baptists assume that Jefferson's policies with respect to religion are dictated by his normative beliefs about the proper role of government toward religion, beliefs that they hope will spread over the whole world because they are destructive of hierarchy and tyranny.

In his response, Jefferson explicitly states his personal belief, which is essentially the same as the belief expressed by the Baptists—"that religion is a matter which lies solely between Man and his God, that he owes account to none other for his faith or his worship, that the legitimate powers of government reach actions only, and not opinions. . . ." The word "government" here appears to refer to any government, not just the federal government. *Given or because of this belief,* Jefferson then says, "I contemplate with sovereign reverence that act of the whole American people which declared that *their* legislature should 'make no law respecting an establishment of religion, or prohibiting the free exercise thereof,' thus building a wall of separation between Church & State." Again, the clear implication is that Jefferson reveres the religion clauses precisely because they express his belief about the proper relationship between government and religion. Finally, in the paragraph's last sentence, Jefferson says that the clauses were adopted "in behalf of the rights of conscience" and that he favors "the progress of those sentiments which tend to restore to man all his natural rights," the implication being that the liberty of conscience protected by the First Amendment is a natural right.[83]

In short, what Jefferson does in his reply to the Baptists is to affirm that they understand him correctly, that he shares their normative beliefs on religion and government, and that those beliefs are expressed in the religion clauses of the First Amendment. There is nothing in his letter that suggests that he was expressing a states' right or federalist interpretation of those clauses.

Nevertheless, some scholars, most notably Daniel Driesbach, argue that in his letter to the Danbury Baptists, Jefferson was expressing a federalist interpretation of the religion clauses. Driesbach, for example, writes:

> It is not self-evident that Jefferson thought the [wall of separation] metaphor . . . described his views on the constitutional and prudential relationship between religion and *all* civil government. . . . A universal principle of church-state separation applicable at all levels of civil government—local, state, and federal—was *not* among the seeds deliberately sown. . . . The "wall" Jefferson erected in his letter to the Danbury Baptist served primarily to separate state and nation in matters pertaining to religion, rather than to separate ecclesiastical and all governmental authorities. The principal importance of his "wall," like the First Amendment it metaphorically represents, is its clear demarcation of the legitimate jurisdictions of federal and state governments on religious matters.[84]

On what basis does Dreisbach say this? He argues that there is more to Jefferson's letter than what meets the eye. He points out that Jefferson originally intended to use the letter as an occasion for explaining why he did not issue religious proclamations, such as designations of days of public fasting, thanksgiving, and prayer, and that the first draft of the letter to the Danbury Baptists contained such an explanation.[85] It was, however, excised from the final version of the letter upon the advice of his Attorney General, Levi Lincoln, who thought it would be politically damaging to the cause of Jefferson's Republican allies in New England.[86] Although Jefferson's explanation of why he refused to issue religious proclamations did not appear in the letter he actually sent to the Danbury Baptists, Dreisbach seizes on it as the basis of his federalist interpretation of the letter. He points out that earlier when Jefferson was a legislator and governor of Virginia he authored or supported laws authorizing the issuance of religious proclamations and on one occasion issued such a proclamation.[87] Dreisbach then asks, "How can one reconcile

Jefferson's record on religious proclamations in Virginia with the position he took in the [first draft of] Danbury letter?"

Dreisbach answers his question as follows:

> A careful review of Jefferson's actions throughout his public career suggests that he believed, as a matter of federalism, that the national government had no jurisdiction in religious matters, whereas state governments were authorized to accommodate and even prescribe religious exercises. Therefore, Jefferson saw no inconsistency in authoring a religious proclamation as a state official and refusing to release a similar proclamation as the federal chief executive. The "wall" metaphor was not offered as a general pronouncement on the prudential relationship between religion and all civil government; rather, it was, more specifically, a statement delineating the legitimate constitutional jurisdictions of the federal and state governments on matters pertaining to religion.[88]

To support this conclusion, Dreisbach cites not only Jefferson's record as a public official in Virginia but other writings that he thinks show that Jefferson subscribed to a federalist interpretation of the religion clauses. He cites the following passage from Jefferson's second inaugural address:

> In matters of religion, I have considered that its free exercise is placed by the constitution independent of the powers of the general government. I have therefore undertaken, on no occasion, to prescribe the religious exercises suited to it; but have left them, as the constitution found them, under the direction and discipline of State or Church authorities acknowledged by the several religious societies.[89]

Dreisbach also quotes from a letter that Jefferson wrote to a Presbyterian minister, Samuel Miller, and that explained why as president he refused to proclaim a national day of religious observance. What Dreisbach quotes is as follows:

> I consider the government of the United States as interdicted by the Constitution from intermeddling with religious institutions, their doctrines, discipline, or exercises. This results not only from the provision that no law shall be made respecting the establishment or free exercise of religion, but from that also which reserves to the States the powers not delegated to the United States. Certainly, no power to prescribe any religious exercise, or to assume authority in religious discipline, has been delegated to the General Government. It must then rest with the States, as far as it can be in any human authority. . . . I am aware that the practice of my predecessors may be quoted. But I have ever believed, that the example of State executives led to the assumption of that authority by the General Government, without due examination, which would have discovered that what might be a right in a State government, was a violation of that right when assumed by another. Be this as it may, every one must act according to the dictates of his own reason, and mine tells me that civil powers alone have been given to the President of the United States, and no authority to direct the religious exercises of his constituents.[90]

After quoting these passages, as well as the passage from the Kentucky Resolution of 1798 discussed earlier,[91] Dreisbach restates his argument about how Jefferson interpreted the religion clauses of the First Amendment. He writes:

> Jefferson's "wall," like the First Amendment, affirmed the policy of federalism. This policy emphasized that all governmental authority over religious matters was allocated to the states. The metaphor's principal function was to delineate the legitimate jurisdictions of state and nation on religious issues. Insofar as Jefferson's "wall," like the First Amendment, was primarily jurisdictional (or structural) in nature, it offered little in the way of a substantive right or universal principle of religious liberty. . . . There is no evidence that Jefferson considered the metaphor the quintessential symbolic expression of his church-state views. There is little evidence to indicate that Jefferson thought the metaphor encapsulated a *universal* principle of religious liberty or of the prudential relationships between religion and *all* civil government (local, state, and federal).[92]

What should one make of this argument and evidence? First, nothing in either draft of Jefferson's letter to the Danbury Baptists supports the argument. The first draft, of course, does contain Jefferson's explanation of why he, as president, does not issue religious proclamations, but his explanation is that the religion clauses, a national expression "in behalf of the rights of conscience," do not allow him to do so. He says nothing about states' rights.[93] In fact, Attorney General Lincoln objected to the first draft on the grounds that it was likely to be "construed into an implied censure of the usages of any of the States." He recommended that the wording be changed to say that religious exercises should be subject not only to the "regulations and discipline" of each sect, but "to the particular situations, usages and recommendations of the several States, in point of time and local circumstances."[94] This, of course, Jefferson refused to do, and to avoid the whole issue, the final draft makes no reference to religious proclamations. The best that Dreisbach can do is point to the fact that in the final draft Jefferson was interpreting the First Amendment and "recognized that . . . [it] was applicable to the federal government only."[95] Moreover, given the fact that he repeats this point many times,[96] Dreisbach apparently assumes that it carries great weight.

This leads to the second problem with Dreisbach's argument. The mere fact that Jefferson recognized that the religion clauses do not apply to the states is logically and clearly no reason for concluding that he did not think the clauses express a moral principle to which states as well as the federal government should adhere. He could have thought that the clauses express a universal moral principle, but because the clauses apply only to the federal government, the states as semi-sovereign entities were constitutionally or legally free to decide for themselves whether to adhere to the principle. In other words, the problem with Dreisbach's reasoning is that it fails to distinguish between what is (and is not) *constitutional* and what is (and is not) *moral,* between what is constitutionally permissible and what is morally permissible. Because the religion clauses originally did not apply to the states, Jefferson naturally thought they had a *constitutional* or *legal* right to establish a religion or prohibit the free exercise thereof, but that certainly does not mean that he thought they had a *moral* right to do so. In this connection, it is misleading for Dreisbach to say that Jefferson believed the "state governments were *authorized* to accommodate and even prescribe religious exercises."[97] *They were "authorized" only in the sense that the Constitution did not prohibit them from doing so.*

Third, because of his failure to distinguish between the constitutional or legal and the moral, Dreisbach misinterprets the passages he quotes from Jefferson's Second Inaugural Address and his letter to Samuel Miller. In the former, Jefferson says only the obvious—that before the Constitution was ratified, the states, as sovereign governments, had the *power* to prescribe religious exercises and that the Constitution gave none of that power to the federal government. Jefferson, however, does not indicate why that power was withheld from the federal government or that he approves of the states' exercising that power. In the latter document, at least the part quoted by Dreisbach, he makes the same argument. Although he comes close to implying that he approves of the states' prescribing religious exercises, he does not actually do so. He says that the power to prescribe such exercises "must then rest with the States, as far as it can be in any human authority." But how far is that? Jefferson does not say, but the implication is that it is not very far. He then cautiously goes on to say regarding religious proclamations that states "*might,*" not *do*, have "a right" to issue them. In short, Jefferson never says that the states have a *moral* right to prescribe religious exercises.

In fact, and fourth, in a part of his letter to Rev. Miller (that Dreisbach does not include when first making his argument), Jefferson clearly implies that *no* government, including a state government, has the moral right to even "*recommend*" a religious observance. He explains why not:

> I do not believe it is for the interest of religion to invite the civil magistrate to direct its exercises, its discipline, or its doctrines; nor of the religious societies, that the General Government should be invested with the power of effecting any uniformity of time or matter among them. Fasting and prayer are religious exercises; the enjoining them an act of discipline. Every religious society has a right to determine for itself the times for these exercises, and the objects proper for them, according to their own particular tenets; and this right can never be safer than in their own hands, where the Constitution has deposited it.[98]

Although in this passage Jefferson refers to the "General Government" as the government that should not enjoin fasting and prayer, at another point he refers to "the civil magistrate," presumably any civil magistrate, and more importantly he says that "[e]very religious society has a right to determine for itself" what its beliefs and practices will be. This clearly suggests that Jefferson here is referring to a natural right that no government should violate. Of course, he goes on to say that because of the religion clauses, this natural right is also a constitutional right. Finally, Jefferson clearly gives a normative reason for religious persons/groups' having such a right. *It is not in the interest of religion or religious societies* for government to issue religious proclamations. Obviously, this is a reason that applies not just to the federal government, but to all governments—a point conceded by Dreisbach.[99]

Moreover, according to James H. Hutson, Jefferson's reason for not issuing presidential proclamations—because they were "religious exercises"—"was conventional Republican doctrine that could be found in any number of party newspapers." He adds that the Republican faithful, outside New England, considered thanksgiving and fast day proclamations, at both the state and national level, as "anathema" and examples of "political exploitation" of religion. They even went so far as to organize street demonstrations and boycotts against them.[100] It is only to be expected, therefore, that Jefferson would express the same normative position.

A fifth weakness in Dreisbach's interpretation of Jefferson's letter to the Danbury Baptists is that even if Jefferson's position on religious proclamations when he was a state official was different from the position he took when he was President, it would not logically follow from that fact that Jefferson had a federalist understanding of the religion clauses—because there are other possible explanations for the different positions. In the first place, Jefferson, like most elected officials, may have been inconsistent for political reasons. As Dreisbach himself points out, in another of his works, both Jefferson and Madison were skillful politicians who often compromised certain positions, including those on church-state relations, in order to attain other objectives or to maintain the support of their constituents.[101] A second possible explanation of Jefferson's apparent inconsistency is that he may indeed have thought that his issuing religious proclamations did not violate the religion clauses or any natural right, and thus he supported and issued them while an elected official in Virginia. At the same time, he could have thought that his issuing them as President violated the Tenth Amendment because the power to issue such proclamations had never been given to the Congress or the President. There would not be anything inconsistent here. In other words, it is possible that Jefferson could have had a normative or principled understanding of those clauses but simply did not believe his issuing religious proclamations violated the clauses as he understood them.

Interestingly, Dreisbach himself notes that even *while acting as President*, Jefferson did things that were inconsistent with his "wall of separation" interpretation of the religion clauses.[102] Obviously, those inconsistencies cannot be explained on the grounds that he thought the states could do some things that the federal government could not do. Although we do not know exactly what accounts for those inconsistencies, whatever they were could also account for the inconsistencies between what Jefferson said/did in Virginia and what he did as President and said in his letter to the Danbury Baptists.

A sixth objection—Dreisbach is unclear and inconsistent on the issue of whether Jefferson had a normative or federalist understanding of the religion clauses. On the one hand, he explicitly says that the religion clauses, as interpreted by Jefferson, have some normative content. For example, in the passage quoted above[103] that concludes and summarizes his jurisdictional interpretation of Jefferson's "wall of separation," he says that Jefferson's "wall" was "*primarily* jurisdictional (or structural) in nature" and "offered *little* in the way of a substantive right or universal principle of religious liberty."[104] In another place, Dreisbach says, "It [Jefferson's wall] had *less* to do with the separation between church and all civil government than with the separation between the federal and state governments."[105] The implication of both sentences is that the religion clauses as understood by Jefferson served, at least *secondarily*, a normative purpose.

At times, Dreisbach even appears to subscribe to a dualistic interpretation of the religion clauses that would give *equal* weight to their normative and federalist content. For example, he writes, "Jefferson believed the First Amendment erected two distinct walls of separation: one between the federal government and religious institutions, thereby preventing the establishment of a national church, and the other between the federal and the state governments on matters pertaining to religion, thereby preventing the federal regime from interfering with religious establishments and practices endorsed by state governments."[106] He goes so far as to concede that "[i]t is plausible, even likely, that Jefferson desired each state . . . to erect its own wall of separation between ecclesiastical and state authorities. . . . There is every reason to believe that he would have wanted the states to follow the model implemented in Virginia with passage in 1786 of his celebrated 'Statute for Establishing Religious Freedom.'" Dreisbach then tacks in the other direction by adding that "these state walls would not be the same First Amendment 'wall' described in the Danbury letter."[107] In any case, even though Dreisbach fails to make clear the relative importance of Jefferson's normative and federalist concerns, all the above-quoted passages indicate that he believes that Jefferson understood the religion clauses as reflecting both concerns.

On the other hand, at the end of his argument, Dreisbach appears to say that Jefferson would have accepted Steven Smith's thesis that neither clause has any normative content. To support his federalist interpretation of Jefferson, he cites Smith's book and adds, "In other words, the First Amendment was calculated not to articulate a principle or theory of religious liberty but *merely* to specify who (or what level or branch of civil government) shall substantively address this subject matter."[108] Does this mean that Dreisbach actually thinks that the religion clauses, as understood by Jefferson, have *no* normative meaning? If so, he should have made this clear instead of saying that they have *primarily* federalist meaning or implying that the normative and federalist meanings are more or less equally important. In any case, the bottom line is that Dreisbach's interpretation of Jefferson's writings on the meaning of the religion clauses is confusing and raises as many questions as it answers.

Finally, the same point can be made about Jefferson's letter to the Danbury Baptists and related writings that was made earlier about the Kentucky and Virginia Resolutions. Were Jefferson's views representative of the general public's views at that time on the meaning of the religion clauses? Even if it were true that Jefferson subscribed to a federalist interpretation of the religion clauses, was such an interpretation generally accepted? Even Dreisbach says it was not. According to him, by telling Levi Lincoln that in his letter to the Danbury Baptists he was expressing "useful truths & principles" that he hoped would "germinate and become rooted" among the people, Jefferson "implicitly conceded that these ideas were not yet political tenets accepted by the people."[109] Dreisbach also writes, "Jefferson took seriously the jurisdictional prohibition on federal involvement with religion, and in this respect he was more separationist [but primarily for federalist reasons] than virtually all of his contemporaries. He went further than most national public figures of his day in limiting the federal government's acknowledgment of, or interaction with, religion. . . . *Indeed, his views on this matter were outside the mainstream*."[110] He goes on to point out that Jefferson's predecessors and other public officials of the time favored religious proclamations issued by and legislative chaplains paid by the federal government, and did not think that such practices violated the religion clauses.[111]

If, however, that is what most public officials thought at that time, it logically implies that they did not subscribe to the federalist interpretation of the religion clauses that Dreisbach attributes to Jefferson, i.e., they did not think that the clauses deprived the national government of *all* power to legislate with respect to religion. They must have thought that the clauses removed from the federal government only the power to establish a religion or to prohibit the free exercise of religion. If, moreover, this is what they thought, it logically implies that they subscribed to a normative understanding of the religion clauses. After all, if the reason for denying the federal government such power had been states' rights, then that same reason would have justified denying it the power to legislate *at all* with respect to religion, but, according to Dreisbach, most Americans did not want to limit the federal government to this extent.[112]

VII. CONCLUSION

This chapter has surveyed most, if not all, of the available evidence pertaining to how early Americans understood the religion clauses after they were drafted and submitted for ratification. It has examined what was said about the clauses by the ratifiers, clergy, authors of commentaries on the Constitution, other lawyers and public officials, and finally James Madison and Thomas Jefferson. The survey has shown that no one from 1790 to around 1830 expressed a federalist or states' rights interpretation of the religion clauses. The judgment appears to be uniform that the religion clauses were intended to protect an individual right—liberty of conscience.

The chapter has also shown, of course, that some persons, most notably Madison and Jefferson, thought that any federal law respecting the establishment of religion or its free exercise violated states' rights, and thus the Tenth Amendment, inasmuch as the federal government had never been granted the power to pass such a law. It shows that they also thought that because the religion clauses applied only to the federal government, the states retained the legal or constitutional right to pass laws establishing or regulating religion. It does not follow from this, however, that Jefferson and Madison thought the religion clauses have no or only little normative content. To the contrary, the evidence presented shows that they valued the religion clauses because they express a normative or moral principle—no direct government involvement with religion—that they thought *all* governments should adhere to in order to avoid infringing on religious freedom. Yes, Jefferson's actions on a few occasions may have been inconsistent with his professed beliefs, but alone those actions do not indicate that he held a federalist understanding of the religion clauses, and "no where in his writings does he indicate any agreement with those who argued that the states had any *legitimate* power over religion."[113]

Although it is possible that there is a quote from some early American in some source somewhere that reflects a federalist understanding of the religion clauses, this author has not been able to find it. Even if there is, it surely would not outweigh all the many passages quoted in this section that reflect a normative understanding of those clauses.

NOTES

1. Chester J. Antieau et al., *Freedom from Federal Establishment: Formation and Early History of the First Amendment Religion Clauses* (Milwaukee, Wisc.: Bruce Pub., 1964), 143–58.

2. See Thomas J. Curry, *The First Freedoms: Church and State in America to the Passage of the First Amendment* (New York: Oxford Univ. Press, 1986), 215–16, and Leonard W. Levy, *The Establishment Clause: Religion and the First Amendment* (Chapel Hill, N. Car.: Univ. of North Carolina Press, 1994, 2d ed. rev.), 108–11. Cf. Antieau et al., *Freedom from Establishment*, 144–46.

3. Quoted in Antieau et al, *Freedom from Establishment*, 153.

4. Quoted in Gerard V. Bradley, *Church-State Relationships in America* (Westport, Conn.: Greenwood Press, 1987), 116.

5. For this point, see Antieau et al., *Freedom from Federal Establishment*, 146–49, 152.

6. Antieau et al., *Freedom from Federal Establishment*, 150–51.

7. "'Nonpreferential' Aid to Religion: A False Claim about Original Intent,"*William and Mary Law Review*, 27 (1986): 901.

8. See "Letter to George Washington," 11/20/1789, in *The Papers of James Madison* [hereafter cited as *PJM*], ed. Robert A. Rutland et al. (Chicago: Univ. of Chicago Press, 1977), 12:453.

9. "The Rights of Conscience Inalienable . . .," 1791, in *Political Sermons of the American Founding Era: 1730–1805*, ed. Ellis Sandoz (Indianapolis, Ind.: Liberty Press, 1991), 1083–99.

10. "The Connecticut Dissenters' Strong Box: No. 1" (New London, CT, 1802), in *American Political Writing during the Founding Era, 1760–1805*, ed. Charles S. Hyneman & Donald S. Lutz (Indianapolis, Ind.: Liberty Press, 1983), II, 1204.

11. Quoted in Philip Hamburger, *Separation of Church and State* (Cambridge, Mass.: Harvard Univ. Press 2002), 171. The equation here of "befriend" with "interference" is striking. For another example of a normative interpretation of the religion clauses by a Baptist minister, see David Austin, "The dance of Herodias, through the streets of Hartford, on election day, to the tune of the Stars of heaven, in the dragon's tail . . . ," (1799) (Early American Imprints, First Series, 35125), 37.

12. Both persons are quoted in William G. McLoughlin, *New England Dissent, 1630–1883: The Baptists and the Separation of Church and State* (Cambridge, Mass.: Harvard Univ. Press, 1971), II: 783–84, 1097.

13. Enos Hitchcock, "An Oration in Commemoration of the Independence of the United States of America," 7/4/1793, in *Political Sermons*, 1181–83.

14. *The Constitution of the Reformed Dutch Church, in the United States* vii–viii, quoted in Philip Hamburger, "Equality and Diversity: The Eighteenth-Century Debate about Equal Protection and Equal Civil Rights," in *1992 Supreme Court Review*, (1993): 355, fn 149.

15. The Sedition Act made seditious libel a federal crime. It outlawed "writing, printing, uttering or publishing any false, scandalous and malicious writing or writings against the government of the United States, or either house of the Congress . . ., or the President . . ., with intent to defame. . . ." Sedition Act of 1798, ch. 74, 1 Stat. 596.

16. 2 *Annals of Congress, 5 th Congress*, 2d Session 2153 (7/10/1798).

17. George Hay, *An Essay on the Liberty of the Press* (New York: Arno Press, 1970 reprint of 1799 ed.), 41. Hay reasoned that if religious speech/publications were protected that much by the First Amendment, then surely other kinds of expression were protected just as much. *Essay on Liberty of Press*, 41–42.

18. Hay, *Essay on Liberty of Press*, 48 (emphasis added). What Granger said however, could have been true only if Jefferson's letter was stating a normative interpretation of religion clauses.

19. "A Solemn Address, to Christians & Patriots, upon the Approaching Election of a President of the United States," 1800, in *Political Sermons*, 1518. Earlier in that same address, at 1484–94, Wortman explained at length why a union of church and state would lead to the mutual destruction of both.

20. For a list of all possible commentaries on the Constitution written before 1860, see Elizabeth K. Bauer, *Commentaries on the Constitution 1790–1860* (New York: Columbia Univ. Press, 1952), 361–66. Whether some of these works should be categorized as constitutional commentaries is questionable, because some are general legal commentaries with scattered references to the Constitution, while others are more in the nature of textbooks to be used in secondary schools.

21. Indianapolis, Ind.: Liberty Fund, 1999 rep. of 1803 ed. This work was originally published as an appendix to Tucker's edition and study of *Blackstone's Commentaries*.

22. Clyde N. Wilson, "Foreword," in Tucker, *View of the Constitution*, vii. Saul Cornell says that "as a comprehensive legal treatise on American constitutionalism, Tucker enjoyed a virtual monopoly until Federalist James Kent published his *Commentaries on American Law* in 1826."*The Other Founders: Anti-federalism and the Dissenting Tradition in America, 1788–1828* (Chapel Hill, N. Car.: Univ. of North Carolina Press, 1999), 263–64.

23. Tucker, *View of the Constitution*, 235–36.

24. Tucker, *View of the Constitution*, 372–76.

25. Tucker, *View of the Constitution*, 373.

26. See Cornell, *Other Founders*, 263–73.

27. Tucker, *View of the Constitution*, 236.

28. Michael Kammen, *A Machine That Would Go of Itself: The Constitution in American Culture* (New York: Vintage Books, 1987), 77.

29. *A View of the Constitution of the United States of America* (New York: Da Capo Press, 1970 rep. of 1829 ed.), 120–23.

30. Melvin I. Urofsky and Paul Finkelman, *A March of Liberty: A Constitutional History of the United States* (New York: Oxford Univ. Press, 2002), 1:178. Kent served as Chancellor of New York from 1814 to 1823.

31. *Commentaries on American Law* (New York: O. Halsted, 1832, 2d ed.), 35–36 (emphasis added).

32. James Bayard, *A Brief Exposition of the Constitution of the United States*, (Littleton, Col.: Fred B. Rothman & Co., 1992 rep. of 1845 ed. first published in 1833), 146–47.

33. *Commentaries on the Constitution of the United States (Abridgement)* (Durham, N. C.: Carolina Academic Press, 1987 rep. of 1833 ed.), 700.

34. This is the way that Gerard Bradley, e.g., reads Story. See his *Church-State Relationships*, 121.

35. *Commentaries on the Constitution*, 701–2.

36. *Commentaries on the Constitution*, 702–3 (emphasis added).

37. Kurt Lash and Jed Rubenfeld argue for the latter interpretation of Story, but ignore the passages that support the former interpretation. See Lash, "Power and the Subject of Religion,"*Ohio State Law Journal*, 59 (1998): 1096, and Rubenfeld, "Antidisestablishmentarianism: Why RFRA Really Was Unconstitutional,"*Michigan Law Review*, 95 (Aug. 1997). 2356 57.

38. *Commentaries on the Constitution*, 701–3.

39. In light of what Story actually wrote, it is not clear why Christopher Grenda cites Story's statement that "[t]he whole power over the subject of religion is left exclusively to the state governments" to support the claim that "the primary if not exclusive purpose of the First Amendment's religion clauses was procedural rather than substantive. . . ." "Revealing Liberalism in Early America: Rethinking Religious Liberty and Liberal Values,"*Journal of Church and State*, 45 (Winter 2003): 134, fn 10. Other scholars who mistakenly interpret Story along these lines include John C. Jeffries, Jr., and James E. Ryan, "A Political History of the Establishment Clause,"*Michigan Law Review*, 100 (Nov. 2001): 293 ("It may be . . . that the original Establishment Clause embraced no substantive conception of the proper relation of church and state, but merely reflected a determination that the issue be settled locally. This was the understanding of Joseph Story. . . ."); William K. Lietzau, "Rediscovering the Establishment Clause: Federalism and the Rollback of Incorporation,"*DePaul Law Review*, 39 (1989–1990): 1202 (Cites Story to support the following: "There is little doubt that the first amendment initially reflected a federalism-based policy of exclusive state authority over the subject of religion."); Kurt Lash, "Power and the Subject of Religion," 1096, fn 102 ("Story thus rejected claims that the Founders meant to express a principle of church-state relationships that should

operate at the state, as well as at the federal level."); and Jed Rubenfeld, "Antidisestablishmentarianism . . .," 2357 (For Story "the core meaning of the Establishment Clause" is that Congress "has no power to dictate church-state relations at all—where 'state' refers to the governments of the several states.") Such statements are not only incorrect, but dishonor Story's commitment to religious freedom.

40. In *Barron v. Baltimore*, 19 32 U.S. (7 Pet.) 243 (1833), the Supreme Court held that the Bill of Rights did not apply to state governments or political entities under their jurisdiction.

41. Akhil Amar, *The Bill of Rights: Creation and Reconstruction* (New Haven, Conn.: Yale Univ. Press, 1998), 145.

42. *Bill of Rights*, 148. Amar qualifies this by saying that it applied only to "those clauses of the First Amendment that spoke of 'rights' or 'freedoms.' (The establishment clause most distinctly did not.)"*Bill of Rights*, 150. Here, in my opinion, Amar is mistaken, for as we have seen above, see pp. 67–70, 73, the rights of conscience or the free exercise of religion meant no establishment of religion. If, therefore, the First Amendment guarantees fundamental rights, as Amar rightly claims, it includes a right to be free of religious establishments.

43. *Bill of Rights*, 145–56.

44. *Bill of Rights*, 152.

45. See above, pp. 66–71, 73–74.

46. *Bill of Rights*, 246 ("We have seen that these words, as originally written, stood as a pure federalism provision. . . . [T]he clause was utterly agnostic on the substantive issue of establishment; it simply mandated that the issue be decided state by state and that Congress keep its hands off, that Congress make no law 'respecting' the vexed question. In short, the original establishment clause was a home rule—local option provision mandating imperial neutrality.") Amar is not alone in asserting this. See the sources cited in *The Bill of Rights*, 324–25, fn 62.

47. Amar relies on two indirect and inconclusive pieces of evidence. The first is the wording of the establishment clause, i.e., what is prohibited is not an establishment of religion, but laws "respecting" such. Although this wording makes it *possible* to interpret the clause as prohibiting the federal government's legislating with respect to state religious establishments, it does nothing more. Most importantly, it does not support the contention that that was *all* it was intended to do. Secondly, Amar, *Bill of Rights*, at 35, cites statements by Jefferson and others to the effect that the states had the right to promote religion, but this only states the obvious—the First Amendment was not intended to apply to the states. Amar fails to explain how that fact alone leads to the conclusion that the establishment clause has *no* normative meaning.

48. "Speech on the Maryland 'Jew Bill'," in *Cornerstones of Religious Freedom in America*, ed. Joseph L. Blau (Boston, Mass.: Beacon Press, 1950), 99.

49. "Speech on Maryland 'Jew Bill,'" at 99–100.

50. See Jefferson's "A Bill for Establishing Religious Freedom," in *The Papers of Thomas Jefferson*[hereafter cited as *PTJ*], ed. Julian P. Boyd (Princeton, N.J.: Princeton Univ. Press, 1950), 2:545–47, and Madison's "A Memorial and Remonstrance Against Religious Assessment" (1785), in *PJM*, 8:298–304.

51. See scholars cited below in notes 56–58.

52. For an account of what happened, see John C. Miller, *Crisis in Freedom: The Alien and Sedition Acts* (Boston: Little, Brown, 1951).

53. "Jefferson's Fair Copy [of the Kentucky Resolutions of 1798]" (before 10/4/1798), in *PTJ*, 30:544.

54. "Jefferson's Fair Copy," 30:544. The last sentence in the above quote refers to the Virginia Statute for Establishing Religious Liberty, which indicates that when Jefferson first drafted this document, he intended for it to be passed by the Virginia General Assembly. How it came to be the basis of the Kentucky Resolutions is explained in "Editorial Note," in *PTJ*, 30:531–34.

55. "Report of 1800" (1/7/1800), in *PJM*, 17:310, 339–40.

56. *Constitutional Opinions: Aspects of the Bill of Rights* (New York: Oxford Univ. Press, 1986), 166 (emphasis added). Also, see Levy, *Emergence of a Free Press* (New York: Oxford Univ. Press, 1985), 266–71.

57. "The Second Adoption . . .," 1114. Also, see 1112.

58. "Taking Liberties with the First Amendment," 1570–71. Also see Walter Berns, "Freedom of the Press and the Alien and Sedition Laws: A Reappraisal," in *The Supreme Court Review 1970*, ed. Philip Kurland (Chicago: Univ. of Chicago Press, 1970), 126–35; Steven D. Smith, *The Constitution and the Pride of Reason* (New York: Oxford Univ. Press, 1998), 56; Daniel Dreisbach, *Thomas Jefferson and the Wall of Separation between Church and State* (New York: New York Univ. Press, 2002), 62–63; Lietzau, "Rediscovering the Establishment Clause," 1202–4; and Amar, *Bill of Rights*, 39–41.

59. "Virginia Resolution" (12/21/1798), in *PJM*, 17:189–90 (emphasis added).

60. "Report of 1800," 17:336–39, 344. Interestingly, Madison also says that the American understanding of *freedom of religion* "will never be admitted" to be the same as that in England. "Report of 1800," 17:339.

61. "Report of 1800," 17:338. Also, see David Rabban, "The Ahistorical Historian: Leonard Levy on Freedom of Expression in Early American History,"*Stanford Law Review*, 37 (Feb. 1985): 818–19.

62. "Report of 1800," 17:339–40, 346 (emphasis in original).

63. "Report of 1800," 17:346–47.

64. Rabban, "Ahistorical Historian," 818–19. Even Leonard Levy admits that Madison's *Report* is a libertarian document. *Emergence of a Free Press*, 315–25. Although Kurt Lash concedes that "Madison argued that the Acts did abridge individual freedom," he contends that for Madison and Jefferson "the central problem with the Acts" was that "they violated the rights of the *states*." "Power and the Subject of Religion," 1108 (emphasis in original).

65. "Jefferson's Draft," 30:537, 540.

66. On this point, see David N. Mayer, *The Constitutional Thought of Thomas Jefferson* (Charlottesville, Va.: Univ. Press of Virginia, 1994), 174–75.

67. This is well explained by Bybee, "Taking Liberties . . .," at 1567–70.

68. "Report of the Minority on the Virginia Resolution" (1/22/1799), in *The Founders' Constitution*, 5:138. The same argument was made by a select committee of the House of Representatives that was appointed to respond to the Kentucky and Virginia Resolutions (3 Annals of Congress, 6th Cong., 1st Sess. 2990 (1799)), and by James Iredell, "Charge to the Grand Jury, in Case of Fries," in *The Founders' Constitution*, 5:140.

69. "Report of 1800," 17:347 (emphasis in original).

70. See Lash, "Power and the Subject of Religion," 1107–8. Jefferson, too, may have understood the words of the First Amendment in this way, for at least on one occasion he described the Amendment as "the provision that no law shall be made respecting the establishment or free exercise of religion. . . ." "Letter to Reverend Samuel Miller" (1/23/1808), in *The Founders' Constitution*, 5:98.

71. "Report of 1800," 17:346 (emphasis in original).

72. See Lash, "Power and the Subject of Religion," 1095–96.

73. See above, pp. 60, 87–88, 89, 107. Later, in 1811, in his message to the House of Representatives explaining why he vetoed an act incorporating an Episcopal Church in Alexandria, Virginia, President Madison said that "the Bill exceeds the rightful authority, to which [all!] Governments are limited by the essential distinction between Civil and Religious functions, and violates, in particular the . . . [establishment clause] of the Constitution. . . ." To the House of Representatives, in *The Papers of James Madison: Presidential Series*, ed. J. C. A. Stagg et al. (Charlottesville, Va.: Univ. Press of Virginia, 1996), 3:176.

74. In contrast to Madison, Jay Bybee stresses the distinctiveness of the establishment clause's wording. "Taking Liberties . . .," 1564–66.

75. Remarks of July 10, 1798, *Annals of Congress*, 5th Congress, 2nd sess., 2144. Also, see 2139–43, 3006–14.

76. Remarks of July 10, 1798, *Annals of Congress*, 5th Congress, 2nd sess., 2164. Also, see 2159–63, 2996.

77. Letter to James Madison, 7/19/1798, in *PJM*, 17:165. Also, see George Hay, *An Essay on the Liberty of the Press*, 33–51, and "Address of the General Assembly to the People of the Commonwealth of Virginia" (1/23/1799), in *The Founders' Constitution*, 5:139–40. (Although the editors of *The Founders' Constitution* attribute this "Address" to Madison, the editors of Madison's papers do not. See "Note on the Virginia Resolutions, 10 January 1799, and the

Address of the General Assembly to the People of the Commonwealth of Virginia, 23 January 1799," in *PJM*, 17:199–206.) Given remarks such as those quoted above, it is difficult to see how Walter Berns can assert that Republicans in Congress "were not contending for free speech and press; they were contending for states' rights, for the right of the states to punish seditious libel." "Freedom of the Press and the Alien and Sedition Laws: A Reappraisal," 121–22.

78. Bybee, "Taking Liberties . . .," 1567.

79. Cornell, *The Other Founders*, 240 ("Madison and Jefferson had hoped that the resolutions would rally opposition to Federalist policy, but they attracted no official support outside their states of origin and drew hostile replies from many legislatures. . . .").

80. The letter, of course, is most famous because it contained Jefferson's assertion that the religion clauses built "a wall of separation between Church & State." For the influence of this phrase and the letter generally, see Dreisbach, *Jefferson and the Wall*, 2–5.

81. See *Reynolds v. United States*, 98 U.S. 145, 164 (1879), and *Everson v. Board of Education*, 330 U.S. 1, 15–16, 18 (1947). For the influence of Jefferson's interpretation on the general public and the Supreme Court, see Dreisbach, *Jefferson and the Wall*, 2–5, 95–128.

82. "Address of the Danbury Baptist Association to Thomas Jefferson" (10/7/1801), in Dreisbach, *Jefferson and the Wall*, Appendix 6, pp. 142–43.

83. "Letter to Danbury Baptist Association" (1/1/1802), in Dreisbach, *Jefferson and the Wall*, Appendix 6, p. 148.

84. Dreisbach, *Jefferson and the Wall*, 50, 53, 56 (emphasis in original). Scholars who appear to agree with Dreisbach include James H. Hutson, *Religion and the Founding of the American Republic* (Washington, D. C.: Library of Congress, 1998), 92–93, and Vincent P. Muñoz, *God and the Founders: Madison, Washington, and Jefferson* (New York: Cambridge Univ. Press, 2009), 78–81.

85. Dreisbach, *Jefferson and the Wall*, 56–57. In the first draft, after giving his "wall of separation" interpretation of the religion clauses, Jefferson wrote, "Congress thus inhibited from acts respecting religion, and the Executive authorized only to execute their acts, I have refrained from prescribing even occasional performances of devotion, prescribed indeed legally where an Executive is the legal head of a national church, but subject here, as religious exercises only to the voluntary regulations and discipline of each respective sect." Quoted in Dreisbach, *Jefferson and the Wall*, 38.

86. Dreisbach, *Jefferson and the Wall*, 38–48.

87. Dreisbach, *Jefferson and the Wall*, 58–59.

88. Dreisbach, *Jefferson and the Wall*, 59–60.

89. Quoted in Dreisbach, *Jefferson and the Wall*, 65.

90. Quoted in Dreisbach, *Jefferson and the Wall*, 63–64.

91. See above, pp. 151, 153, 155. He also quotes from a letter Jefferson wrote in 1804 to Abigail Adams, in which he said, "While we deny that Congress have a right to control the freedom of the press, we have ever asserted the right of the States, and their exclusive right, to do so." Quoted in Dreisbach, *Jefferson and the Wall*, 62.

92. Dreisbach, *Jefferson and the Wall*, 69–70. Phillip Muñoz also says that Jefferson's Second Inaugural Address and his letter to Samuel Miller reflect a jurisdictional or non-principled understanding of the religion clauses. *God and Founders*, 78–80. Akhil Amar also appears to agree with Dreisbach's interpretation of Jefferson. See *The Bill of Rights*, 34–35. Compare Dreisbach's interpretation of Jefferson's letter with that of David Barton, "The Image and the Reality: Thomas Jefferson and the First Amendment,"*Notre Dame Journal of Law, Ethics & Public Policy*, 17 (2003), who, although agreeing, at 408, with Dreisbach that "it was Jefferson's understanding of federalism and separation of powers that was largely behind his refusal to issue a national prayer proclamation," argues, at 428–32, that the letter to the Danbury Baptists expresses a normative understanding of the religion clauses.

93. For the complete first draft, see Dreisbach, *Jefferson and the Wall, 144*–45.

94. Quoted in Dreisbach, *Jefferson and the Wall*, 146–47.

95. Dreisbach, *Jefferson and the Wall*, 53–54.

96. See, e.g., Dreisbach, *Jefferson and the Wall*, at 65, 68, and 69.

97. Dreisbach, *Jefferson and the Wall*, 60 (emphasis added).

98. Quoted in Dreisbach, *Jefferson and the Wall*, Appendix 9, 153–54.

99. Dreisbach, after making his case that Jefferson subscribed to a federalist interpretation of the religion clauses, later concedes that in his letter to Miller, Jefferson "ardently defended the rights of conscience with arguments applicable, it would seem, to both state and federal magistrates."*Jefferson and the Wall*, 69. Also, see 199–200, fn 65.

100. James H. Hutson, "Thomas Jefferson's Letter to the Danbury Baptists: A Controversy Rejoined,"*William and Mary Quarterly*, 3rd ser., 56 (Oct. 1999): 781, 783.

101. *Real Threat and Mere Shadow: Religious Liberty and the First Amendment* (Westchester, Ill,: Crossway Books, 1987), 108. Even Madison, perhaps as principled a public servant as anyone in American history, took inconsistent positions on the issue of public aid to religion. While President, he issued Thanksgiving proclamations, but later regretted doing so. See his "Detached Memoranda," in *The Founders' Constitution*, 5:105. According to Gerard Bradley, Madison was inconsistent on other church-state issues. See *Church-State Relationships*. . ., 86–87.

102. Dreisbach, *Jefferson and the Wall*, 57–58, and *Real Threat and Mere Shadow*, 127–31.

103. See above, p. 160.

104. (Emphasis added). Dreisbach, in *Jefferson and the Wall*, also uses the word *primarily* in a sentence on p. 56.

105. *Jefferson and the Wall*, 60 (emphasis added). For similar statements, see p. 61.

106. *Jefferson and the Wall*, 68.

107. *Jefferson and the Wall*, 68–69. Unfortunately Dreisbach fails to explain this last assertion. In what normative way is the "wall" erected by Jefferson's Virginia statute different from the "wall" he thought was erected by the First Amendment?

108. *Jefferson and the Wall*, 69, 200, fn 66 (emphasis added).

109. *Jefferson and the Wall*, 44.

110. *Jefferson and the Wall*, 66–67 (emphasis added). On the other hand, Dreisbach may be wrong in stating that Jefferson's views were not widely accepted. After all, Jefferson's Postmaster General and political adviser, Gideon Granger, to whom Jefferson had given the first draft of his Danbury Baptist letter, had this to say about the letter: "The answer will undoubtedly give great Offence to the established Clergy of New England while it will delight the Dissenters as they are called. *It is but a declaration of Truths which are in fact felt by a great Majority of New England, & publicly acknowledged by near half of the People of Connecticut*. . . ." Quoted in Dreisbach, *Jefferson and the Wall*, 147 (emphasis added) What Granger said, however, could have been true only if Jefferson's letter was stating a normative interpretation of the religion clauses.

111. *Jefferson and the Wall*, 67.

112. Of course, another explanation is that those early Americans who wanted the government to issue religious proclamations and provide chaplains for Congress could have subscribed to a federalist interpretation of the religion clauses and simply been inconsistent, for one reason or another, in their application of that interpretation.

113. Lash, "Power and the Subject of Religion," 1126, fn 208.

Chapter Eight

The Federalist Interpretation of the Religion Clauses: A Concluding Assessment

This book has examined the thesis that one or both of the religion clauses of the First Amendment have little or no normative meaning, but were intended to protect states' rights by giving the state governments exclusive jurisdiction over issues regarding the proper relationship between government and religion. It has attempted to present every piece of available historical evidence that might or might not support the thesis. Specifically, the book has examined (1) what the proponents of religious liberty amendments sought to accomplish by such amendments and why, (2) the various drafts in the First Congress of what came to be the religion clauses and the debate that accompanied them, and (3) how Americans during the first few decades after their ratification understood or interpreted the religion clauses. The major findings of this examination are as follows:

First, those who thought the Constitution should be amended to protect religious freedom, the members of the First Congress who commented on the drafting of the religion clauses, and the "public intellectuals" (clergy, lawyers, judges, legislators, legal scholars) who commented on their meaning after they were ratified ALL had a normative understanding of the clauses, in both their proposed and final versions. In other words, they all thought that the purpose of the clauses was to protect religious freedom or liberty of conscience, which they strongly believed to be an inalienable natural right that *no* government has the moral right to abridge or violate. Moreover, they all assumed that traditional European-style establishments of religion and laws characteristic of ("respecting") such establishments inherently threaten, if not abridge, religious liberty. In their minds, therefore, the protection of religious liberty requires the prohibition of such establishments and laws. Many of them also considered such establishments and laws to be divisive and a threat to American national unity. In short, all the persons surveyed in this book thought that the establishment and free exercise clauses had not only a normative meaning, but essentially the same meaning.

Ironically, Steven Smith, the leading proponent of the federalist interpretation of the religion clause, agrees that the two religion clauses originally had a unitary meaning, i.e., were two different ways of saying the same thing. He agrees that early Americans equated an establishment of religion with persecution and that the clauses did not serve conflicting, or even distinct, purposes, but expressed one principle. More specifically, he uses the fact that the two clauses had the same meaning to argue against the dualistic interpretation of the clauses, i.e., that the establishment clause protects states' rights and the free exercise clause individual rights.[1] Strangely, however, he concludes that the one principle that they both express is that of federalism or states' rights. It does not follow, however, that just because the clauses have the same meaning, they are federalist and not normative in content. It is just as possible, and what the historical evidence actually shows is, that they express one normative principle, e.g., that government should be neutral, i.e., not take a position, on essentially religious issues.

Second, all of the evidence that supports a federalist reading of the religion clauses is indirect and circumstantial in nature, which in turn means that all the arguments for such a reading are speculative in nature. There is no evidence, for example, that *anyone* before, during, or after their drafting (until the twentieth century?) understood the clauses as guarantees of federalism or states' rights, nor is there any evidence that anyone understood the establishment clause as intended to protect the remnants of religious establishments that existed in a few New England states. At best, certain pieces of evidence, such as the existence of the remnants of established religions in a few states, are consistent with a federalist reading of the clauses, but they certainly do not require such a reading.

Yes, the Anti-federalists and, later, Jefferson, Madison, and their Democratic-Republican allies were very much committed to states' rights and especially to the principle enunciated in the Tenth Amendment, i.e., that the powers of the federal government were limited to those delegated to it and those not delegated to it remained with the states or the people thereof. Yes, they also stated that the religion clauses were intended to affirm that no power to legislate on the rights of conscience had ever been delegated to the national government and, consequently, to the extent that any government legally possessed such a power, it was the state governments. They believed, therefore, that if Congress were to pass a law respecting an establishment of religion or prohibiting the free exercise of religion, it would constitute a violation of states' rights.

These facts, however, do not show that these same individuals believed that the purpose of the religion clauses was to enable states to legislate as they please with respect to religion. When they said the religion clauses left the states with the legal right to legislate on religion, they did so not because of the *content* of the clauses themselves but simply because the clauses did not apply to the states. Moreover, the fact that they thought the states have a legal or constitutional right to legislate on religion does not mean that they thought the states have a moral right to do so; in fact, all the evidence indicates they believed the contrary. The evidence, in other words, shows that the reason Jefferson, Madison, and their allies believed that no power to legislate on religious matters had been or should be delegated to the national government was because the exercise of such a power by *any* government would pose a direct threat to religious liberty, which they considered to be a natural right.

Third, as for the establishment clause, its wording alone, if taken literally, does prevent Congress from legislating against existing establishments of religion in one or more of the states, but it also prevents it doing anything like establishing a religion at the national level or in the states. This raises an obvious question about the purpose of the clause. Was it to protect existing state establishments of religion, to protect a states' right (to protect disestablishments as well as establishments), to prevent anything like a national establishment, or some combination of the above? Although many, if not most, federalist interpreters of the clause contend that it was intended solely to protect establishments of religion that existed in some of the states, that interpretation is certainly not dictated by the wording of the clause.

More importantly, there is simply NO evidence that explicitly or directly shows that the reason for the clause and its "respecting" wording was to prevent federal laws aimed at state laws dealing with religion. In the first place, no one, either during or several years after its drafting, publicly interpreted the clause in this way. Moreover, at the time of the drafting of the religion clauses, most persons in the states that had some laws aiding religion did not consider those laws to constitute an establishment of religion. If they had wanted to protect such laws from national legislation, they would not have wanted an amendment that referred to those laws as establishments of religion. By definition, language protecting establishments of religion from Congressional action would not protect laws that were not considered to be establishments of religion.

Defenders of the view that the establishment clause was meant to protect the remnants of religious establishments in New England might respond that the literal wording of the establishment clause, i.e., the word "respecting," is alone enough to show that the clause has that purpose. This would be true, however, only if that were the only way of explaining the meaning of the clause, but as shown earlier,[2] "respecting" could have been used to express

Madison and others' view that the federal government, like any government, should have no authority to pass any sort of law associated with traditional establishments of religion. More importantly, as Thomas Curry has so eloquently argued, the meaning of a constitutional provision "must arise out of its historical context rather than from a literalist reading."[3]

In this regard, it is particularly disturbing that so many constitutional law scholars have routinely and even brazenly asserted that the establishment clause was intended to prevent federal legislation aimed at state laws aiding religion, but have failed to support their claim with any direct historical evidence other than its "respecting" language. Instead of historical evidence, what they have cited is one or more secondary sources, which they imply contain the historical evidence.

For example, after stating that the establishment clause "prohibited the national legislature from interfering with, or trying to *dis* establish, churches established by state and local governments," Akil Amar begins his citation following that claim with the words, "For more support and elaboration, see" and then lists thirteen *secondary* sources.[4] Not one of them, however, contains any evidence, other than the wording of the clause and the existence of so-called religious establishments in some states,[5] that directly or explicitly supports Amar's interpretation of the establishment clause. Some mention only circumstantial evidence, such as the alleged lack of a consensus on the correct relationship between government and religion,[6] or irrelevant evidence, such as the fact that the states had the power to legislate on religion, because no power to do that had ever been delegated to the national government and the religion clauses confirmed that denial of power.[7] One scholar alleges that during the ratification controversy many American objected to the Constitution because it contained no provision protecting state establishments of religion, but he provides no example of such objections.[8] Others simply *assume*, with no supporting evidence, that the final wording had the same meaning as the earlier version proposed by Samuel Livermore that prohibited laws "touching" religion, that Livermore's version had the same meaning as New Hampshire's proposed amendment, and that New Hampshire's proposal was intended to protect state establishments of religion.[9] Three of the scholars cited by Amar contend that the debates in the First Congress were over how best to protect state policies on religion from federal legislation. One cites no evidence to support the contention,[10] and two rely on Representative Benjamin Huntingdon's comments, which they misinterpret as expressions of concern about possible *Congressional* action against state laws aiding religion.[11] Finally, Amar cites Steven Smith's book, *Foreordained Failure*, about which enough has already been said.

Surely this kind of history is unacceptable and inexcusable. It is simply not enough to cite secondary sources, especially when those sources cite only other secondary sources. At some point, some scholar or source must present primary documents or writings, and *those primary sources must actually support the point or conclusion that they are alleged to support.* This is especially important in the field of constitutional history where the original meaning of a constitutional provision is often the basis for a judge or court's decision in a constitutional law case.

One other point—even if there was direct or explicit evidence that conclusively demonstrated that the establishment clause was drafted and then understood to protect state laws aiding religion, that would not be enough to show that the religion clauses in toto have such a purpose. After all, there is the free exercise clause. For this reason, some scholars argue that the religion clauses together have a dual purpose. The establishment clause, they say, was intended to protect certain state laws, and the free exercise clause to protect the individual right of conscience.[12] Such a purpose, however, would have been most anomalous. It would mean or at least suggest that the framers were trying to accomplish (simultaneously) contradictory objectives—to prevent religious establishments (by means of the free exercise clause) and to protect them (by means of the establishment clause).

Of course, it can be replied that such an argument does not follow because establishments of religion are not inherently or necessarily inconsistent with religious freedom. That, however, is precisely the issue. More precisely, the issue is what position did early Americans take on this issue. The evidence presented in this book shows unmistakably that those early Americans who wanted a religious liberty provision added to the Constitution believed that religious establishments and religious freedom were simply incompatible.[13] Although there may have been a few persons at that time who thought that religious establishments, if slim or mild enough, do not necessarily threaten religious freedom,[14] there is no evidence that they caused the establishment clause to be adopted in order to protect such establishments or even that they understood the clause in this way. This is hardly surprising, however, because in order to have done this, they would have had to be able to show just how slim or mild a religious establishment would have to be in order not to be a threat to religious freedom, and this would have required the most subtle kind of "hair-splitting," which would not have appealed to most persons' way of thinking. In short, a dualistic interpretation of the religion clauses is just not credible. It pits two normative principles against each other. It is no wonder, therefore, that Steven Smith, the most committed of the federalist interpreters of the religion clauses, rejects the dualistic interpretation.[15]

Fourth, much of the circumstantial evidence on which the exponents of a federalist interpretation rely does not work to support their interpretation of the clauses. Its use, in other words, reflects fallacious or illogical reasoning. The most obvious example of this failing is the argument that because the religion clauses (and the Bill of Rights in general) originally applied only to the federal government (and not to the states), *the clauses themselves* are expressions of federalism, i.e., they give the states the constitutional right to establish religions and even deny the free exercise of religion. On its face, this is simply an illogical argument.

Moreover, if it were valid, it would mean that the framers were simply contradicting themselves when they proposed or adopted an amendment that would have prohibited the states from abridging the freedoms of religion, speech, press, and assembly. In other words, if the religion clauses themselves were intended to allow the states to do as they pleased with respect to religion, it would have made no sense for the first House of Representatives to have adopted a version of those clauses and then soon thereafter to have adopted an amendment that would have prevented the states from doing as they pleased with respect to religion. This, however, is exactly what the House did when it voted in favor of Madison's proposal to prohibit the states from infringing "the equal rights of conscience . . . the freedom of speech or of the press, . . . the right of trial by jury in criminal cases."[16]

Moreover, the House voted for Madison's proposal without the slightest awareness that it was being inconsistent. Although one member of the House objected to Madison's proposal, he did so on the grounds not that it was inconsistent with the previously adopted religion clauses that applied to Congress, but that it interfered with the state governments, which he thought should be left to themselves. Madison's response, of course, was that if it was wrong for the federal government to infringe these essential rights, it was also wrong for the states to do so.[17] Obviously Madison, and by implication the two-thirds majority of the House that sided with him, did not consider the religion clauses then under consideration to be guarantees of states' rights.

Another example of a premise illogically used by some scholars to support a federalist interpretation of the religion clauses is the idea that, as the Federalists had argued, the original Constitution never gave the federal government jurisdiction over religion and, thus, the religion clauses were meant simply to make that lack of jurisdiction clear.[18] Again, such a premise, even if valid, does not by itself indicate that the religion clauses have little or no normative meaning. Whether that is true depends on *why* the Constitution never gave the federal government jurisdiction over religion and *why* so many persons thought it was important to add an amendment to make clear that lack of jurisdiction.[19] When answers to those questions are sought, the findings are clear. *No one* at the time gave as the reason for denying the federal government jurisdiction over religion the argument that states were better qualified than the federal government was to address church-state issues or that state establishments of religion needed to be protected. To the contrary, the reason universally given was that if the federal government had power to legislate on religious issues, it would threaten religious freedom, degrade religion, and lead to conflict and instability in the nation—all normative reasons.

A third example of fallacious reasoning is Steven Smith's argument that because the debates in the First Congress over the religion clauses were "desultory and superficial," there must have been no dispute over their meaning, which could have been the case only because their meaning was understood to be federalist and not normative in nature.[20] As explained earlier,[21] there could have been several reasons for the quality of the debates, some of which applied to the Bill of Rights as a whole and not just to the religion clauses. Above all, this kind of reasoning overlooks the possibility that a consensus existed at the time on the core or essential meaning of religious liberty, a consensus that many, if not most, scholars believe did exist.

A fifth finding—some of the circumstantial evidence, although relevant, is by itself not enough to support a states' right interpretation of the religion clauses. For example, it is true that many, if not most, Anti-federalists were concerned that the proposed national government had been given too much power and would take away too many of the states' traditional powers, and that they sought amendments that would reduce the powers of the national government vis-à-vis those of the states. From that fact, however, one cannot conclude or assume that the religion clauses (or, for that matter, other provisions in the Bill of Rights) were sought mainly to protect the states' traditional powers to legislate on religion and other matters, as opposed to being sought to prevent the national government from violating individual, natural rights. More evidence is needed.

A second example—some states (mostly in New England) had laws that had the practical effect of financially and symbolically supported a particular denomination or part of the Christian religion. It is not unreasonable, therefore, to assume that some persons in those states would not have wanted Congress to pass laws that eliminated those state laws. Moreover, even if it did not go so far as to prohibit a state's laws favoring a certain denomination or religion, Congress might still threaten or undermine them if it established or in other ways favored a religion or denomination other than the one being supported in a particular state. Again, therefore, it is not unreasonable to assume that persons in those states would have wanted to prevent Congress from taking such action—not because they were opposed to all laws promoting or favoring a particular religion, but because they wanted to protect their state's laws that promoted or favored their brand of Christianity.[22] Is, however, this "reasonableness" enough to demonstrate that the religion clauses originally had little or no normative meaning? Again, the answer is, No; more evidence is needed.

Are these two pieces of circumstantial evidence *together* enough to warrant the conclusion that the religion clauses were originally meant to protect states' rights rather than individual rights? Obviously two pieces of circumstantial evidence supporting a conclusion are more persuasive than just one is, but by themselves are surely not enough to constitute a compelling case.

Again, what is missing are statements by some early Americans that the sole or primary purpose of the religion clauses is to protect the states' power to legislate as they pleased on the subject of religion.

Sixth, some of the historical evidence has been misconstrued, if not distorted, by those favoring a federalist interpretation of the religion clauses. Perhaps the clearest example of this is their argument that the Federalists believed and stated that the original Constitution gave the central government no jurisdiction over *religion.* As explained earlier, however, what the Federalists actually said in most cases (and implied in the others) was that the central government had no jurisdiction over *religious freedom or the rights of conscience*. This is important distinction, for if the Federalists thought it was religious freedom (and not religion in general) over which the federal government had no jurisdiction, then they must have had a normative reason, like protecting individual rights, for taking such a position. If their reason had been to protect states' rights, then they would have taken the position that *all* legislation having to do with religion, and not just legislation that threatens religious liberty, should be placed outside the jurisdiction of the federal government. There is little evidence, however, to show that such was their position.

A second example of evidence misunderstood is the contention that in the First Congress, Benjamin Huntington expressed concern that Congress might legislate against Connecticut's system of public financing of churches. Such an interpretation of what he said, if accurate, could be used as evidence that at least some persons in the First Congress wanted the religion clauses worded in a way that would protect the church-state arrangements that existed in some states from federal legislation.[23] As we have seen, however, what Huntington actually expressed concern over was the possibility of the federal *courts'* misinterpreting and using the religion clauses to attack church-state arrangements in the states. What he actually wanted, therefore, was for the religion clauses to be worded so that it would be quite clear that they restricted only the national government and not the states, and, of course, he got what he wanted. The First Amendment begins, "Congress shall make no law . . . ."

Third, there is the misinterpretation of Justice Joseph Story's understanding of the religion clauses. In his *Commentaries on the Constitution,* Story explicitly and clearly gives a normative or principled interpretation of the religion clauses. Although he says that the clauses were intended to deprive the federal government of "all power to act upon the subject" (whether the subject is religion or establishment of religion is unclear) and to leave it with the states, he unmistakably says that this was done to prevent an establishment of religion, which he condemns in the harshest of terms as leading to religious persecution and social conflict. Nevertheless, far too many scholars have said that Story had a federalist interpretation of the religion clauses.[24]

Finally, there is the misinterpretation of Madison and Jefferson's writings, i.e., those written in response to the Sedition Act, those written by Jefferson to the Baptists in Danbury, Connecticut, and those explaining why he, as President, did not issue religious proclamations. Here the main problem has been the conflating of two different reasons the two men gave for opposing certain laws or actions, the two reasons being to protect states' rights and to protect individual rights. In other words, too many scholars have illogically concluded that because Jefferson and Madison opposed the Sedition Act and the issuing of religious proclamations on the grounds that they violated both states' rights and the religion clauses, Jefferson and Madison must have understood those clauses as guarantees of states' rights. At the same time, these same scholars have ignored passages from those same writings that explicitly stated that the religion clauses, as well as the free speech and press clauses, were meant to protect individual rights. The fact is that Jefferson and Madison opposed the Sedition Act and the issuing of religious proclamations on two different and independent grounds, neither of which takes away from the strength of the other.

The other mistakes, noted earlier,[25] pertain to Jefferson's Letter to the Danbury Baptists and other writings in which he explains why he did not issue religious proclamations. The first mistake was to focus on Jefferson's first draft of his Danbury letter instead of his final draft or the letter actually sent to the Baptists, which unmistakably conveys a normative or principled interpretation of the religion clauses. The second mistake was to *assume* that because in that first draft and in other writings Jefferson expressed his opposition to Presidents' issuing religious proclamations AND because earlier while in Virginia he had supported and issued such proclamations, he must have had a federalist understanding of the religion clauses. Otherwise, one would have to conclude that Jefferson was being inconsistent, God forbid! That conclusion, however, is certainly a possibility, and there are ways of explaining away what appears to be an inconsistency besides attributing to Jefferson a federalist interpretation of the religion clauses. In short, Jefferson's apparent inconsistency on the issue of religious proclamations is a reed too slender to support the thesis that he subscribed to a federalist interpretation of the religion clauses.

The seventh and final finding of this book is that, in spite of all their shortcomings, the federalist interpreters of the religion clauses deserve credit for establishing one very important point about the clauses, namely, that they are jurisdictional in nature. In other words, the clauses prohibit the national legislature, Congress, from legislating on a particular subject or area of life. For this reason, the religion clasues, including the free exercise clause, are best understood *not as statements about what private individuals and groups are free to do, but as statements about what government is not free to do. As a matter of constitutional law, religious liberty means that government may not pass certain kinds of laws, rules, or regulations*. The religion clauses are, therefore, a "meta-law"—a law about laws, a law for lawmakers, and not a law for judges to apply in specific cases or situations.[26] In short, although the federalist scholars may be mistaken as to exactly what kinds of laws Congress is forbidden to pass and why, they are correct in saying the religion clauses deprive Congress (and after incorporation, the state legislatures) of jurisdiction over certain kinds of laws.

Where the federalist interpreters go wrong is in *assuming* two other points. First, they assume that if the religion clauses were intended to deny the national government jurisdiction over a certain subject, that subject must have been religion. Although that comes close to being correct, the evidence presented in this book shows that the clauses prohibit not all laws that pertain to religion in any way, but only laws that take a position on religious issues, i.e., beliefs and practices, and thus threaten religious freedom. The clauses prohibit the national government from discriminating for or against a particular religion, doctrine, or practice, or for or against any person because of his/her religion. *In short, the religion clauses prohibit laws of the sort associated with traditional establishments of religion, and to early Americans, the right of conscience, the free exercise of religion, simply meant the absence of such laws.* What, however, about a law that attempts to prevent state governments or private individuals or groups from discriminating on the basis of religion or in other ways violating religious liberty? There is no reason for thinking that the religion clauses were intended to prohibit Congress from passing such a law. One can, of course, argue that Congress cannot pass such a law because it was never given the authority to do so, but that is quite different from saying that the religion clauses themselves prohibit such a law.

Secondly, the federalist interpreters of the religion clauses mistakenly assume that if the clauses were intended to deny the national government jurisdiction over religious issues, they must have done so because their framers/ratifiers wanted the states to have jurisdiction over that subject. They fail to consider that the framers/ratifiers of the religion clauses may have denied the national government jurisdiction over religious issues because they believed that *no government* should have jurisdiction over such matters. The advocates of a federalist interpretation assume that the Anti-federalists were concerned only about states' rights and not about individual rights. If only they had read the arguments made by the Anti-federalists for adding a religious liberty amendment to the Constitution (arguments presented in chapter four), they would have known better. They would have known that the Anti-federalists considered the creation of the new national government to be analogous to the creation of a government from a state of nature and that they wanted to make sure that this government, like any government so created, was prohibited from violating certain fundamental natural rights.

Given the preceding points, it follows that what the Supreme Court did when it incorporated the religion clauses into the due process clause of the Fourteenth Amendment and, thereby, applied the clauses to the state governments was not inconsistent with the original meaning of the religion clauses. If the clauses were not intended to protect states' rights or state establishments of religion, but rather to protect religious liberty and preserve the harmony of the nation, then it is perfectly appropriate for the Court to use the Fourteenth Amendment to overturn state as well as federal laws that threaten those interests. Although there may be other grounds for challenging the incorporation of the religion clauses into the Fourteenth Amendment, such as the argument that that amendment was not intended to apply the Bill of Rights to the states, it cannot be challenged on the grounds that the clauses were originally meant to protect states' rights and, thus, have no normative content.

Perhaps the best way to describe the states' right interpretation of the religion clauses of the First Amendment is to say that it was a plausible hypothesis, but one that needed to be tested against the historical data. What made it plausible were the following facts: most Anti-federalists were concerned that with the new Constitution, the states would be giving up too much of their power to the federal government; some states, mostly in New England, had laws or policies regarding religion that they would not have wanted the federal government to eliminate; and because of the word "respecting," the establishment clause on its face appears to prohibit laws both establishing and disestablishing a religion. Plausibility by itself, however, is not enough to establish the truth of an hypothesis. In this case, what has been needed is a testing of the hypothesis against the historical facts, which, before now, had never been done.

This book has presented those facts. The evidence is overwhelmingly clear. All the proponents, drafters, and subsequent interpreters of the clauses, including the establishment clause, understood them as guarantees of individual rights, not states' rights. In short, the federalist hypothesis, although plausible, is simply not supported by the evidence. Like all hypotheses that have failed the empirical test, it deserves to be relegated to the past as an interesting footnote in American constitutional history. Its time has come and gone.

NOTES

1. Steven D. Smith, *Foreordained Failure: The Quest for a Constitutional Principle of Religious Freedom* (New York: Oxford Univ. Press, 1995), 36–37.
2. See above, pp. 103, 107.
3. *The First Freedoms*, 222.

4. *The Bill of Rights: Creation and Reconstruction* (New Haven, Conn.: Yale Univ. Press, 1998), 32, 324, fn 62. In an earlier version of the same material, Amar's citation began with the words, "For much more support and elaboration than is possible here, see. . . ." "The Bill of Rights as a Constitution," in *The Bill of Rights: Government Proscribed*, ed. Ronald Hallman and Peter J. Albert (Charlottesville, Va.: Univ. Press of Virginia, 1997), 311, fn 127.

5. This is the only "evidence" presented by Edward S. Corwin, "The Supreme Court as National School Board,"*Law & Contemporary Problems*, 14 (1949): 3, 11–12; William W. Crosskey, *Politics and the Constitution in the History of the United States*, 2 vols, (Chicago: Univ. of Chicago Press, 1953), 2:1057, 1060, 1072–74; and William C. Porth and Robert P. George, "Trimming the Ivy: A Bicentennial Re-Examination of the Establishment Clause,"*West Virginia Law Review*, 90 (1987): 109, 136–39.

6. William K. Lietzau, "Rediscovering the Establishment Clause: Federalism and the Roll-back of Incorporation,"*DePaul Law Review* 39 (1990): 1191, 1200; Michael A. Paulsen, "Religion, Equality, and the Constitution: An Equal Protection Approach to Establishment Clause Adjudication,"*Notre Dame Law Review*, 61 (1986): 311, 321–23; and Daniel O. Conkle, "Toward a General Theory of the Establishment Clause,"*Northwestern University Law Review*, 82 (1988): 1113, 1132–35.

7. Kurt T. Lash, "The Second Adoption of the Establishment Clause: The Rise of the Nonestablishment Principle,"*Arizona State Law Journal*, 27 (1995): 1085, 1089–99; Joseph M. Snee, "Religious Disestablishment and the Fourteenth Amendment,"*Washington University Law Quarterly*, 1954 (1954): 371; Edward Dumbauld, *The Bill of Rights and What It Means Today* (Westport, Conn.: Greenwood Press, 1979 rep. of 1957 ed.), 104 & fn. 5; and Lietzau, "Rediscovering," 1200–01. Dumbauld, however, says only that "[r]ecognition of the rights of the several states to regulate religious matters *may* have influenced the choice of words used in the First Amendment."*Bill of Rights*, 104 (emphasis added).

8. Jed Rubenfeld, "Antidisestablishmentarianism: Why RFRA Really Was Unconstitutional,"*Michigan Law Review*, 95 (Aug. 1997): 2354. Although Rubenfeld cites three secondary sources, none of them presents any evidence to support his claim. He also cites the remarks of Iredell at the North Carolina ratifying convention (discussed above at p. 62), but Iredell was not objecting to the lack of such a provision in the Constitution. He was merely explaining, in response to another delegate's question, why there was not a provision in the Constitution guaranteeing religious freedom in the states!

9. See Wilbur Katz, *Religion and American Constitutions* (Evanston, Ill.: Northwestern Univ. Press, 1964), 8–10; Rubenfeld, "Antidisestablishmentarianism," 2354–55; Snee, "Religious Disestablishment," 378–79, 385–86 (but Snee, at 378, admits that the "reported debates shed no light on why New Hampshire chose this phrasing. . . ."); and Gerard V. Bradley, *Church-State Relationships in America* (Westport, Conn.: Greenwood Press, 1987), 76, 92, 94–95. As explained earlier p. 84), although Bradley cites a primary source, it does not contain any evidence to support his interpretation of New Hampshire's proposed amendment or of the final wording of the religion clauses.

10. Conkle, "Toward a General Theory," 134.

11. Lash, "Second Adoption," 1091, and Snee, "Religious Disestablishment," 385.

12. See above, chapter 1, p. 11.

13. On this point, see Thomas J. Curry, *The First Freedoms: Church and State in America to the Passage of the First Amendment* (New York: Oxford Univ. Press, 1986), 216–17, and Noah Feldman, "The Intellectual Origins of the Establishment Clause,"*New York University Law Review*, 77 (May 2002): 350–52.

14. As Steven Smith points out, the Massachusetts Constitution of 1780 seems to manifest just such a position. *Foreordained Failure*, 7.

15. *Foreordained Failure*, 36–37.

16. *Documentary History of the First Federal Congress of the United States of America*, vol. 11, *Debates in the House of Representatives*, ed. Charlene B. Bickford et al. (Baltimore, Md.: Johns Hopkins Univ. Press, 1992), 1292.

17. *Documentary History*, vol. 11, *Debates in House*, 1292.

18. See, e.g., Smith, *Foreordained Failure*, 47.

19. Steven Smith seems unaware of the importance of this question. He simply assumes that if it can be shown that "the religion clauses did no more and no less than confirm the constitutional allocation of jurisdiction over religion to the states," that fact alone automatically and "rudely refuses to satisfy the judges' and scholars' hunger for a substantive [normative] right or principle of religious freedom." *Foreordained Failure*, 47.

20. *Foreordained Failure*, 26–27, 39.

21. See above, pp. 46, 119–20.

22. For this argument, see Ira C. Lupu and Robert W. Tuttle, "Federalism and Faith,"*Emory Law Journal*, 56 (2006): 19, 104–5.

23. This misinterpretation most likely was innocently made because it was stated most influentially, but not first, in *The First Freedoms* by Thomas J. Curry, who clearly does not subscribe to a federalist interpretation of the religion clauses. Then other scholars, without carefully examining the original debates in Congress, simply accepted Curry's interpretation because his work on the religion clauses is so authoritative.

24. See above, p. 147.

25. See above, pp. 157–64.

26. For an elaboration of this important point, see John Harrison, "The Free Exercise Clause as a Rule about Rules," *Harvard Journal of Law and Public Policy* 15 (1992): 169–74.

Bibliography

PRIMARY SOURCES

Abington School District v. Schempp, 374 U.S. 203 (1963).
Agostini v. Felton, 521 U.S. 203 (1963).
2 *Annals of Congress*, 5th Congress, 2nd Session (1798).
3 *Annals of Congress*, 6th Congress, 1st Session (1799).
Bailyn, Bernard, ed. *The Debate on the Constitution: Federalist and Antifederalist Speeches, Articles, and Letters During the Struggle over Ratification*. 2 vols. New York: Library of America, 1993.
Barron v. Baltimore, 32 U.S. 243 (1833).
Bayard, James. *A Brief Exposition of the Constitution of the United States*. Littleton, Col.: Fred B. Rothman & Son., 1992 rep. of 1845 ed. (first published in 1833).
Blakely, William A., ed. *American State Papers and Related Documents on Freedom of Religion*. 4th ed. Washington, D. C.: Religious Liberty Association, 1949.
Blakely, William A., and Willard A Colcord, eds. *American State Papers Bearing on Sunday Legislation: Legislative, Executive, Judicial*. New York: Da Capo Press, 1970 ed., rev. and enl., of 1911 ed.
Blau, Joseph L., ed. *Cornerstones of Religious Freedom in America*. Boston, Mass.: Beacon Press, 1950.
Cantwell v. Connecticut, 310 U.S. 296 (1940).
Carroll, John. *The John Carroll Papers*, edited by Thomas O. Hanley. 3 vols. Notre Dame, Ind.: Univ. of Notre Dame Press, 1976.
City of Boerne v. Flores, 521 U.S. 507 (1997).
Collin, Nicholos. "Remarks on the Amendments to the Federal Constitution . . .," Philadelphia *Federal Gazette*, (11/18/1788): 2.
Cutter v. Wilkinson, 544 U.S. 709 (2005).
Davis, Augustine, compiler and printer. "The Ratification of the New Foederal Constitution, Together with the Amendments, Proposed by the Several States." Pp. 43–68 in *Contexts of the Bill of Rights*, edited by Stephen L. Schechter and Richard B. Bernstein. Albany, N. Y.: New York State Commission on the Bicentennial of the United States Constitution, 1990.
De Pauw, Linda G., et al, eds. *Documentary History of the First Federal Congress of the United States of America, March 4, 1789–March 3, 1791*. 17 vols. Baltimore, Md.: Johns Hopkins University Press, 1971.
Elk Grove Unified School District v. Newdow, 542 U.S. 1 (2004).

Elliot, Jonathan, ed. *The Debates in the Several State Conventions on the Adoption of the Federal Constitution*. New York: Burt Franklin, 1965 rep. of 1888 ed.
Everson v. Board of Education, 330 U.S. 1 (1947).
Hay, George. *An Essay on the Liberty of the Press*. New York: Arno Press, 1970 rep. of 1799 ed.
Hyneman, Charles S., and Donald S. Lutz, eds. *American Political Writing during the Founding Era, 1760–1805*. 2 vols. Indianapolis, Ind.: Liberty Press, 1983.
Jefferson, Thomas. *The Papers of Thomas Jefferson*, edited by Julian P. Boyd. Princeton, N.J.: Princeton University Press, 1950.
Jensen, Merrill, et al, ed. *The Documentary History of the Ratification of the Constitution,* Vols III, VIII, IX, X, XIII, XIV, XV, XVI, XVIII. Madison, Wis.: State Historical Society of Wisconsin, 1976.
Kent, James. *Commentaries on American Law*. 2d ed. New York: O. Halsted, 1832.
Kurland, Philip B., and Ralph Lerner, eds. *The Founders' Constitution*. Chicago: University of Chicago Press, 1987.
Lee v. Weisman, 505 U.S. 577 (1992).
Leland, John. *The Writings of John Leland*, edited by L. F. Greene. New York: Arno Press, 1969 rep. of 1845 ed.
Lemon v. Kurtzman, 403 U.S. 602 (1971).
Madison, James. *The Papers of James Madison*, edited by Robert A. Rutland et al. Chicago: University of Chicago Press, 1977.
Madison, James. *The Papers of James Madison: Presidential Series*, edited by Robert A. Rutland et al. Charlottesville, Va.: University Press of Virginia, 1983.
Madison, James, et al. *The Federalist Papers*, edited by Isaac Kramnick. London: Penguin Books, 1987, orig. pub. 1788.
Perry, Richard L., ed. *Sources of Our Liberties: Documentary Origins of Individual Liberties in the United States Constitution and Bill of Rights*. Chicago: American Bar Foundation, 1959.
Rawle, William. *A View of the Constitution of the United States of America*. New York: Da Capo Press, 1970 rep. of 1829 ed.
Religious Freedom Restoration Act, 42 U.S.C. sec. 2000 bb (1993).
Reynolds v. United States, 98 U.S. 145 (1879).
Sandoz, Ellis, ed. *Political Sermons of the American Founding Era, 1730–1805*. Indianapolis, Ind.: Liberty Press, 1991.
Sedition Act of 1798, ch. 74, 1 Stat. 596.
Storing, Herbert J., ed. *The Complete Anti-Federalist*. 7 vols. Chicago: University of Chicago Press, 1981.
Story, Joseph. *Commentaries on the Constitution of the United States (Abridgement)*. Durham, N. C.: Carolina Academic Press, 1987 rep. of 1833 ed.
Thorpe, Francis N., comp. and ed. *The Federal and State Constitutions, Colonial Charters, and Other Organic Laws of the States, Territories, and Colonies*. Vol. IV. Washington, D. C.: Government Printing Office, 1909.
Tucker, St. George. *View of the Constitution of the United States: With Selected Writings*. Indianapolis, Ind.: Liberty Fund, 1999, orig. pub. 1803. *United States Constitution.*
Washington, George. *The Papers of George Washington: Presidential Series*, edited by Dorothy Twohig et al. Charlottesville, Va.: University Press of Virginia, 1987.
Wilson, John E., and Donald L. Drakeman, eds. *Church and State in American History*. 3rd ed. Boulder, Col.: Westview Press, 2003.

SECONDARY SOURCES

Adams, Arlin M., and Charles J. Emmerich. *A Nation Dedicated to Religious Liberty: The Constitutional Heritage of the Religion Clauses*. Philadelphia, Penn.: University of Pennsylvania Press, 1990.

Alexander, John K. "Pennsylvania, Pioneer in Safeguarding Personal Rights." Pp. 308–32 in *The Bill of Rights and the States: The Colonial and Revolutionary Origins of American Liber ties*,edited by Patrick T. Conley and John P. Kaminski. Madison, Wis.: Madison House, 1992.

Amar, Akhil. "Anti-Federalists, *The Federalist Papers*, and the Big Argument for Union."*Harvard Journal of Law & Public Policy*, 16 (1993): 111–18.

———. "The Bill of Rights and the Fourteenth Amendment."*Yale Law Journal*, 101 (April 1992): 1193–1284.

———. "The Bill of Rights as a Constitution." Pp. 274–386 in *The Bill of Rights: Government Proscribed*, edited by Ronald Hoffman and Peter J. Albert. Charlottesville, Va.: University Press of Virginia, 1997.

———. *The Bill of Rights: Creation and Reconstruction*. New Haven, Conn.: Yale University Press, 1998.

Anderson, David A. "The Origins of the Press Clause."*U.C.L.A. Law Review*. 30 (1983): 455–541.

Anglim, Christopher T. *Encyclopedia of Religion and the Law in America*. 2d ed. Amenia, N. Y.: Grey House Pub., 2009.

Antieau, Chester J. et al., *Freedom from Federal Establishment: Formation and Early History of the First Amendment Religion Clauses*. Milwaukee, Wis.: Bruce Publishers, 1964.

Ariens, Michael S., and Robert A. Destro. *Religious Liberty in a Pluralistic Society*. Durham, N.C.: Carolina Academic Press, 1996.

Banning, Lance. *The Sacred Fire of Liberty: James Madison and the Founding of the Federal Republic*. Ithaca, N. Y.: Cornell University Press, 1995.

———. "Virginia: Sectionalism and the General Good." Pp. 261–99 in *Ratifying the Constitution*, edited by Michael A. Gillespie and Michael Lienesch. Lawrence, Kan.: University Press of Kansas, 1989.

Barlow, J. Jackson et al. *The American Founding: Essays on the Formation of the Constitution*. New York: Greenwood Press, 1988.

Bartolomucci, Chris. "Rethinking the Incorporation of the Establishment Clause: A Federalist View."*Harvard Law Review*, 105 (May 1992): 1700–20.

Barton, David. "The Image and the Reality: Thomas Jefferson and the First Amendment."*Notre Dame Journal of Law, Ethics & Public Policy*, 17 (2003): 399–460.

Bauer, Elizabeth K. *Commentaries on the Constitution 1790–1860*. New York: Columbia University Press, 1952.

Berg, Thomas C. "Religion Clause Anti-Theories."*Notre Dame Law Review*, 72 (1997): 693–752.

Bernhard, Winfred E.A. *Fisher Ames, Federalists and Statesman, 1758–1809*. Chapel Hill, N. C.: University of North Carolina Press, 1965.

Berns, Walter. *The First Amendment and the Future of American Democracy*. New York; Basic Books, 1976.

———. "Freedom of the Press and the Alien and Sedition Laws: A Reappraisal."*1970 Supreme Court Review*,(1970): 109–59.

Bickford, Charlene B., and Kenneth R. Bowling. *Birth of the Nation: The First Federal Congress 1789–1791*. Madison, Wis.: Madison House Publishers, 1989.

Borden, Morton. "Federalists, Antifederalists, and Religious Freedom."*Journal of Church and State*, 21 (Autumn 1979): 469–82.

———. *Jews, Turks and Infidels*. Chapel Hill, N. C.: University of North Carolina Press, 1984.

Bork, Robert H. *The Tempting of America: The Political Seduction of the Law*. New York: Free Press, 1990.

Bowling, Kenneth R. "'A Tub to the Whale': The Founding Fathers and the Adoption of the Federal Bill of Rights."*Journal of the Early Republic*, 8 (Autumn 1988): 223–51.

Bradley, Gerard V. "Beguiled: Free Exercise Exemptions and the Siren Song of Liberalism."*Hofstra Law Review*, 20 (1991): 245–320.

———. *Church-State Relationships in America*. Westport, Conn.: Greenwood Press, 1987.

Brose, Jonathan P. "In Birmingham They Love the Governor: Why the Fourteenth Amendment Does Not Incorporate the Establishment Clause."*Ohio Northern University Law Review*, 24 (1998): 1–30.

Butler, Jon. "Why Revolutionary America Wasn't a 'Christian Nation'." Pp. 187–202 in *Religion and the New Republic*, edited by James H. Hutson. Lanham, Md.: Rowman & Littlefield, 2000.

Bybee, Jay S. "Common Ground: Robert Jackson, Antonin Scalia, and a Power Theory of the First Amendment."*Tulane Law Review*, 75 (Dec. 2000): 251–336.

———. "Taking Liberties with the First Amendment: Congress, Section 5, and the Religious Freedom Restoration Act."*Vanderbilt Law Review*, 48 (Nov. 1995): 1539–1633.

Cahn, Edmond. "The 'Establishment of Religion' Puzzle."*New York University Law Review*, 36 (Nov. 1961): 1274–97.

Conkle, Daniel O. *Constitutional Law: The Religion Clauses*. New York: Foundation Press, 2003.

———. "Toward a General Theory of the Establishment Clause."*Northwestern University Law Review*, 82 (1988): 1113–94.

Cord, Robert L. *Separation of Church and State: Historical Fact and Current Fiction*. New York: Lambeth Press, 1982.

Cornell, Saul. "Mere Parchment Barriers? Antifederalists, the Bill of Rights, and the Question of Rights Consciousness." Pp. 175–208 in *The Bill of Rights: Government Proscribed*, edited by Ronald Hoffman and Peter J. Albert. Charlottesville, Va.: University Press of Virginia, 1997.

———. *The Other Founders: Anti-Federalism & the Dissenting Tradition in America, 1788–1828*. Chapel Hill, N. C.: University of North Carolina Press, 1999.

Cortner, Richard C. *The Supreme Court and the Second Bill of Rights*. Madison, Wis.: University of Wisconsin Press, 1981.

Corwin, Edward S. "The Supreme Court as National School Board."*Law and Contemporary Problems*, 14 (Winter 1949): 3–22.

Crosskey, William W. *Politics and the Constitution in the History of the United States*. 2 vols. Chicago: University of Chicago Press, 1953.

Curry, Thomas J. "Church and State in Seventeenth and Eighteenth Century America."*Journal of Law and Religion*, 7 (1989): 261–73.

———. *Farewell to Christendom: The Future of Church and State in America*. New York: Oxford University Press, 2001.

———. *The First Freedoms: Church and State in America to the Passage of the First Amendment*. New York: Oxford University Press, 1986.

Davis, Derek H. *Religion and the Continental Congress 1774–1789: Contributions to Original Intent*. New York: Oxford University Press, 2000.

Denbeaux, Mark P. "The First Word of the First Amendment."*Northwestern University Law Review*, 80 (Spring 1986): 1156–1220.

Destro, Robert A. "The Structure of the Religious Liberty Guarantee."*Journal of Law & Religion*, 11 (1994–95): 355–409.

Drakeman, Donald L. *Church-State Constitutional Issues: Making Sense of the Establishment Clause*. New York: Greenwood Press, 1991.

———. *Church, State, and Original Intent*. New York: Cambridge University Press, 2010.

———. "Religion and the Republic: James Madison and the First Amendment."*Journal of Church and State*, 25 (Autumn 1983): 427–46.

Dreisbach, Daniel. *Thomas Jefferson and the Wall of Separation between Church and State*. New York: New York University Press, 2002.

———. *Real Threat and Mere Shadow: Religious Liberty and the First Amendment*. Westchester, Ill.: Crossway Books, 1987.

Dumbauld, Edward. *The Bill of Rights and What It Means Today*. Westport, Conn.: Greenwood Press, 1979 rep. of 1957 ed.

Duncan, Kyle. "Subsidiarity and Religious Establishments in the United States Constitution."*Villanova Law Review*, 52 (2007): 67–134.

Esbeck, Carl. "Dissent and Disestablishment: The Church-State Settlement in the Early Republic."*Brigham Young University Law Review*, (2004): 1385–1592.

Eubanks, Cecil L. "New York: Federalism and the Political Economy of Union." Pp. 300–40 in *Ratifying the Constitution*, edited by Michael A. Gillespie and Michael Lienesch. Lawrence, Kan.: University Press of Kansas, 1989.

Feldman, Noah. "The Intellectual Origins of the Establishment Clause."*New York University Law Review*, 77 (May 2002): 346–428.

Finkelman, Paul. "Between Scylla and Charybdis: Anarchy, Tyranny, and the Debate over a Bill of Rights." Pp. 123–36 in *The Bill of Rights: Government Proscribed,* edited by Ronald Hoffman & Peter J. Albert. Charlottesville, Va.: University Press of Virginia, 1997.

———. "James Madison and the Bill of Rights: A Reluctant Paternity."*1990 Supreme Court Review*, (1990): 301–47.

———. "The Ten Amendments as a Declaration of Rights."*Southern Illinois University Law Journal*, 16 (Winter 1992): 351–96.

Gedicks, Frederick M. "The Establishment Clause Gag Reflex."*Brigham Young University Law Review*, 2004 (2004): 995–2004.

Gillespie, Michael A. "Massachusetts: Creating Consensus." Pp. 138–67 in *Ratifying the Constitution,* edited by Michael A. Gillespie and Michael Lienesch. Lawrence, Kan.: University Press of Kansas, 1989.

Glendon, Mary Ann, and Raul F. Yates. "Structural Free Exercise."*Michigan Law Review*, 90 (1991): 477–550.

Glenn, Gary D. "Forgotten Purposes of the First Amendment Religion Clauses."*Review of Politics*, 49 (Summer 1987): 340–67.

Goldstein, Leslie F. "Popular Sovereignty, the Origins of Judicial Review, and the Revival of Unwritten Law."*Journal of Politics*, 48 (Feb. 1986): 51–71.

Graham, George J., Jr. "Pennsylvania: Representation and the Meaning of Republicanism." Pp. 52–70 in *Ratifying the Constitution*, edited by Michael A. Gillespie and Michael Lienesch. Lawrence, Kan.: University Press of Kansas, 1989.

Green, Steven K. "'Bad History': The Lure of History in Establishment Clause Adjudication."*Notre Dame Law Review*, 81 (June 2006): 1717–54.

———. "Federalism and the Establishment Clause: A Reassessment."*Creighton Law Review*. 38 (2004–2005): 761–98.

———. "Religion Clause Federalism: State Flexibility over Religious Matters and the 'One-Way Ratchet'."*Emory Law Journal*, 56 (2006): 107–24.

Greenawalt, Kent. "Common Sense about Original and Subsequent Understandings of the Religion Clauses."*University of Pennsylvania Journal of Constitutional Law*, 8 (2006): 479–512.

Grenda, Christopher S. "Revealing Liberalism in Early America: Rethinking Religious Liberty and Liberal Values."*Journal of Church and State*, 45 (Winter 2003): 131–63.

Guinness, Os. "Tribespeople, Idiots or Citizens?: Religious Liberty and the Reforging of the American Public Philosophy."*Journal of Law and Religion*, 8 (1990): 33–55.

Gunn, T. Jeremy. *A Standard for Repair: The Establishment Clause, Equality, and Natural Rights*. Hamden, Conn.: Garland Pub. Co., 1992.

Hamburger, Philip. "A Constitutional Right of Religious Exemption: An Historical Perspective."*George Washington Law Review*, 60 (1992): 915–48.

———. "Equality and Diversity: The Eighteenth-Century Debate about Equal Protection and Equal Civil Rights."*1992 Supreme Court Review* (1993): 295–392.

———. *Separation of Church and State*. Cambridge, Mass.: Harvard University Press, 2002.

Handy, Robert T. "The American Tradition of Religious Freedom: An Historical Analysis."*Journal of Public Law*, 13 (1964): 247–66.

Harrison, John. "The Free Exercise Clause as a Rule about Rules."*Harvard Journal of Law & Public Policy*, 15 (1992): 169–79.

Hitchcock, James. *The Supreme Court and Religion in American Life*. 2 vol's. Princeton, NJ: Princeton University Press, 2004.

Howe, Mark DeWolfe. *The Garden and the Wilderness: Religion and Government in American Constitutional History*. Chicago: University of Chicago Press, 1965.

Hutson, James H. "The Bill of Rights and the American Revolutionary Experience." Pp. 62–97 in *A Culture of Rights: The Bill of Rights in Philosophy, Politics, and Law*, edited by Michael J. Lacey & Knud Haakonssen. New York: Cambridge University Press, 1991.

———. "The Birth of the Bill of Rights: The State of Current Scholarship."*Prologue*, 20 (Fall 1988): 143–61.

———. "The Creation of the Constitution: The Integrity of the Documentary Record." Pp. 151–78 in *Interpreting the Constitution: The Debate over Original Intent*, edited by Jack N. Rakove. Boston, Mass.: Northeastern University Press, 1990.

———. *Religion and the Founding of the American Republic*. Washington, D. C.: Library of Congress, 1998.

———. "Thomas Jefferson's Letter to the Danbury Baptists: A Controversy Rejoined."*William and Mary Quarterly*, 3rd ser. 56 (Oct. 1999): 775–90.

Ireland, Owen S. *Ethnicity, and Politics: Ratifying the Constitution in Pennsylvania*. University Park, Penn.: Pennsylvania State University Press, 1995.

Ivers, Gregg. *Redefining the First Freedom: The Supreme Court and the Consolidation of State Power*. New Brunswick, N.J.: Transaction Publishers, 1993.

Jeffries, John C., and James E. Ryan. "A Political History of the Establishment Clause."*Michigan Law Review*, 100 (Nov. 2001): 279–370.

Jellinek, George. *The Declaration of the Rights of Man and of Citizens*, trans. by Max Farrand. Westport, Conn.: Hyperion Press, 1979 reprint of 1901 ed.

Kaminski, John P. "The Making of the Bill of Rights: 1787–1792." Pp. 18–64 in *Contexts of the Bill of Rights,* edited by Stephen L. Schechter and Richard B. Bernstein. Albany, N. Y.: New York State Commission on the Bicentennial of the United States Constitution, 1990.

———. "Rhode Island: Protecting State Interests." Pp. 368–90 in *Ratifying the Constitution*, edited by Michael A. Gillespie and Michael Lienesch. Lawrence, Kan.: University Press of Kansas, 1989.

Kamman, Michael. *A Machine That Would Go of Itself: The Constitution in American Culture*. New York: Vintage Books, 1987.

Katz, Wilber G. *Religion and American Constitutions.* Evanston, Ill: Northwestern University Press, 1964.

Kauper, Paul G. *Religion and the Constitution*. Baton Rouge, La.: Louisiana State University Press, 1964.

Ketcham, Ralph. *James Madison: A Biography*. New York: Macmillan, 1971.

Klein, Milton M. "Liberty as Nature's Gift: The Colonial Origins of the Bill of Rights in New York." Pp. 215–45 in *The Bill of Rights and the States: The Colonial and Revolutionary Origins of American Liberties*, edited by Patrick T. Conley and John P. Kaminski. Madison, Wis.: Madison House, 1992.

Kruse, Clifton B. "The Historical Meaning and Judicial Construction of the Establishment of Religion Clause of the First Amendment."*Washburn Law Journal*, 2 (Winter 1962): 65–141.

Lambert, Frank. *The Founding Fathers and the Place of Religion in America*. Princeton, N. J.: Princeton University Press, 2003.

Lash, Kurt T. "Power and the Subject of Religion."*Ohio State Law Journal*, 59 (1998): 1069–1154.

———. "The Second Adoption of the Establishment Clause: The Rise of the Nonestablishment Principle."*Arizona State Law Journal*, 27 (1995): 1085–1154.

———. "The Second Adoption of the Free Exercise Clause: Religious Exemptions Under the Fourteenth Amendment."*Northwestern University Law Review*, 88 (Spring 1994): 1106–56.

———. "Two Movements of a Constitutional Symphony: Akhil Reed Amar's *The Bill of Rights*."*University of Richmond Law Review*, 33 (May 1999): 485–510.

Laycock, Douglas. "Individual Liberty and Constitutional Architecture: The Founders' Prompt Correction of Their Own Mistake."*Harvard Journal of Law & Public Policy*, 16 (Winter 1993): 75–86.

———."'Nonpreferential' Aid to Religion: A False Claim about Original Intent."*William & Mary Law Review*. 27 (1986): 875–924.

———. "Regulatory Exemptions of Religious Behavior and the Original Understanding of the Establishment Clause."*Notre Dame Law Review*, 81 (2006): 1793–1842.

———. "Theology Scholarships, the Pledge of Allegiance, and Religious Liberty: Avoiding the Extremes but Missing the Liberty."*Harvard Law Review*, 118 (Nov. 2004): 155–246.

Leibiger, Stuart. "James Madison and Amendments to the Constitution, 1787–1789: 'Parchment Barriers'."*Journal of Southern History*, 59 (1993): 441–68.

Levy, Leonard. "The Bill of Rights." Pp. 295–327 in *The American Founding: Essays on the Formation of the Constitution*, edited by J. Jackson Barlow et al. New York: Greenwood Press, 1988.

———. *Constitutional Opinions: Aspects of the Bill of Rights.* New York: Oxford University Press, 1986.

———. *Emergence of a Free Press*. New York: Oxford University Press, 1985.

———. *The Establishment Clause: Religion and the First Amendment*. Chapel Hill, N. C.: University of North Carolina Press, 1994, 2d ed. rev.

———. *Legacy of Suppression: Freedom of Speech and Press in Early American History*. Cambridge, Mass.: Harvard University Press, 1960.

Lienesch, Michael. "North Carolina: Preserving Rights." Pp. 343–67 in *Ratifying the Constitution*, edited by Michael A. Gillespie and Michael Lienesch. Lawrence, Kan.: University Press of Kansas, 1989.

———. "Reinterpreting Rights: Antifederalists and the Bill of Rights." Pp. 245–73 in *The Bill of Rights: Government Proscribed*, edited by Ronald Hoffman and Peter J. Albert. Charlottesville, Va.: University Press of Virginia, 1997.

Lietzau, William K. "Rediscovering the Establishment Clause: Federalism and the Rollback of Incorporation."*DePaul Law Review*, 39 (1990): 1191–1234.

Lippy, Charles H. "The 1780 Massachusetts Constitution: Religious Establishment or Civil Religion."*Journal of Church and State*, 20 (Autumn 1978): 534–49.

Lupu, Ira C., and Robert W. Tuttle. "Federalism and Faith."*Emory Law Journal*, 56 (2006): 19–105.

Lutz, Donald S. "Religious Dimensions in the Development of American Constitutionalism."*Emory Law Journal*, 39 (Winter 1990): 21–40.

———. "The States and the United States Bill of Rights."*Southern Illinois University Law Journal*, 16 (1992): 251–62.

———. "The U.S. Bill of Rights in Historical Perspective." Pp. 3–17 in *Contexts of the Bill of Rights,* edited by Stephen L. Schechter and Richard B. Bernstein. Albany, N. Y.: New York State Commission on the Bicentennial of the United States Constitution, 1990.

McAffee, Thomas B. "The Federal System as Bill of Rights: Original Understandings, Modern Misreadings."*Villanova Law Review*, 43 (1998): 17–154.

McClellan, James. "Hand's Writing on the Wall of Separation: The Significance of *Jaffree* in Future Cases on Religious Establishment." Pp. 43–68 in *How Does the Constitution Protect Religious Freedom?,* edited by Robert A. Goldwin and Art Kaufman. Washington, D. C.: American Enterprise Institute, 1987.

———. *Joseph Story and the American Constitution*. Norman, Okla.: University of Oklahoma Press, 1971.

McConnell, Michael W. "The Origins and Historical Understanding of Free Exercise of Religion."*Harvard Law Review*, 103 (1990): 1409–1517.

McConnell, Michael W., John H. Garvey, and Thomas C. Berg. *Religion and the Constitution*. 2d ed. New York: Aspen Publishers, 2006.

McGarvie, Mark D. *One Nation Under Law: America's Early National Struggles to Separate Church and State*. Dekalb, Ill: Northern Illinois University Press, 2004.

McGraw, Barbara A. *Re-Discovering America's Sacred Ground: Public Religion and the Pursuit of the Good in a Pluralistic Society*. Albany, N.Y.: SUNY Press, 2003.

McLoughlin, William G. *New England Dissent, 1630–1883: The Baptists and the Separation of Church and State*. Cambridge, Mass: Harvard University Press, 1971.

Malbin, Michael. *Religion and Politics: The Intentions of the Authors of the First Amendment*. Washington, D. C.: American Enterprise Institute, 1978.

Martin, Richard W. T. *The Free and Open Press*. New York: New York University Press, 2001.

Mayton, William T. "Seditious Libel and the Lost Guarantee of a Freedom of Expression."*Columbia Law Review*, 84 (Jan. 1984): 91–142.

Mayer, David N. *The Constitutional Thoughts of Thomas Jefferson.* Charlottesville, Va.: University Press of Virginia, 1994.

Merriam, Jesse R. "Finding a Ceiling in a Circular Room: Locke v. Davey, Federalism, and Religious Neutrality."*Temple Political & Civil Rights Law Review*, 16 (Fall 2006): 103–44.

Michaelson, Sherryl E. "Religion and Morality Legislation: A Reexamination of Establishment Clause Analysis."*New York University Law* Review, 59 (May 1984): 301–409.

Miller, John C. *Crisis in Freedom: The Alien and Sedition Acts*. Boston: Little, Brown, 1951.

Miller, Robert T. "Religious Conscience in Colonial New England."*Journal of Church and State*, 50 (Autumn 2008): 661–76 (orig. pub. 1959).

Miller, William L. *The First Liberty : Religion and the American Republic.* New York: Alfred Knopf Inc., 1986.

Munoz, Vincent P. *God and the Founders: Madison, Washington, and Jefferson*. New York: Cambridge University Press, 2009.

———. "The Original Meaning of the Establishment Clause and the Impossibility of Its Incorporation."*University of Pennsylvania Journal of Constitutional Law*, 8 (2006): 585–640.

Murray, John Courtney. *We Hold These Truths: Catholic Reflections on the American Proposition*. Garden City, N. Y.: Doubleday & Co., 1964.

Myers, Frank C. "New Hampshire Accepts the Bill of Rights." Pp. 162–81 in *The Bill of Rights and the State: The Colonial and Revolutionary Origins of American Liberties*, edited byPatrick T. Conley and John P. Kaminski, Madison, Wis.: Madison House, 1992.

Nelson, William E. *Americanization of the Common Law: The Impact of Legal Change on Massachusetts Society, 1760–1830*. Cambridge, Mass.: Harvard University Press, 1975.

Nelson, William E., and Robert C. Palmer. *Liberty and Community: Constitution and Rights in the Early American Republic*. New York: Oceana Publishers,1987.

Noonan, Jr., John T. *The Lustre of our Country: The American Experience of Religious Freedom*. Berkeley, Calif.: University of California Press, 1998.

———. "Quota of Imps." Pp. 171–99 in *The Virginia Statute for Religious Freedom: Its Evolution and Consequences in American History*, edited by Merril D. Peterson and Robert C. Vaughn. New York: Cambridge University Press, 1988.

O'Brien, F. William. *Justice Reed and the First Amendment: The Religion Clauses*. Georgetown University Press, 1958.

Paulsen, Michael A. "Religion, Equality, and the Constitution: An Equal Protection Approach to Establishment Clause Adjudication."*Notre Dame Law Review*, 61 (1986): 311–71.

Perry, Michael J. "The Legitimacy of Particular Conceptions of Constitutional Interpretation."*Virginia Law Review*, 77 (1991): 669–719.

Peters, Ronald M. *The Massachusetts Constitution of 1780.* Amherst, Mass.: University of Massachusetts Press, 1978.

Peterson, Walfred H. "The American Federal System and Church-State Relations."*Western Political Quarterly*, 16 (Sept. 1963): 598–609.

Pfeffer, Leo. "The Case for Separation." Pp. 52–94 in *Religion in America: Original Essays on Religion in a Free Society*, edited by John Cogley. New York: Meridian Books, 1958.

Porth, William C., and Robert P. George. "Trimming the Ivey: A Bicentennial Re-examination of the Establishment Clause."*West Virginia Law Review*. 90 (1987): 109–70.

Rabban, David. "The Ahistorical Historian: Leonard Levy on Freedom of Expression in Early American History."*Stanford Law Review*, 37 (Feb. 1985): 795–856.

Rakove, Jack. "The Madisonian Theory of Rights."*William and Mary Law Review*, 31 (1990): 245–66.

Ridgway, Whitman H. "Popular Sentiment and the Bill of Rights Controversy." Pp. 209–44 in *The Bill of Rights: Government Proscribed*, edited by Ronald Hoffman and Peter J. Albert. Charlottesville, Va.: University Press of Virginia, 1997.

Rogers, Melissa. "Traditions of Church-State Separation: Some Ways They Have Protected Religion and Advanced Religious Freedom and How They Are Threatened Today."*Journal of Law & Politics*, 18 (2002): 277–321.

Rosen, Mark D. "Establishment, Expressivism, and Federalism."*Chicago-Kent Law Review*. 78 (2003): 669–716.

Rossum, Ralph A. "*The Federalist's* Understanding of the Constitution as a Bill of Rights." Pp. 219–33 in *Saving the Revolution: The Federalist Papers and the American Founding*, edited by Charles R. Kesler. New York: 1987.

Rubenfeld, Jed. "Antidisestablishmentarianism: Why RFRA Really Was Unconstitutional."*Michigan Law Review*, 95 (August 1997): 2347–84.

Rutland, Robert. "The Trivialization of the Bill of Rights."*William and Mary Law Review*, 31 (1990): 287–94.

Scalia, Antonin. *Matter of Interpretation: Federal Courts and the Law: An Essay*. Princeton, N.J.: Princeton University Press, 1997.

———. "Originalism: The Lesser Evil."*Cincinnati Law Review*, 57 (1989): 849–65.

Schragger, Richard C. "The Role of the Local in the Doctrine and Discourse of Religious Liberty."*Harvard Law Review*, 117 (2003–04): 1810–92.

Schwartz, Bernard. *The Great Rights of Mankind: A History of the American Bill of Rights*. New York: Oxford University Press, 1977.

Semonche, John E. *Keeping the Faith: A Cultural History of the U. S. Supreme Court*. Lanham, Md.: Rowman & Littlefield, 1998.

Shain, Barry. "Religious Conscience and Original Sin." Pp. 161–86 in *Liberty and American Experience in the Eighteenth Century*, edited by David Womersley. Indianapolis, Ind.: Liberty Fund, 2006.

Shiffrin, Steven H. "Liberalism and the Establishment Clause."*Chicago-Kent Law Review*. 78 (2003): 717–28.

Sky, Theodore. "The Establishment Clause, the Congress and the Schools: An Historical Perspective."*Virginia Law Review*, 52 (Dec. 1966): 1395–1466.

Smith, Steven. *The Constitution and the Pride of Reason*. New York: Oxford University Press, 1998.

———. *Foreordained Failure: The Quest for a Constitutional Principle of Religious Freedom*. New York: Oxford University Press, 1995.

———. "The Jurisdictional Establishment Clause: A Reappraisal."*Notre Dame Law Review*, 81 (2005–06): 1843–93.

———. "The Religion Clauses in Constitutional Scholarship."*Notre Dame Law Review*, 74 (March 1999): 1033–54.

Smylie, James H. "Protestant Clergy, the First Amendment and Beginnings of a Constitutional Debate, 1781–91." Pp. 116–53 in *The Religion of the Republic*, edited by Elwyn A. Smith. Philadelphia, Penn.: Fortress Press, 1971.

Snee, Joseph M. "Religious Disestablishment and the Fourteenth Amendment."*Washington University Law Quarterly*, (1954): 371–407.

Steinberg, David. "Gardening at Night: Religion and Choice."*Notre Dame Law Review*, 74 (March 1998): 987–1032.

Steiner, B. C. "Maryland's Adoption of the Constitution."*American Historical Review*, 5 (Oct. 1899): 22–44, 207–24.

Strang, Lee J. "The (Re)turn to History in Religion Clause Law and Scholarship."*Notre Dame Law Review*, 81 (2005–2006): 1697–1716.

Tinling, Marion. "Thomas Lloyd's Reports of the First Federal Congress."*William and Mary Quarterly*, 3d ser., 18 (Oct. 1961): 519–45.

Tushnet, Mark. "The Origins of the Establishment Clause."*Georgetown Law Journal*, 75 (April 1987): 1509–18.

Urofsky, Melvin I., and Paul Finkelman. *A March of Liberty: A Constitutional History of the United States*. 2 vols. New York: Oxford University Press, 2002.

Waldman, Steven. *Founding Faith: Providence, Politics, and the Birth of Religious Freedom in America*. New York: Random House, 2008.

Weir, Robert M. "South Carolina: Slavery and the Structure of the Union." Pp. 201–34 in *Ratifying the Constitution*, edited by Michael A. Gillespie and Michael Lienesch. Lawrence, Kan.: University Press of Kansas, 1989.

Werline, Albert W. *Problems of Church and State in Maryland During the Seventeenth and Eighteenth Centuries*. South Lancaster, Mass.: College Press, 1948.

West, Ellis M. "The Case Against a Right to Religion-Based Exemptions."*Notre Dame Journal of Law, Ethics & Public Policy*, 4 (1990): 591–638.

———. "The Right to Religion-Based Exemptions in Early America: The Case of Conscientious Objectors to Conscription,"*Journal of Law and Religion*, 10 (1993–94): 367–401.

———. "Religious Tests for Office-holding (Article 6, Cl. 3)." Pp. 1314–15 in *Encyclopedia of American Civil Liberties,* edited by Paul Finkleman. 3 Vols. New York: Routledge, 2006.

"The Williamsburg Charter."*Journal of Law and Religion*, 8 (1990): 5–22.

Wilson, John. F. "Religion, Political Culture, and the Law."*DePaul Law Review*, 41 (1992): 821–40.

Wingate, Charles E. L. *Life and Letters of Paine Wingate*. 2 vols. Medford, Mass.: Mercury Printing Co. 1930.

Witte, Jr., John. "Facts and Fiction about the History of Separation of Church and State."*Journal of Church and State*, 48 (Winter 2006): 15–46.

———."A Most Mild and Equitable Establishment of Religion': John Adams and the Massachusetts Experiment."*Journal of Church and State*, 41 (Spring 1999): 213–52.

———. *Religion and the American Constitutional Experiment*. 2d ed. Boulder, Col.: Westview Press, 2005.

Wood, James E., Jr., ed. *The First Freedom: Religion & the Bill of Rights*. Waco, Tex.: Baylor University Press, 1990.

Yarbrough, Jean. "New Hampshire: Puritanism and the Moral Foundations of America." Pp. 235–58 in *Ratifying the Constitution*, edited by Michael A. Gillespie and Michael Lienesch. Lawrence, Kan.: University Press of Kansas, 1989.

Index

Breinigsville, PA USA
16 February 2011
255651BV00003B/1/P